P9-CFY-783

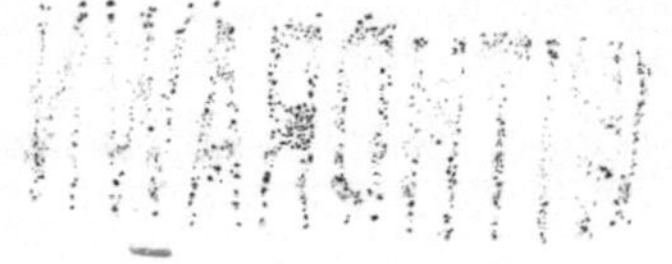

Grandeur and Illusion

Literature and Society

General Editor: Herbert Tint

Grandeur and Illusion

French Literature and Society 1600–1715

Antoine Adam

Translated by Herbert Tint

Basic Books Inc., Publishers
New York

Library of Congress
Catalog Card Number: 74-187000

SBN 465-02697-4

Printed in Great Britain

Contents

Preface

This is a history of French literature in the seventeenth century. It is not, and is not meant to be, a history of French civilisation, for that would allow literature to be treated merely as an illustration of that civilisation. In any case, such a history would be an altogether too ambitious project, and would also have the unfortunate result of abstracting from the masterpieces of the period their aesthetic value by reducing them to simple specimens of history.

This book attempts something quite different. It seeks to exhibit as clearly as possible the fundamental relationships that existed between French society in the seventeenth century and the literature it created. The most original masterpiece is not born in a vacuum. It is society which determines its subject-matter and the way it is shaped. It fulfils the expectations and interprets the conceptions of that society. It may transcend its social environment, but it is nevertheless rooted within it.

One of the most valuable aspects of history in our time is its full awareness of these relationships, and it is these which provide the main subject-matter for this volume. It is hoped that a better understanding of the masterpieces of French classical literature will be gained through their being illuminated by the social context that gave them life. The structure of this book reflects the desire to bring out these relationships. The first chapter discusses the social structure of France in the seventeenth century, with a view to showing its evolution during that period. Similarly, the roots of French culture will be analysed in terms of the cultures of the major social groups that made up the French nation. The culture of the nobility was different from that of the bourgeoisie, and at that time there was also a popular culture which had little to do with either of the others. Then, once the century as a whole has been examined, a closer look will be taken at the periods into which it may usefully be divided. Of course the same social classes will again be encountered, but they will be shown in their evolution or, rather, they will be examined in terms of the decisive changes they underwent. The political causes of these changes will be carefully analysed, as well as the efforts of statesmen who did not merely wish to fashion a new society but also a culture – and consequently a literature – that was radically different from the culture and literature of earlier periods. But the facts of politics will not be discussed for their own sake; they will only be treated where they are relevant to the evolution of society and its culture.

The succeeding chapters are also designed to portray the period in terms of historical change rather than as a static entity. Belles-lettres, philosophical thought and literary forms could hardly remain static while society was changing. Indeed these art forms may well be no more than expressions, in language and outlook, of the attempts of a new society to come into being and, gradually, to take the place of the old.

Part I

Social Structure and Political Change

I

Social structure

The structure of French society in the seventeenth century was, basically, very much like that of the preceding centuries. The king, at its head, was not a head of state in the modern sense, but he was held to be the representative of God, and his authority had a sacred character. He was the father of the different orders that made up the nation. The religious origins of his authority gave him the right to speak to the bishops as their equal while, so far as the nobility was concerned, he was the first gentleman of the kingdom; for the third estate, he was the leader of the administration and the guarantor of justice.

Royal authority, thus understood, was absolute in the sense of being of divine origin, but limited in practice through its being exercised in a nation that was composed of different, firmly established orders, each of which had its proud traditions, privileges and franchises. The king's authority was not exercised through passive agents; he had to assert it and, in the end, to impose it in the face of all kinds of opposition which he could not afford to ignore. Of course, French kings were not happy about the limits imposed upon their powers and, gradually, they emancipated themselves from outside restraints so that the intendants of police, justice, and finance became civil servants in the modern sense of the term, acting solely on the wishes of the government. Until Richelieu's time the 'intendants' were entrusted only with temporary tasks, but by the end of the century they had become the permanent organs of the royal power.[1]

The 'Orders'

United by their common allegiance to the monarchy, there were three social orders that, traditionally, made up the nation: the clergy, the nobility, and the third estate. As a speaker at the Estates General of 1614 put it: 'The clergy is the oldest, the nobility the younger, and the third estate the youngest'. It would be wrong to talk of social classes; 'orders' is the right word, for it renders better the nature of the three groups, their traditional character, and the desire for organisation that underlay them.[2]

The clergy occupied the supreme position in French society because France is, above all, a Catholic country, and the elder daughter of the Church. Moreover, the economic power of the Church was considerable, and its immense possessions had in time become benefices which gave a living to a large number of Frenchmen. These benefices were in the gift of the king or of the bishops (or, as was said, '*à la collation*' of those two) and, while a few benefices were opulent, many of them were modest but adequate for a decent life and could, in any event, be combined with others by the beneficiaries. Since they entailed no real duties, not even the beneficiaries' presence, a cleric resident in Paris, for example, could live off several benefices from various parts of the kingdom with which no other contact was needed than that required by the termly collection of prebends. There were, of course, benefices which carried with them spiritual responsibilities, and in their case the presence of the beneficiary was clearly required. However, a very large number of livings went to men who might have been in minor orders, but who neither were, nor were called upon to be, priests. Their only obligation was celibacy, but this was an obligation which ceased the moment they renounced their living and returned to the secular world.

During the seventeenth century, many Catholics were scandalised by this state of affairs. The most ardent supporters of the Church were very unhappy that so many clerics should have entered holy orders 'without vocation'. But neither the Church of France nor the court felt able to give up a system which guaranteed the social supremacy of the clergy as well as the dependence of that clergy upon the authority of the court.[3]

The nobility thought of itself as providing the foundation for the monarchy, or at least as much as the clergy. It was proud of its hereditary character, which was reasonable at a time when it was thought that virtue is transmitted through the blood. It was also proud of its social role, which was to serve the king with the sword. For, above all, the nobleman was a soldier, and he had privileges that were to compensate him for his readiness to sacrifice his life. These meant that he could only be judged by his peers and that he and his lands were exempt from the direct taxes imposed upon the third estate. Yet his prestige and privileges must not be exaggerated. The position of the nobility was dramatically described in an address to the king in 1627, drawn up by the Comte de Cramail; it said that the nobility[4] 'finds itself in the most pitiable state of all time. It is crushed by poverty, robbed of its virtue by idleness, made almost desperate by oppression'. Repeated accounts throughout the century testified to the continuing accuracy of that picture.

It was the religious wars that had ruined most of the nobility. Already in 1605 François Miron, provost of the Paris merchants, estimated that half their lands had passed into other hands,[5] because the impoverished nobility had to sell them to bourgeois businessmen and lawyers. An additional new factor which finally sealed the economic fate of the nobility was a concomitant of the changes in the economic structure of France. Traditionally, the income of a nobleman came from farm and ground rents, a fact quite unconnected with his spirit of initiative but the consequence of French law which forbade the nobility all forms of activity bringing pecuniary gain. A nobleman who had involved himself in a commercial activity would have been excluded from his order. The expansion of industry and trade during the seventeenth century necessarily brought with it the contraction of wealth based on the land, and it was the nobility which was the first victim of that change.

Some noble families, however, were immensely rich and thus escaped the fate of the majority. They were called 'Les Grands' and were in fact the successors of the feudal lords, reigning over entire provinces where their authority was more in evidence than that of the king;[6] the gentry and the bourgeoisie in the towns recognised their authority. At the beginning of the century they were so conscious of their own power that they were always ready to contest that of the king, who then had to send an army to impose his will. Richelieu seemed to have broken the power of the great noble families, but then the

Fronde proved that it was not quite so simple to make them renounce their old habits. In fact they were not finally subdued until Louis XIV made them take up residence near him at Versailles, and thus deprived them of all political power.[7] By way of compensation, the king showered them with honours and lavish gifts which allowed them to preserve a princely way of life. The brilliance of the court, at which they occupied the most prominent positions, was the most visible characteristic feature of the monarchic society at the end of the seventeenth century.

The third estate was the third order of the kingdom. Hitherto inferior to the other two, its importance grew in the course of the seventeenth century. It was the most active and liberally-minded part of the nation, and the political changes of the century turned it into a most efficient instrument for the monarchy. It was, however, a heterogeneous group and its constituent parts have to be carefully examined.[8]

At the top were the members of the parlements, who were in fact closer to the nobility than to the third estate; presidents and counsellors of the parlements had created dynasties in which, from generation to generation, offices were handed down within the same families like any other family possession. They were very rich and bought estates which gave them the status of noblemen; they also married their daughters to members of the best aristocracy. Their connections with the world of finance were to bring upon them the anathemas of the democratic Fronde, which claimed that these false Brutuses and Catos were often in collusion with the worst extortioners of taxes. Even so, their authority in French society was considerable. The Paris Parlement at that time tended to look upon itself as the heir to the Roman Senate; its counsellors called themselves *senatores* and acted, for a while, as if it was their duty to ratify or reject the decisions of the royal government. The fact that laws and decrees had to be registered by them had persuaded them that it was within their authority either to accept or refuse to register them altogether. However, the government constantly contested that claim, recalling that the only function of the various parlements was that they should dispense justice to the private citizen. The king – whether he be Louis XIII or Louis XIV – constantly held to the view that it was neither 'permitted nor desirable for the courts of parlement or any of their officers to concern themselves with affairs of state or with the administration and government of the kingdom, [and] that these were matters only for the king who had been appointed and recommended by God and to whom alone he was responsible'.[9] The court lost no opportunity to humiliate these proud and inconvenient members of the parlements, and by appointing unsuitable maîtres des requêtes in fact debased the existing offices so that their prestige as well as their income declined. Thus, during most of the reign of Louis XIV, the Paris Parlement had a rather wretched existence. Nevertheless its traditions persisted and when, during the last years of the reign, the authority of the government no longer made itself felt as firmly as before, the magistrates showed that they were still ready to prevent the exercise of arbitrary power. Their courageous conduct during the quarrel about the Bull *Unigenitus* showed the strength of the opposition the magistracy were able to put up against arbitrary royal acts.[10]

The offices of president, counsellor, and maître de requête were the most prestigious of the parlements. There were, however, many other offices, and these too conferred prestige. Their holders were bourgeois who had decided to give up commerce to buy themselves their offices; they made up the bulk of the presidials, councils, and requêtes de l'hôtel. They were a kind of bourgeois aristocracy of judicial and financial officers, and from them were drawn also, in the provinces, the consuls, and town magistrates. Moreover, like the officers of the parlements, they liked their daughters to marry into the gentry. That they were numerous is shown by the fact that of the 192 deputies of the third estate who attended the States General of 1614, 131 were royal officers of that kind.[11]

Among the groups of the third estate that held no royal office there was one which had nevertheless acquired great importance. This was the group of tax-farmers (variously known as financiers, fermiers, traitants, or partisans). Except for the taille, which was levied by the royal officers, who were its proprietors, taxes were levied by businessmen who 'farmed' them out. Their leases entitled them to do whatever they thought necessary to collect their taxes, and they used their position as masters of the administration to make enormous profits.[12] The traites, i.e. customs and town duties, were also farmed out to businessmen; the latter were called traitants. Despite the government's distrust, the nobility's jealousy, and the hatred of the bourgeoisie and the people, the financiers were untroubled as they collected their money. They knew that the king, who was always short of money, needed them, and that the great noblemen felt very honoured at being able to marry one or other of their daughters to a financier's son.[13]

Population changes in the wake of early industrial development accompanied the growing power of the financiers. Besides the traditional corporations of artisans in the towns, there were now factories which foreshadowed the large industries of the nineteenth century. This kind of change began before Colbert, but was considerably speeded up by the impetus he gave it. There were then businesses employing up to 1,500 workers, and these were no longer run by a 'master' who was bound to his workmen by the rules of a corporation, but by a director and his clerks and offices. The real employers, who had put up the money to bring the business into being, remained unseen by the workers.[14]

Thus was created a mass of rootless workers, making their way from town to town to find employment – however temporary – and without any kind of permanent home or stable environment. However, secret links were created between them that were kept alive through exchanges of letters.[15] Now and again such workpeople drew attention to themselves through 'coalitions', i.e. strikes.[16] Their conditions were hard, but industry had been ruined by the religious wars. To take an example, in the first part of the century cloth manufacturers produced only about one-eighth of the amount of the previous period. Workers in many towns had become unemployed, and this meant they had been reduced to beggary. Although it might have been expected that this situation would improve later in the century, especially since Richelieu and in particular Colbert were inclined to favour industrial expansion, the war policies and the drive for prestige did much to minimise progress. Moreover, Colbert's system could only have produced results in the long term, after the necessary investments. In the event, the subsidies to factories ceased very quickly. The figures show that the textile industry made immense progress, but not until many years after Colbert's death.[17] But the Frenchman of the seventeenth century saw nothing of the rewards of the birth of modern industry.

The workers in the towns had indeed a difficult time, but the poverty of the peasants assumed dreadful proportions. At the beginning of the century there was still a class of prosperous peasants whose perpetual leases (censives) made them virtually owners of their land. But the endless wars and punishing taxation, which fell particularly heavily on them, gradually ruined them. They left their lands 'to withdraw from the desolation of the countryside',[18] and were replaced by labour that was given little security by its exploiters.[19] Reports of the living conditions of these peasants show that they ate bread made from acorns and roots, and even had to make do with grass from the fields and bark from the trees; they slept on straw. An investigation made in 1687 in Maine and the Orléanais had references to ruined houses that no one was rich enough to repair; it also spoke of the disappearance of the prosperous peasants, and of the countryside in many provinces as being no more than 'a morass of poverty and misery'.[20]

These atrocious conditions, which marked the decline of an important section of the population, were not the inevitable consequence of progress, but the results of a political régime dedicated to war and prestige. In his travels through France, Locke was struck by the difference between the countryside in England and the misery of the French peasantry. The decline was there for all to see, and Vauban estimated that the value of the land had dropped by one-third in thirty years; Boisguilbert thought that revenue from the land had decreased by half since 1660.[21] In such circumstances the peasantry forever had to face the threat of famine, and one bad harvest was enough to decimate the population of the provinces. There were, indeed, bad harvests in 1603–5 and 1609, and again in 1637, 1638, and 1660; a particularly bad one occurred in the winter of 1663–4 which, in Chateauroux alone, orphaned two hundred children. According to the Bishop of Montauban in 1694, four hundred persons were dying of hunger each year in his diocese.[22] Sometimes the peasants revolted against their misery, as in the uprisings of the Croquants and the Va-nu-pieds at the end of Louis XIII's reign. Similar revolts occurred during the time of Louis XIV; for example, there was, in 1674, trouble in Guyenne where armed peasants roamed the countryside, and 1707 as well as 1709 brought other uprisings. On each occasion the peasants were pitilessly suppressed. But their despair reached its peak at the end of Louis XIV's reign, which coincided with the war of the Spanish Succession.

Although the modern reader is scandalised by such misery, which was the lot of a large part of the population of France, there is enough evidence to show that those who lived at that time were also disturbed by it. It is quite remarkable how often official reports spoke of the ill-concealed sympathy of the bourgeoisie of the towns for the insurgents of the countryside.[23] There was clearly a new spirit in the making which showed itself, among the preachers, but particularly in some of the writings of La Bruyère.[24] It amounted to a kind of protest against the state of society at that time, to a fatalistic refusal to accept the misery of the peasantry.

But it must be clearly understood that this new outlook did not lead to a questioning of the social order as such: for instance, at the end of the seventeenth century there was no trace of the millenarianism which had exercised its influence over large parts of Europe from the end of the Middle Ages to the beginning of the sixteenth century. All that was left of it in the age of Louis XIII and Louis XIV was confined to small circles of visionary mystics or, in literary and harmless form, to utopian and poetic works which extolled the joys of the golden age.[25] Frenchmen of that period thought that the social order accorded with the wishes of God, and that in France it was based on the authority of the king, on the laws of the land, and on the hierarchy of the system of orders.

But though it is true that the social order was not called into question, there was considerable animosity and conflict between the different groups of Frenchmen. Ever since the time of Henry IV, the provincial nobility objected to seeing the state being governed 'by lawyers and attorneys' and, as was derisively said, 'by gentlemen of the pen and ink'. On the other hand, the bourgeoisie did not take kindly to the haughtiness of the nobility, nor, above all, to the privileges of the nobility which exempted it from paying talliage. In fact, the bourgeoisie looked upon the nobility as a useless and witless class. The significance of the changes that were beginning to occur in French society can be seen from the fact that, while earlier States General had never brought out serious conflicts between the social orders, that of 1614 was almost exclusively preoccupied with such conflicts.

Social classes and their culture

It was already at this time possible to speak of a national French culture because the French by then had created a wealth of works in literature and the other arts and were the possessors of an impressive intellectual tradition. It was however a very varied culture and within it could be distinguished elements which were contributed at different social levels.

For example, there was a popular culture. In Paris, as well as in the provinces, there was a public for short books, booklets and pamphlets printed on rough paper which provided useful information, told edifying or fantastic stories, or dealt with some recent event. In Paris, such publications were mainly hawked on the Place Dauphine and on the Pont-Neuf. In the provinces, however, there was an organised system of hawkers which saw to it that such books were carried even into the villages. An analysis of this literature has enabled us to learn what subjects were of interest to the majority of the population.[26] First, there were of course practical matters which the public wanted to know about, and these were of the kind that would interest a mainly agricultural population. Calendars and almanacks were particularly in demand, and some hundred different ones have been counted for the course of the seventeenth century; the most widely read had about one hundred pages, and listed the feastdays on which no work had to be done, the dates of the seasons, the phases of the moon, the signs of the zodiac; it also gave mottoes in verse for each month of the year. Some books provided information about remedies for certain illnesses. It goes without saying that the information in these books came from traditional medieval sources and not from the new scientific discoveries. For example, they provided a list of saints to be invoked for particular illnesses, and the saint was selected simply on the basis of the consonance of his name with that of the illness. Other books were based on white magic, and they gave recipes for cures as well as for the correct use of the stars. Then there were books which taught how one could always be successful in lotteries, or how hidden treasures might be discovered.

The public which believed in all this was avid for stories of the fantastic. In their reading matter people learned of battles that had been witnessed in the sky, marvels of all kinds, and stories about monsters; there were also tales about Satan's intervention in the world of the living, telling of crimes too horrible to be explained in natural terms. This kind of literature, with its supernatural emphasis, obviously had deep roots in the people, and it showed how strongly very ancient beliefs were still entrenched in the seventeenth century. Nor was it only in written form that this mentality showed itself, but it was also to be found in nursery tales and stories told at the veillées which were transmitted by oral tradition. Little is known of these tales today, except for the titles of some of them, but that they existed is certain. It would also be a mistake to assume that these tales only reached the ears of poor peasants: they were also told to the children of rich families of the nobility or of the bourgeoisie who were, in their early years, looked after by nurses. Thus, during the first eight or ten years of his life, a nobleman or a bourgeois of the seventeenth century had his mind filled with an entirely popular culture.[27] This is how the sudden fashion, at the end of the seventeenth century, for fairy stories can be explained. If this fashion surprises us today, it is because we have become accustomed to thinking of the period in terms of classicism, Cartesianism, and Greco-Roman culture, and have been unaware that the contemporaries of Perrault saw in his stories, in a somewhat sophisticated form, the old tales which had enthralled them in their childhood.

Satirical catéchismes – and patenôtres, credos, de profundis which contained amusing paraphrases of liturgical texts and applied them to recent events – also represented a national tradition, like the complaintes which had become satirical a century earlier. And the so-called esprit gaulois appeared in a large number of books which inveighed against 'the imperfection and spite of women'.[28] None of these books dealt seriously with contemporary politics nor, *a fortiori*, criticised the institutions of the monarchy. But there was another kind which did, and this was specifically aimed at the people of Paris. In these publications ministers were taken to task, misdeeds denounced, and the policies of the government criticised. Already numerous at the time of Marie de Médicis, Concini, and de Luynes, such booklets or pamphlets appeared in an unending stream during the period of Mazarin and the Fronde; the later period knew them as mazarinades.[29] As many as 230 publishers are known to have had such booklets and pamphlets printed, and according to the historians 4,000 of them were printed between January 1649 and October 1652. A pamphlet of four pages would sell for two liards or six sous. If it dealt with a recent event it would be written in a few hours, and printed during the night so that it could be sold in the streets of Paris 'like hot cakes straight from the oven'; some might be printed in editions of 5,000 copies. It is believed that Paris alone had between 800 and 1,000 pamphlet-sellers (colporteurs).

This kind of popular literature, whether political or not, seemed to be of interest also to some of the educated bourgeoisie. L'Estoile's *Journal* provides evidence for that: even though he often calls the pamphlets 'twaddle' (fadaises), it is clear that he was looking out for them, bought them, and put them into his library. The same was true, a little later, of Naudé and Guy Patin. The great French libraries contain a large number of manuscripts that are in fact copies of topical pamphlets made by interested observers of the contemporary scene. The cultured bourgeois of the seventeenth century was therefore not the blinkered and narrow person many historians have made him, but he was as interested in public opinion as in the events around him. This kind of literature ceased, however, after the defeat of the Fronde, at least in its printed form. But popular literature continued to thrive, and its main readership was to be found in the country. Large publishing houses promoted it, the oldest of which (Oudot in Troyes) went back to about 1606; there were others in Lyon, Rouen, and Epinal. Oudot's booklets formed the *Bibliothèque bleue* and appealed to a wide public; they ranged from burlesque stories to *Passions de Jésus-Christ*, or from lives of saints and moral dialogues to bawdy tales.[30] Surprisingly, the series contained only a few novels; it was only during the following century that the *Bibliothèque bleue* brought them out in greater numbers.

These literary forms provide a good indication of the tastes of the very large part of the population which, though unmoved by recent changes in literary fashion, was certainly not without culture. But it would be false to suppose that this public did not know about those changes, for some of the tragedies of Corneille and Tristan had also been published in the *Bibliothèque bleue*, along with adaptations of Ariosto and Tasso.

Apart from the traditional culture which was being kept alive by the least privileged sections of French society, another culture was emerging in the seventeenth century whose roots were in the French Renaissance. Already in the sixteenth century that culture had created masterpieces in literature as well as in the other arts. It was based on the traditions of Greece and Rome, and was to become the foundation for the education of later generations. But its great prestige should not mislead one into thinking that it was of significance for more than the small social group of educated bourgeois – rich merchants, doctors, lawyers, and university professors. It was this group which insisted that Ronsard be regarded as the summit of French literary achievement (whatever may be said to the contrary by people who mistake the disdain in Boileau's famous lines for the real position of Ronsard in the eyes of the educated bourgeoisie of the seventeenth century). Every piece of evidence points to the fact – as will be shown later – that during the first part of the century Ronsard remained the most admired of French poets. And this admiration was based on the belief that he personified the real Renaissance, that is the Greco-Roman tradition as it had been rediscovered after centuries of gothic barbarism.[31] It was a tradition which, for the French bourgeoisie, was a culture and not merely a subject for scholars. They saw it as providing the right notions of beauty as well as of morality, and it gave them a conceptual framework. It would be difficult for a historian to exaggerate the degree to which those who came under its spell in the seventeenth century were transformed by it. The Greek poets themselves were certainly not neglected, but their importance decreased as that of Virgil, Cicero, Seneca, and Tacitus increased. Virgil was admired because he was taken to be the master of all poetry, Cicero because he was the sovereign model for all eloquence (eloquence being an art much needed by the French bourgeoisie), and Seneca because he advocated a morality that was based on universal reason; finally, Tacitus was loved because he was thought to have revealed the fundamental maxims of politics. For the French bourgeoisie Greco-Roman culture was definitely not a mere passing or academic interest.

The thoroughness with which the men of the seventeenth century knew their Greco-Roman culture is, in fact, quite extraordinary. This is not particularly well brought out in any study of the ancient models for one of the tragedies of the period, because there is really nothing remarkable about a dramatist who takes his subjects from Greek or Roman plots and then turns them neatly into plays for his own time. What is much more significant is the kind of surprise one gets on reading, say, the letters of Guy Patin. He was Dean of the Faculty of Medicine and spontaneously quoted from ancient writers, used Greek expressions, a phrase from Athenaeus, or a verse from Virgil. Only on reading this kind of evidence is it possible to understand to what degree the culture of the ancients was alive for the bourgeois of the seventeenth century.

By contrast, most of the nobility was, at the beginning of the century, abysmally uncultured. In a later chapter a good deal of contemporary evidence will be given which will leave no doubt on that score. During the first quarter of the century there were of course still great ladies and gentlemen of the nobility who remained faithful to the traditions of the Renaissance, and who perpetuated them in a new and difficult social climate.[32] But there were very few of them and, as the brutal manners that were the outcome of the long religious wars gradually softened, there was no returning to the times of Francis I and Henry II. At that stage a new, modern culture took over which owed little to the traditions of antiquity and which, in fact, set itself up in opposition to them. The manner in which the opposition between these two cultures manifested itself, and what its consequences were, will be discussed later. What matters here is that we recognise the co-existence of two very different cultures, and that they belonged to different, though leading, social classes of the French nation.

From 1630 onwards there was certainly nothing uncultured

about the fashionable aristocracy. But the young noblemen had been educated in Jesuit colleges and were afterwards unlikely to look for intellectual inspiration in the writings of antiquity. Just as the young bourgeois of the nineteenth century were still compelled to learn Latin, but secretly read Eugène Sue or Edmond About, so the nobility of the seventeenth century were much less interested in Homer and Virgil than in tales of chivalry, adaptations of *Lancelot*, and the *Amadis de Gaule*.[33] Rather than Ronsard, who was still being obstinately admired by the bourgeoisie, they liked Marot and the quality of his wit; and they adored Ariosto, whom many of them read in the original. Epic poetry, for them, meant Tasso and not Homer, while the literary forms they liked best (and often tried their hand at themselves) were sonnets and madrigals and, from about 1640 onwards, the rondeau or énigme.

As might be expected, the more modern culture of the aristocracy also, in time, influenced parts of the bourgeoisie. This was particularly true of the financiers and businessmen, who were won over to the new culture in literature as well as in the fine arts. The bourgeoisie of the parlements and the lawyers were less attracted to it, even though from the beginning of the reign of Louis XIV lawyers took an increasingly active part in society life.[34]

The social status of writers

In the changing class patterns and relationships of the seventeenth century, the place of writers was no more stable than the society in which they lived. At the beginning of the century it would be difficult to assign them to any particular class, although noblemen and soldiers who wrote verse or novels were remarkably common. The fact that they nearly all had links with a great patron is of greater social significance.

Indeed, poets and novelists could hardly have made a living from their earnings, and the printers themselves paid very little.[35] Their protectors, however, paid better, whether they were the king or Marguerite de Valois (back in Paris after 1605) or some of the great noblemen; a little later, the Duc de Montmorency alone protected or subsidised a whole group of writers which was as great as – or even greater than – that which was working for the king; the Guise and Condé families also looked after men of letters. But this kind of patronage should not mislead one, for the majority of writers were still living in precarious material conditions. Despite the court's benefactions, and his own prestige, Malherbe was poor, and there were many others who knew real misery.[36] There was much talk at that time of 'starveling poets',[37] who spent their days in taverns and their nights in hovels.

Richelieu changed a good deal of this once he had taken over the government. No doubt there continued to be poets who starved, as well as poets who avoided starvation only by going into the service of some great nobleman; for example, Saint-Amant had the protection of the Maréchal de Créquy, and Tristan worked for Gaston d'Orléans and later for the Duc de Guise. But the greatest successes at this time were won by men of good bourgeois stock, sons of bourgeois parents who remained within the social framework of their class: Colletet, Malleville, and L'Estoile were typical examples. Similarly, the most respected critics (Chapelain, Conrart, Balzac) were bourgeois. The way of life of these men was far removed from the freer and rather bohemian existence of some of the writers of the previous generation. Some of the first members of the Académie française were rich, like Conrart for instance; and Chapelain was prosperous enough; Godeau is known to have had thirty thousand écus, and Serizay was the Duc de la Rochefoucauld's administrator (intendant).[38]

Apart from the new kind of writer, created through the direct influence of Richelieu, there soon appeared another kind who came to be known as the poète galant, i.e. the poet who frequented the aristocratic salons of the period rather than the taverns. Voiture was the first of them, and was followed by many others, like Benserade and Abbé Cotin. It was henceforth their verses that filled the anthologies and provided the ethos of French writing. The change had begun under Richelieu and very soon engulfed nearly the entire domain of French literature.[39] It would be false to think of the poètes galants as poor men received by the upper classes in their large houses for fun, but despised. Most of these poets were comfortably prosperous, many of them belonging to the clergy and endowed with benefices; Montplaisir was a marquis and a marshal of the king's armies. Clearly poets no longer had to live always in hovels.

But it was at least as significant that the new economic aristocracy played a much greater rôle in these changes than the old, authentic aristocracy. The time of the Hôtel de Rambouillet was over after 1645, the marquise refusing to receive more than a handful of visitors thereafter. Mazarin's period, from the point of view of social history, was that of Nicolas Foucquet, for writers in search of money turned to him. Foucquet made Pellisson his secretary, Scarron referred to Foucquet as his 'patron', and even Gombauld, for all his pride, forgot his republican principles to enter Foucquet's service. La Fontaine only seemed to follow the fashion when he, too, began to work for him.[40]

From the beginning of the personal reign of Louis XIV a new policy for artists and writers was, not surprisingly, inaugurated. Henceforth the royal government was to be the patron of all the arts and, at the same time, take over their control. A policy of systematic subsidies was begun in 1663, and a list of their recipients was published. Poets, historians, and scholars were among those who received between 800 and 3,000 livres.[41] It would, however, be a mistake to think that this apparently generous policy met with universal acclaim. Lest it be thought that the desire for free speech is a phenomenon of the present century, it should be noted that already at that time there were critics of the scheme. Thus, Daniel Huet wrote to Ménage, 'It is in a sense shameful to write verse for money', and saw in it 'shame and ignominy'.[42] But Colbert, taking note of this kind of reaction, signified that those who showed reluctance 'would be noticed'. In fact, however, the policy of official and interested support for writers and artists did not last long. The requirements of the wars used up the resources of the treasury and, already by 1676, subsidies had fallen to the derisory level of 4,900 livres. War was indeed expensive.

Thus, as before under Mazarin, the aristocracy, both traditional and financial, resumed its rôle as patron of the arts. The great families once again gave employment to writers, and in that way La Bruyère lived at Chantilly as tutor to Monsieur le Prince, and then as librarian of the Château. Often, too, writers would now be staying with great families as honoured guests incarnating a sophisticated culture, and were thus no longer looked upon as in any way inferior; they were, as was said, 'beaux esprits'. The philosopher and poet Malézieu and Abbé Genest, for example, were the cultural arbiters at Sceaux, and Chaulieu was the trusted friend of the Vendôme family, and was also to be seen at the dinners of the Temple with Palaprat, Brueys, Du Boulay and La Chapelle.

The literature of France in the seventeenth century will not be properly understood unless account is taken of the kindness and delicacy with which men of letters were welcomed into the houses of the great noble families who had a sincere respect for what would today be called 'culture'.

2

The social implications of political history[1]

The first point to note about the seventeenth century in France is that it did not have that changelessness about it that certain historians seem to attribute to it. If the France of 1600 is compared with that of 1715 the differences are enormous, and it would be correct to say that a great gulf separates these two moments in history. We may deduce from this that literature, which is so closely linked with society, changed with it. As the expression of a nation that was undergoing rapid and profound changes, literature itself changed rapidly and profoundly.

To get a clear picture of this transformation one may distinguish within it a number of stages each of which is closely related to those contiguous with it.

During the early years of the century the powerful monarch Henry IV concentrated upon restoring order to the kingdom, and appeared to be succeeding. He maintained the unity of the various political, social and religious forces which made up the nation. When he was assassinated (14 May 1610) his widow, Marie de Médicis, took over the regency. Then, as a result of a coup d'état (24 April 1617), her son Louis XIII tried to govern with a few favourites and successive ministers. This second period (1610–24) was marked by a state of semi-anarchy which seemed incurable.

But in 1624 Louis XIII called upon a strong man, Cardinal Richelieu, to govern and he remained the real power in France until his death (2 December 1642). His genius left a lasting impact upon his country.

Louis XIII outlived Richelieu by only a few months. After his death the kingdom was again entrusted to a regent, Anne of Austria, who called upon the assistance of Mazarin. The latter lacked the vigorous firmness of Richelieu and, in 1648, there began the troubles known as the Fronde. These lasted from 1648 to 1652 and ended with the return to Paris of the young King Louis XIV and of Mazarin. Mazarin thereafter governed with absolute authority. He died in 1661.

It was then that the personal rule of Louis XIV began. His was to be one of the longest reigns in French history, lasting until 1715. But it cannot be appraised properly unless one distinguishes within it two very different periods. From 1661 until about 1680 the policies of the crown brought victory after victory abroad and splendid achievements at home, particularly in the realms of administration, public works, the fine arts and literature.

From 1680 to 1715 the cumulative results of interminable wars, religious conflicts at home, financial ruin, the use of power that grew increasingly tyrannical as the gravity of the situation became clear, all these created within the kingdom a new state of mind which was to make itself strongly felt after the death of the old king and left its mark on the following century.

These main trends in the political history of the period also mark out developments in the social and literary history. The impetus given by Richelieu and by Louis XIV had its effect on the life of French society as well as on the activities of artists and writers. Periods of war diminish the importance of some sections of society and increase that of others. At the same time they create a general state of mind which has a profound effect upon the products of literature.

Henry IV and the recovery of France

The peace concluded at Vervins in 1598 marked the end of a period of wars and unrest which had lasted forty years. The kingdom of France emerged from this ordeal with its foundations badly shaken. The countryside was ruined, the soil untilled, and the roads in disrepair. In the towns business was partly at a standstill and commerce depressed by debt. As usually happens in such cases, the ruin of the many coincided with the concentration in a few hands of immense fortunes ostentatiously enjoyed. Those who had thus profited from the disorders were called financiers, that is men who had lent money to the state at rates inflated by the very scarcity of money.

To the general ruin was added the serious breakdown of discipline. The fact that for forty years a large part of the nation had devoted its efforts to making war had its pernicious results. Demobilised soldiers were incapable of putting up with the normal tasks of peace. They complained that Henry IV was doing nothing for them although they had served him faithfully. It took ten years to subdue the rebellious bands of ex-soldiers which had formed in some of the more remote provinces. This helps to explain the outbreak of banditry at this time. Country roads were not very safe. The streets of Paris were taken over at night by well-organised robbers. Given the state of the kingdom in those days one can well understand the remark made by Chancellor Pasquier that anyone who woke up after having slept for forty years would have seen 'not France but the corpse of France'.

It was Henry IV who undertook to restore life to France. He made it his task to pacify the fanatics, to return to the rule of law, to put the economy on a sound footing, and to ensure the improvement of agriculture, the manufacturing industries, and commerce.

In order to succeed, he had first of all to restore life to the idea of the monarchy, its function, and its rights. It had been opposed, and in fact was still being opposed, by some of the followers of the Reformation as well as by the theologians of the League and Spain. The Protestants had not forgotten the works of Théodore de Bèze and Du Plessis-Mornay, according to which subjects have the right to revolt against usurpers and tyrants. The propagandists of the League for their part continued to sing the praises of Jacques Clément, the monk who had assassinated Henry III. They called his crime 'a truly heroic and divine act'. They maintained that the civil power must be rigorously subordinated to the Catholic hierarchy, to the pope and bishops; that the principal function of kings was the carrying out of decisions made by the hierarchy; that the pope had the power to depose kings, abolish their laws and promulgate new ones. These were not the pretensions of just a few ultramontane theologians. The entire episcopate, the

Faculty of Theology of the University of Paris and several provincial parlements agreed with them. A fact which epitomises the degree to which the pretensions of the ultramontanes were continuing to upset the moral and political climate of France is that during twelve years of peace there were at least twelve attempts on the life of the king.

Henry IV was not well-equipped to deal with a doctrine which denied his authority and encouraged his assassins. To become king of France he had to abandon Protestantism, which meant that he had to submit his hereditary right to the will of the pope and the episcopate. Throughout his reign he practised a policy of appeasement. He even recalled the Jesuits and made one of them his confessor. One gains the impression that he wanted it to be forgotten that he had ever been the leader of the Protestant party.

Nor did he make any attempt to invoke a theory of the state against the theologians and propagandists of the ultramontanes. Such a doctrine was not sufficiently formulated at that time to provide a policy. He based his authority on the traditional notion of the monarchy. Now that he was legitimate king of France it was his task (he thought) to give his kingdom order, prosperity and peace: this was a task imposed on him by God. Those who questioned his orders were reminded of the prerogatives of his charge and the extent of the powers it carried with it. It seems certain that this was not merely for him an opportunistic argument. He was fully convinced by it.

In this way he re-established peace, but it remained precarious. Political ambitions and religious fanaticisms were submerged rather than suppressed: bad habits were not very easily cured. Causes for disorder remained all the more active since the international situation favoured them. The followers of the Reformed Church were aware that England was still ready to help them. The Catholics were still looking to Spain. The king had to put down sporadic outbreaks of trouble which reflected the deep and lasting uneasiness in peoples' minds.

The return of anarchy

On 14 May 1610 Henry IV was stabbed to death by a religious fanatic. His assassination showed how precarious peace and order still were, and it marked the beginning of a period of weakness and uncertainty which lasted fourteen years.

Henry IV's widow, Marie de Médicis, was entrusted with the regency of the kingdom and governed for her son Louis XIII. It appeared that the new government was continuing the policies of the dead king, and the ministers of Henry IV for a while retained responsibility for the running of affairs. But the man who had been his right hand, Sully, who would have been the only man capable of stemming the rising tide of disorder, was ousted almost at once.

Marie de Médicis seemed to have made up her mind to buy peace with the big feudal lords the moment they became threatening. The Prince de Condé, the Guises, the Duc de Bouillon all soon saw the benefit they could obtain from indiscipline, and they plundered the treasury of France.

To protect herself against them the regent relied on Concini, an Italian of unknown origins. He was perhaps only an adventurer. When Henry IV had seen him in the queen's entourage he had been repelled by him. But in order to ensure his own position Concini defended that of the regent, and for some years he was the prop of royal authority.

He liked pomp and the royal entertainments of 1612 were particularly splendid. They were spread over several days and two hundred thousand Parisians crowded the path of the cavalcade. The poets were invited to celebrate the splendours of the régime. Malherbe, in the verses for a ballet, called Concini 'l'Esprit sacré'. On 24 April 1617 Concini was assassinated at the gates of the Louvre.

A new government took over with Luynes at its head who remained in office for five years. During that time he succeeded in maintaining his authority over the great families. But this apparent restoration of order deceived no one. With Concini gone, France now obeyed Luynes; in other words, government by one favourite had been replaced by that of another. Like Concini, Luynes received advice from Madrid and Rome. The papal nuncios Ubaldini, Bentivoglio, and Corsini could be considered to be the real masters of French policy. It was no longer simply a question of concessions being made to the ultramontanes as used to be the case under Henry IV. They now had charge of all the affairs of government. Marie de Médicis, who was Italian and devout, found it natural to obey the injunctions of the royal confessor. It was Luynes' wish that the prelates should have precedence in the governmental council of which Cardinal de Retz was president.

Luynes had vowed to work as hard as he could for the ruin of the Huguenots, even to the point of making war on them if he found an opportunity. In 1620, at the behest of his favourite, Louis XIII marched on the Béarn at the head of his army. There he restored Catholicism and returned to the clergy the property and privileges it had possessed before the wars of religion. Then, in 1621, Luynes organised a second military campaign against the Protestant strongholds in the Garonne region. In December 1621, he died ingloriously before the small stronghold of Monheur.

The three years that followed were marked by a series of tentative policies through which France vainly hoped to define her aims. For some time the kingdom was administered by Chancellor Brulart de Sillery and his son Paisieux. They felt powerless in the midst of intrigues over which they had no control. In January 1624 Louis XIII dismissed them. The superintendent of finance La Vieuville tried to reorganise the government, but fared no better and in August he was arrested and imprisoned in the castle at Amboise. Pressed by his mother, the king made Cardinal de Richelieu the head of his council. The period of indecision and weakness was over.

Richelieu

For the first six years the cardinal had to play it by ear and maintain his position by scheming. Since he had been placed in his position of eminence by Marie de Médicis, he had to rely for his support on the Catholic party, and consequently to carry out its wishes. There was no question of his having a personal policy.

To begin with he contented himself with suppressing some intrigues at court, but with a severity to which the French were not accustomed.

Then Richelieu turned on the Protestants, and laid siege to

their best defended stronghold, La Rochelle. He set about this task with extreme vigour, in sharp contrast to the weakness which had marked the sieges of Montauban and Montpellier. La Rochelle capitulated (October 1628) and the king, with the cardinal at his side, entered the town, in which fifteen thousand people had lost their lives.

Richelieu was no less anxious to tame the Catholic faction than he had been to reduce the Protestants. The leaders of the faction were Bérulle and Marshal de Marillac who relied for their support on the queen mother who still exercised a powerful influence on her son. Since the siege of La Rochelle Marie de Médicis had turned against Richelieu. She got on well with Gaston, whom she no doubt preferred to Louis. She inclined more and more towards a policy that would have ensured for Spain hegemony in Europe. The tension which had been noticeable since 1629 led the following year to the decisive crisis which has gone down in history as the Day of the Dupes (10 December 1630). Richelieu emerged from it as the victor, and Marie de Médicis was relegated to Compiègne and finally fled abroad (1630).

The great families considered themselves threatened; so did Gaston, who incited the Duc de Montmorency, governor of the Languedoc, to revolt. He was overcome, tried and executed (1632), and Gaston fled to the Netherlands. The Duc de Guise went to Italy for a holiday.

Richelieu had made it his objective to promote not only the internal cohesion of the kingdom but also its prestige in Europe. To achieve both these aims he had to humble Spain and the Holy Empire, and to prevent them from achieving a dominant position in Europe. He would, however, have preferred to avoid open war, but he was very soon led into it. In May 1635 he declared war on Spain. The following year the Emperor in his turn declared war on France.

The French armies were not ready, and the frontiers were badly defended. During the very first campaign it became obvious that the French generals were incapable even of feeding their armies or of paying them. The soldiers were leaving their units and deserting *en masse*. The following year the Spaniards, coming from Belgium, only had to attack the Picardy border with one cavalry corps to enable them to cross the Somme, take Corbie, and drive forward as far as Pontoise. The roads in the west were crowded with refugees from Paris. Nevertheless Richelieu managed to organise resistance and raise morale, and finally the Spanish cavalry withdrew. But the French were not to forget the 'year of Corbie' for a long time. By the time Richelieu died Artois and Rousillon had both been conquered.

He had fought this war in spite of the opposition of the Catholic faction, which entirely supported the interests of Spain. He had also fought it against the wishes of the queen, who could not forget that she was the sister of the king of Spain. Richelieu even had her searched one day to make sure that she was not hiding a note in her bodice. He had, therefore, many enemies hatching plots. Gaston, who had returned to France, could not bring himself to give up his intrigues. Most of the great families openly opposed Richelieu's policies. The majority of those who had sought refuge abroad, mainly in Brussels and in London, retained informants within the kingdom.

This opposition was not confined to idle chatter. It sought to assassinate the tyrant and to liberate France from him. In 1636 Gaston and the Duc de Soissons decided to have Richelieu killed by their men in the middle of his headquarters. The details of the attempt were agreed, but at the last moment Gaston refused to give the signal.

The royal house, the great families, and the religious faction were not alone in condemning the cardinal's policies. Those in official positions, and in particular the magistrates, knew that Richelieu handled them with care but that he had no love for them: he disliked their spirit of independence and their formalism. They were aware that, if he could, he would suppress their privileges, including the paulette which was the most debatable of all. Parlement, therefore, decided to be difficult. If the royal court failed to respect the strict forms of the law, parlement refused to register. The king would then be obliged to ignore its deliberations. At times he was also led to relieve counsellors of their duties and to exile them to the provinces. On each such occasion their esprit de corps was stronger than their awareness of the requirements of the state, and parlement would side with its more turbulent members against the authority of the court.

The opposition of the parlement to the decisions of the cardinal emerged mainly when it was a matter of new taxation or the creation of new officers, because the more of the latter that were created the less value remained in the existing judicial duties.

The doctrine of Les Politiques

Richelieu had not only imparted to French policy a measure of firmness and coherence unknown in previous governments.[2] His career was also distinguished by the fact that it consisted of something more than a series of decisions imposed by circumstances. It saw the implementation of a systematic doctrine. Henry IV had not possessed a coherent political theory. He had contented himself with resolving difficulties as they arose and recurred, thereby creating an equilibrium that was forever threatened. On the other hand, Richelieu had a firm doctrine on the state, its function, and the extent of its competence. At the very least he acted as if he had such a doctrine, and he supported writers and publicists who expounded it.

He did not have to invent this doctrine. It had been developed in the preceding century by thinkers whom their enemies called 'les Politiques'. It was the counterpart of the theory of the reason of state elaborated by the Italians. As early as 1627 a *Recueil de Lettres* published by a group of writers[3] extolled the merits of the concept of the reason of state, demanded that everyone should align himself with the state and act in accordance with its needs, and that in general all energies should be bent on serving the state. The years that followed saw the development of a literary movement which expounded the same themes. One can understand how a writer of the religious faction could, in 1637, speak of *statolatrie.*[4] It was, he said, 'the name which it was best and most proper' to apply to that sect. It was composed of men who adulated what the ancients called the City. The latter was the only deity these 'Politiques' recognised.

To understand the scandal aroused at that time by the doctrine of the state one has to remember that political notions until then had been essentially of a theological character.

Received opinion believed that the end of human society was to accomplish God's will, that it was on the authority of God that leaders exercised their power, that royal power was akin to that of the father of a family, and that it was founded in the divine order of things. More explicitly, it was the *ordo christianus* which had to be brought about in the Catholic states of Europe. This Christian order was consequently thought of as being founded in the pope and in the emperor, the latter being the heir of Charlemagne.

Nothing of this thesis remained in the doctrine of the state which was taking root in France at this time with the approval of Richelieu. The state was said to have only terrestrial ends. Its task is to safeguard the terrestrial interests of the nation, public peace, the development of commerce, the increase of prosperity, and the independence and prestige of the kingdom in relation to other countries. As one historian has put it, the state appears in the literature inspired by the policies of the cardinal as a rational and secular creation designed to defend and promote the terrestrial interests of its members.

The doctrine was far-reaching; it did not just exclude theological considerations, it also brushed aside the views of the humanist tradition on natural rights. It did not admit that there exists an eternal and universal law, over and above particular laws, which could constitute the foundation of justice and injustice and which would thus be superior to positive laws and the decisions of heads of state. The noble doctrine of Erasmus had recently been the inspiration of *De jure belli at pacis* by Grotius, and the author, like his book, was greatly revered by the Paris humanists.[5] The doctrine professed by the writers who promoted the cause of Richelieu either ignored this political philosophy or expressly combated it. The interest of the state was for them the supreme law. Thus, since de Thou did not report what he knew of Cinq-Mars' plot, he was guilty and deserved to die. The excuse of the law of friendship is meaningless in this context.

Mazarin

Richelieu had been ill for a long time. He died on 2 December 1642, and Louis XIII survived him by only five months. The new king, Louis XIV, was still a child, aged only seven and the regency was entrusted to the widow of Louis XIII. She put the government into the hands of Mazarin, who had been one of the ablest of Richelieu's collaborators.[6] He did not conceive the ends and means of politics in a way that was, in principle, different from his predecessor's. But he thought it cleverer to use more subtle means to gain his ends, and to wear down his opponents through the exercise of patience. Above all, he thought he could win over his enemies by making concessions to them. It soon became evident that these tactics were of no avail.

Mazarin emptied the Bastille of the political prisoners whom the preceding régime had put there without bothering to have them tried. He allowed the exiles to return from London and Brussels and these people filled Paris with their ferment. They belonged to the upper reaches of the nobility, and proceeded to show the same political ineptitude that they had proved so abundantly to possess in the past. The Rohans, the Vendômes, the Longuevilles, the Bouillons fought among themselves, quarrelled over silly points of etiquette or about the tabourets, and calmly planned armed revolt each time the state appeared to resist their demands. They remembered nostalgically the days of the first regency when a few threats were enough to draw from Marie de Médicis enormous sums of money and the promise of the dismissal of a government. The desire to exploit the weakness of the state was in any case the only point on which these nobles could agree, and on which they were not disposed to quarrel.

Unhappily for the nation the royal officers, particularly the parlement of Paris, were equally opposed to any kind of collaboration with the ministers. There was no lack of good excuses for resisting them. The financial edicts did not spare the officers. They also knew that the government worked hand in glove with the financiers, and that the latter could without difficulty pillage the country's treasury. They put up such strong opposition that the court was often forced to yield. Most of the time they obtained concessions in which public opinion saw so many successes against tyranny. The people of Paris followed the debates of parlement with passionate attention.

At the beginning of 1648 the conflict between the court and the sovereign courts became extremely acute. In April Mazarin wanted to have an edict passed which would have hit them hard. Parlement refused to recognise it. It thus gained the support of the magistrates of the Cour des Comptes, the Cour des Aides, and the Grand Conseil, that is the bodies most essential to the monarchy. They all met in one assembly, and on 19 June 1648 they drew up a form of manifesto which demanded that the freedom of the individual be guaranteed, that parlement should necessarily have to confirm fiscal edicts, and that the intendants, who were in the eyes of the country symbols of tyranny, be disbanded.

Mazarin pretended to agree. He was waiting for news from the army. When he knew that Condé had smashed the Spaniards at Lens (20 August 1648) he ordered the arrest of some of the members of parlement. The most popular of these agitators was counsellor Broussel (26 August 1648).[7] When the people of Paris heard of this they filled their city with barricades. The coadjutor of Paris, who was later to be Cardinal de Retz, openly encouraged the unrest. Most of the members of parlement did not hide their sympathy for those involved in it.

Once again Mazarin retreated. He was waiting for the rainy season to interrupt the war on the frontier. He then ordered Condé to bring his troops closer to Paris. Condé detested parlement and the great families. He despised the people. He showed a preference for strong and brutally applied power. He himself was universally feared and detested. As he approached Paris its people rose up in rebellion. The regent, fearing for her very life, fled during the night and with the young king sought refuge at Saint-Germain-en-Laye (5 January 1649).

Condé then organised the blockade of Paris. Within the capital parlement, the princes and the municipal authorities flapped about and revealed their inability to do anything. The people of Paris were beginning to laugh at them.[8] Then the inhabitants of the capital became hungry, and they forced their leaders to open the gates of the city (30 March 1649). The royal government, instead of hitting back hard, tried measures of pacification, but the habit of indiscipline had taken root. Condé humiliated Mazarin and it was to be feared that he might try to usurp the throne. Everyone was against him. When

Mazarin realised that he could do it without risk, he had Condé arrested (18 January 1650). He then relied on the princes. But they, in their turn, intended to have Mazarin pay a heavy price for their support, and they united against him. The cardinal had to flee to Germany (February 1651). Before leaving, however, he had taken care to open the doors of Condé's prison himself. He knew very well that Condé could never come to an understanding with the princes.

His predictions were soon confirmed. Condé retired to Guyenne and raised an army there. Mazarin was then able to return to France. He himself raised an army and entrusted its command to Turenne. After a series of encounters the two armies met under the walls of Paris, at the Porte Saint-Antoine (2 July 1652). Condé would have been badly defeated had it not been for the intervention of Mademoiselle. She ordered the cannon of the ramparts to fire on the royal army; then the gates of Paris were opened and Condé installed himself in Paris as its master.[9]

The rabble was with him. The bourgeoisie was hostile to him. He had his partisans murder some of the most justly esteemed worthies at the Hôtel de Ville (4 July 1652) – an act which dishonoured him and finally lost him his cause. These horrible events finally opened the eyes of the French. The good citizens of Paris united to put an end to such senseless violence and on 21 October 1652, the young king entered his capital in triumph.

It marked the end of the Fronde. Condé found refuge in the Spanish Netherlands. Cardinal de Retz was arrested without any fuss from the people of Paris (December 1652). Mazarin, who had remained on the fringe of these developments, then saw that he could return, and he openly took over the government again (February 1653). Some local resistance in the Bordeaux region was quickly overcome (August 1653).

The Fronde had thus been conquered. Historians still see in its defeat the victory of order over anarchy, without any nuance or qualification. It is indeed true that the poor quality of the leaders of the Fronde and their divisions had finally brought about chaos. But it is much more important to see beyond these lamentable convulsions, and recognise the deeper reasons that were their cause. The people of Paris had risen not because they wanted a revolution but because they saw their traditions threatened. For them it was the tradition of the kingdom that power should be in the hands of the king. But, since the death of Henry IV, power had been handed over to some all-powerful minister or favourite. It was also a tradition that the lives of Frenchmen should be protected against arbitrarily exercised power by means of a whole corpus of precise legal provisions, for example, the privileges of various social groups, of towns and provinces, all of which made up a system of justice that could be known with precision. Richelieu, in the name of the interest of the state, had begun to whittle away these privileges; Mazarin had continued this process. Publicists in the pay of those in power maintained that the prince had the right of life and death over his subjects and the right of property over what they owned.[10] In practice, royal governments had handed over the kingdom to the interests of the financiers. The luxury in which the latter lived contrasted scandalously with the impoverishment of the rest of the country. A good deal of the political literature of the period of the Fronde denounced the financiers, traders, and individual businessmen by name, and cited the extent of their fortunes as well as the size of their misappropriations.

Things were seen in a different light after the defeat of the Fronde. Certainly no Frenchman still thought of an uprising. The lesson had been too severe, and the people knew that it had nothing to gain from Condé, or the princes, or the parlements. As one informant wrote, no one wanted 'to hear any more about any kind of unrest'. No doubt Mazarin remained a despised figure, but public opinion detested even more those who had been responsible for the most recent upheavals.

Nevertheless there were many among the bourgeoisie and the enlightened classes who continued to be faithful to the spirit that had inspired the early phases of the Paris Fronde. They were convinced that parlement was the guarantor of the safety of persons and property; they believed that Frenchmen were born free, and that while despotism might well be suitable for Italy or Spain it was not so for France. They detested the financiers. They countered the Machiavellian doctrine of the court with the maxims of what they called a Christian policy. The most respected personality among them was Pomponne de Bellièvre.[11] But some members of the old nobility, for instance the Duchesse de Chevreuse, who did not base their case on the triumphant progress of the financiers, thought back nostalgically to the Fronde and did not give up their desire for revenge.

Mazarin took the country in hand again, without violence. He introduced a number of reforms which, though small, were of decisive importance. The nobility was told that it could no longer hold assemblies, the intendants were brought back. Parlement lost its right to discuss financial edicts.

If there remained one weak spot in the régime it was in the financial sphere. Mazarin was unable to bring any kind of order to it. Foucquet, the chief of the intendants, was allowed to do as he saw fit, and Foucquet had recourse to all kinds of expedients in order to procure ready cash. He created jobs, tampered with the currency or, as we would say today, introduced a series of devaluations. He sold the king's lands. Chiefly, however, he relied on the issuing of loans and bonds. But since the state was a very bad risk it had to borrow at disastrously high rates of interest.[12]

For these reasons Foucquet needed the financiers. They knew that he would refuse them nothing. Soon they constituted an extremely rich and powerful social class, a new bourgeoisie that had nothing in common with the old, traditional bourgeoisie. Its members loved spending money, adored ostentation and luxury. Foucquet himself set them an example. His Château de Vaux was famous for its display of regal magnificence. But his contemporaries were not all impressed. They noted the decadence of the great families, comparing the decline of the Hôtel de Chevreuse and the Hôtel de Soissons with the splendours of Amelot de Bisseuil, La Bazinière, Monnerot, and many others.[13]

It was the wars continuing abroad that absorbed the resources of the state. The war with the Empire had ceased with the treaties of Westphalia in 1648, but Spain had not given up fighting. The operations dragged on, punctuated sometimes by victories, sometimes by defeats. There was fighting all along the border, from Dunkirk to Catalonia. Mazarin, however, wanted peace, and this was finally signed on the banks of the

Bidassoa (7 November 1659). France could consider herself victorious since she acquired Artois, Roussillon, and a number of towns in the Spanish Netherlands. To mark the end of the old conflict between the French and Spanish monarchies, it was decided to arrange a marriage between the Infanta Marie-Thérèse and Louis XIV.

Louis XIV: the glorious period

Mazarin died on 9 March 1660. Louis XIV was then only twenty-two, but he already had clear-cut ideas about the policies he was going to follow. He knew that the French detested government by favourites. He was determined to govern himself. He gathered around him three men, Foucquet, Le Tellier, and Hugues de Lionne, but he relied chiefly on Colbert, whom Mazarin had recommended to him. Colbert advised that, above all else, the finances had to be put straight. This implied the eclipse of Foucquet. The *fêtes* at Vaux (16 August 1661) succeeded in arousing the irritation of the king. On 5 September 1661 Foucquet was arrested at Nantes. At the trial the judges knew that the king wanted the death sentence, but the case dragged on, having begun in March 1662 it did not finish until December 1664. Foucquet defended himself well. The sentence he received was only exile, but by an arbitrary decision of the king he was sent to Pignerol, where he died in 1680.

The period which then opened was one in which the king himself governed; it was one of the most brilliant of the French monarchy. It was marked by victorious wars and conquests, by a policy of prestige which made itself felt all over Europe. Within the kingdom it was a period which saw the creation of a modern administration and an extraordinary expansion of industry and commerce.

Louis XIV wanted war.[14] He wanted it to be simple and overwhelming. At a time when Europe was disarmed he provided himself as fast as he could with all the arms he could get. Then, on unlikely judicial pretexts, his armies entered Flanders (24 May 1667) and quickly occupied several towns. The following year they invaded Franche-Comté and conquered it without meeting serious resistance. Peace was signed at Aix-la-Chapelle and a large part of Flanders remained in the hands of the king (May 1668). These conquests had been made without any real shedding of blood, and French opinion applauded them. Louis XIV then decided to strike at Holland. Here, too, he made careful and unhurried preparations. In May 1672, 120,000 well-equipped men proceeded to the Rhine. The river was crossed without difficulty on 12 June 1672, in the presence of some Dutch militiamen who took to their heels. It seemed as if the Netherlands would be conquered within a few days, but the States decided to impede the progress of the French army by inundating the country.

This was the end of easy conquests. The states of Western Europe were beginning to worry about the increasing power of France. The Empire and Brandenburg formed a coalition and Spain was preparing to join them. In 1674 the whole of Germany made common cause with them. The war lasted until 1678. Finally the belligerents resigned themselves to the prospects of peace. It was signed at Nymwegen in 1678.

Louis XIV could be satisfied with the results of the war, but he was dreaming of other conquests, of a kind that would not require military campaigns. In the midst of peacetime he began to annex (*réunir*) towns in Alsace, Lorraine and Barrois. Thus menaced, Europe decided to band together to put a stop to these constant violations of its traditional frontiers. The emperor, Spain, Sweden, and Holland formed an alliance in 1682. To break it up Louis XIV signed, with the empire on the one hand and Spain on the other, the diplomatic instruments of what was to become known as the truce of Ratisbon (15 August 1684). This was the high water mark of French power in the seventeenth century, the culmination of the period of glorious conquests. But soon came longer and more exhausting wars, and they brought the country moments of despair.

The victorious wars were proof of the new strength of the French monarchy. They were the result of the now disciplined concentration of power, the introduction of order into the administrative machine, the development of the manufacturing industries, of dockyards, and of commerce.

With the active approval of the king, Colbert introduced into the administration a degree of order to which it had not been accustomed. At the top were the councils. There was the

Conseil d'En Haut composed only of the ministers gathered around the king. Then there was the Conseil des Dépêches presided over by the king, the Conseil des Finances, of which Colbert was the chief inspiration but also presided over by the king, and the Conseil des Parties. Executive functions were exercised by four state secretaries, acting upon orders issued directly by the king. The sovereign courts were now merely institutions that carried out the wishes of the ministry.[15]

In the provinces, the intendants – created by Richelieu, abolished through pressure of the parlement only to be brought back by Mazarin – were the representatives of the central authority. There were still some governors who had been chosen from among the aristocracy, but real power was completely in the hands of the intendants. Like the king, they were universally competent. They were, as their title stated, 'intendants de justice, police et finances'.[16]

The new, modern state that Colbert was fashioning with the support of the king did not merely curtail or suppress the political competence of the various institutions of ancient France, such as the sovereign courts and the municipalities. Since the beginning of the reign the power of the financiers had been broken too. Foucquet was not the only one to have been hit. The Cour de Justice had imposed enormous fines on those who had profited from Mazarin's régime. In addition, Colbert had dealt severely with the rentiers.

By this time, even the world of business and the prosperous bourgeoisie had taken fright. Moreover, an economic crisis had broken out which lasted a number of years. The prices of goods were rising. The bourgeoisie was heard protesting against arbitrary government. It was being said that the government was treating the French not as Christians but as Turks.[17] Irritation even gained a foothold at court.

As time went on this kind of opposition ceased, because the government showed that it knew its business. The French recognised that the new administration was acquiring stature, and from this moment order finally prevailed. Moreover, a new impetus was being imparted to industry. Joint stock companies, or 'companies' as they were then simply called, were being formed with the careful backing of the government. Factories were replacing small workshops, indeed real consortia were coming into existence. Some of them, particularly in the manufacture of cloth, were composed of a number of subscribers drawn from among the most powerful businessmen; one had brought in a million livres. It was not unusual to find factories employing several hundred workers.[18]

At the same time the government actively encouraged the creation of companies to promote trade with distant countries. For example, the East India Company and the Near East Company were intended by Colbert to bring about a considerable increase in the prosperity of the kingdom. It was through his determination that the French came to understand the forms of modern economic life.

Colbert could see well enough that his policies were meeting with all kinds of resistance. He tried to overcome these, but he was faced with the difficulties created by his master's war and prestige policy which cost an enormous amount of money. In the end he had to have recourse to the very expedients he had condemned when Foucquet had used them: the creation of new posts for cash payments, more selling of royal land and the manipulation of the currency. The treasury had again fallen into debt. Colbert came to see that the king was no longer much interested in his views. His programme of large-scale economic activity, which was the very essence of his policy, could not be carried out in such circumstances. The subsidies which the policy required were either cut or abolished, while the entire resources of the state were devoted to war. All Colbert's energies had to be spent on dealing with the day-to-day difficulties of the treasury. On 6 September 1683 he died, and his death marked the end of an era in Louis XIV's reign.

Louis XIV: the end of the reign

The Ratisbon truce of 1684 had initially given the government the illusion that it had succeeded in imposing its hegemony upon a divided Europe. But it was only an illusion. The very next year the powers signed a treaty at Augsburg which, without actually saying so, constituted a defensive league against French encroachments. William of Orange in Holland and the Emperor Leopold in Vienna were the chief architects of this policy.

It was from this moment that, until the end of the reign,

France found herself involved in a struggle which all but caused her downfall and which, at the very least, must be said to have put an end to the constant expansion she had known since the days of Richelieu. Victories and defeats followed each other without providing any decisive results. In France the misery of the people worsened. There was no money. Bad harvests brought the country to the verge of famine. The financial deficit was enormous. Louis XIV wished to find a way out of this disastrous situation. At last a peace conference was convened at Ryswyck and peace was signed (September and October 1697). Louis XIV gave up a number of towns his armies had occupied and made important concessions to the coalition. But the real victor of this war was England. She could be pleased with herself. She now held the balance of power in Europe.

But the peace France needed so badly only lasted four years. On 1 November 1700 the death of Charles II of Spain created the conditions for a new and more terrible war: he had died childless. By his will he appointed the Duke of Anjou his universal heir. The latter was his grand-nephew, but also the grandson of Louis XIV. The whole of Europe recognised the danger of being confronted with an enormous power founded upon the combined resources of France, Spain and the Spanish possessions in America. While it is true that Charles II had tried to prevent, through an explicit clause in his will, that the crowns of France and Spain should ever be upon a single head, this was not enough to reassure those who foresaw an excessive increase in the power of France.

On 15 May 1702 England, Holland and the emperor simultaneously declared war on France. It was not long before other states joined the coalition. The war was waged on the plains of the north, in Italy, and in Spain. Although the armies of France had a number of successes, the overwhelming defeat of Hochstaedt was a tremendous blow to French military power (13 August 1704). After the battle of Malplaquet (1709), the coalition was able to contemplate the invasion of France and an advance on Paris. Louis XIV had only the army of de Villars to put against them. It so happened that the latter discovered a weak spot in the ranks of his enemies, attacked it and broke through at Denain. That brought him a victory which was the salvation of France (24 July 1712). Negotiations had already been under way with the coalition for some time, but they had been protracted. The victory of Denain made sure of peace. The treaty of Utrecht was signed on 14 April 1713 between France, England, and Holland. Emperor Leopold concluded peace a little later through the treaty of Rastadtt (March 1714).

France had escaped what looked like imminent catastrophe.

The country came out of the war profoundly shaken. The French had lost confidence. Songs were to be heard which spared neither the king nor his court nor his ministers. Even at Versailles and in Paris society, people were prepared to voice the opinion that such a large number of failures could only be explained by the dreadful crowd that the king had chosen to have around him, time-servers and flatterers to a man. Among the generals it was the inept Villeroy who was quoted and lampooned, and among the ministers it was Chamillart; though certainly honest, he was very narrow and unimaginative. In any case, it was said reproachfully of the king that as he grew older he was ever more inclined to decide things for himself. After the death of Louvois, Louis XIV had got into the habit of dictating or even writing important letters himself to the commanders of the army, and of drawing up in his study the plans for operations on faraway battlefields. He had taken over responsibility for the entire administration and for policy. It was an impossible task, and a method which explained the many failures in diplomacy, in war and in the internal affairs of the kingdom.[19]

The financial situation, already dangerous by the time Colbert died, had become frightening. Between 1700 and 1706, for example, expenditure was well in excess of one thousand million livres while receipts barely reached 350 million. From 1708 to 1715 expenditure amounted to four times the receipts. At the death of Louis XIV the state's debt had risen to the unprecedented figure of two thousand million livres. In the circumstances the government relied on sheer opportunism. From 1701 the treasury issued money bills (billets de monnaie). From 1704 these were issued with increasing frequency. They carried seven-and-a-half per cent interest. But since the state was bad at paying out they quickly lost part of their value. By the end of 1706 they had depreciated by fifty-four per cent.[20]

It is not surprising that the French, who witnessed these failures of the king's policies, and were seriously affected by them in their standard of living, had lost that heady feeling of self-confidence which they had enjoyed during the first fifteen years of the government of Louis XIV. The mood of the nation had changed. Observers of the period tell us that the French were becoming gloomy and distrustful. Ménage said, 'Depuis trente ans, on ne rit plus ici que du bout des lèvres.' The Genoese Marana used a whole letter of his *Espion turc* to depict the disappearance of the old gaiety. This feeling of gloom even reached those in positions of power. Le Verrier wrote to the Duc de Noailles, 'Il me semble que tout se décourage dans ce pays.' He also said, 'Tous nos gens gardent un morne silence.' Madame de Maintenon herself admitted it. She wrote, in 1708, 'Tout est affliction d'esprit dans les affaires temporelles, dans celles de l'Eglise. . . .'[21] Later, in fact as early as the time of Voltaire, the French were to forget these sad days. They wanted to remember only the prestigious parts of the reign. But it is the duty of history not to forget.

This period was no doubt marked by the consequences of hateful policies, by a despotism which stifled the spirit. But these obvious vices of the régime must not hide from us the profound transformation which the nation was then undergoing. While it is true that there were some members in the king's entourage whose vision was not outstanding, there were others who laboured to create, down to the smallest detail, an administration befitting a modern state. The most powerful personality among these was the lieutenant general of police d'Argenson. He was entirely free from any prejudice or preconceptions, but was an extremely efficient organiser. He had no love for the parlement. In Jansenism he saw the germs of an opposition which could become dangerous for the state. He was brutal. His duty, as he saw it, was not to judge the measures decided upon by the king but simply to carry them through. He had made the police an impressive instrument of power. It found out for him what people were saying and doing, and even provided him with the names of individuals entering Paris and with their addresses in the capital. Intelligent Frenchmen were able to distinguish between the kind of stupid despotism that tried to impose upon them dogmas and bulls, and enlightened despotism whose sole aim was the well-being of the state, i.e. order and reason. The philosopher Fontenelle sang the praises of d'Argenson, who fully deserved them.

Moreover, the progress and even the crises of the industries that Colbert had created, the ever more complex commercial operations, the issue of money bills (billets de monnaie), the various kinds of loans to which the government had recourse, all these gave to the economic sphere a degree of importance it had never had before. New areas were thus opened up for the French, aroused their interest, and gave them food for thought. Economic questions now also found their way into literature because French society was just beginning to understand their importance for the future.

There was at that time, in Paris, a circle in which there was a clear awareness of this new reality, and which even gave one hope that the French government would one day adapt itself to its exigencies. It was centred on the Palais-Royal. Historians, philosophers and economists met there in the presence of the Duc d'Orléans, the man who, on the death of Louis XIV, would take over the regency. Paris referred to the circle as the 'Orléans party'. It was known that its members completely condemned the errors, stupidity and violence of the régime, but that they wanted strong government against the rather tentative approach of parlement and the egoism of business. They did not hide their admiration for England, whose régime had just proved its efficacy in time of war. It seemed reasonable to believe that French policy would change after the death of the old king.

Changes in society at the beginning of the century

The nobility. When Henry IV began his reign, forty years of wars and unrest had wrought havoc not only with the political structure of the state; the social structure had also been deeply affected and its balance changed.

At the summit of French society were the great families; they came immediately below the king. There were only a few of them, and among the most important were the Rohans, the

Retz, the Guises, the Nevers, and, nearer the throne, the princes of the blood, the Condés and the Soissons. These families were a survival of feudal times. They possessed vast lands on which their authority counted for more than that of the king. Their power was enhanced by the fact that the provincial 'governments' were in their hands too. The Duc de Montmorency was, to all intents and purposes, viceroy of Languedoc. The Condés had been given the government of Burgundy by successive French kings, which meant that, in this province, not a single office nor any kind of responsibility was given to anyone who was not bound up with that family and tied to it in terms of the utmost dependence.

It had not occurred to Henry IV to change this order of things. He had been content with keeping the great families docile. After his death they soon brought back disorder to the kingdom. The history of France between 1610 and 1624 is dominated by their agitation and unrest. Neither Concini nor Luynes managed to subdue them. France had to wait for Richelieu before these feudal lords could be brought to submit to the will of the central authority.

Below the great families came the nobility. It had been in the forefront of the military campaigns, and it had been ruined by them. According to the testimony of a contemporary, the nobility lost almost half its lands, which were bought up by the bourgeoisie. Moreover, in the course of these wars, the nobility had become used to habits of which it was later unable to rid itself. Whether they had been fighting for Henry of Navarre or for the League or in the Protestant ranks, they shared and indulged a taste for brutality and violence. They missed the life of the military encampments. And it was this bellicose nobility which grumbled about 'la paix qui l'empêchait de mettre au jour ce qu'elle avait de bon dans l'âme'.[22] Their behaviour was generally deplorable. L'Estoile wrote in 1610, 'Notre jeune noblesse d'aujourd'hui est aussi mal embouchée qu'elle est sotte et malapprise.'[23] They were quite incapable of doing anything useful and spent their days in gambling houses and inns.

They also liked to give themselves military airs. Even when they were going about on foot they insisted on wearing boots and, of course, they never went without their swords. They were particularly pleased with themselves when they were beating up some peasant or bourgeois. Mlle de Gournay summed up the characteristics of the nobleman of her time in one word: 'C'est un fou.'[24]

The nobility of this period was, on the whole, uncultured and completely indifferent to things of the spirit. In fact, these pugnacious noblemen actually bragged about not knowing anything, since they were convinced 'que la science et l'étude affaiblissent le courage et rendraient la générosité lâche et poltrone.' The moral law amounted in their eyes to 'points of honour'. This they pushed to ludicrous extremes. The duel, introduced into France from Italy, had become a favourite pursuit. On the slightest pretexts swords were drawn, and every year saw the stupid death of a great number of these men.

The bourgeoisie looked upon this brutish nobility with a mixture of indignation and disdain. One of them, Charles Sorel, wrote in his novel *Francion* in 1623: 'La plupart des seigneurs sont plus chevaux que leurs chevaux mêmes.'[25] He showed them as spending their days throwing dice and, as he put it, 'à remuer trois petits os carrés sur une table'.[26] He accused them of knowing nothing and gave the example of one of the greatest noblemen in the kingdom 'qui peut-etre ne savait pas lire'. This was precisely what Tallemant des Réaux alleged of the High Constable Montmorency.[27]

These noblemen, who despised intelligence, would happily have demanded all the offices in the state, without apparently realising that these might require some measure of ability and certain intellectual qualities. But they came up against Henry IV and his administration. The reconstruction of France, which was his aim, was accomplished without them.

The rise of the bourgeoisie. It was thus the bourgeoisie which, gradually, became the most active and influential class in the nation. But the term is very imprecise and covers a variety of social strata. At the top were the presidents and counsellors of the sovereign courts, i.e. of parlement, the Cour des Comptes, the Cour des Aides, the Grand Conseil, as well as persons appointed to official posts. In fact, for the most highly placed among these the term bourgeois is inappropriate. They really constituted a new nobility, the noblesse de robe. An important innovation for this class was that, during the reign of Henry IV, a royal proclamation instituted what was called the paulette (1604). This transformed the posts and offices held by these people into a kind of personal property, which could be handed down to the widows and heirs of the royal officers.[28]

Thus a new social class came into being. Veritable dynasties of magistrates were created, and it is at this time that the Phélipeaux, the Séguiers, the De Mesmes and the Daguesseaus rose to a rank that was in no way inferior to that of the old aristocracy. This new class was not content merely to bask in the prestige, and carry out the duties, that its position brought with it. It also rapidly acquired considerable financial power. During the Fronde it became evident just how enormous were the fortunes which a large number of members of the parlements and officers of the sovereign courts had amassed.[29]

This class, with its bourgeois roots, on the whole retained the moral and intellectual traditions of the old bourgeoisie. Most of the members of the parlements were very cultured men, educated in the colleges. They knew their Greek and Latin authors. Their education contrasted with the general lack of culture of the nobility and so they constituted the intelligent and active part of the nation. But in the course of the century the hereditary character of the paulette was to have undesirable consequences for the economic development of France. It did not merely bestow upon the office-holders a political importance of the first order. It also encouraged the French to invest their fortunes in the acquisition of offices rather than in commercial and industrial development. The moment a bourgeois had acquired sufficient money he bought himself an office. This would provide him with an honourable rank in society and ensure that his daughter would make a good marriage. Of course such offices were expensive, but it was up to the bourgeois to see that they paid. When, in later days, Colbert tried to turn France into a manufacturing and commercial state, he came up against these inveterate habits which hardly made up for a spirit of enterprise.

Below these counsellors of the sovereign courts there was the vast crowd of lawyers, petty judges, prosecutors, minor palace officials, and court clerks. Still within the bourgeoisie, there were also other social groups; doctors and college heads, for example. There were also the rich merchants who were concentrated in the area around the rue Saint-Denis. As a group, these middle-rank bourgeois were very conscious of their importance and of their traditions, as well as of the unique position they occupied within the kingdom. They despised the nobility because it was uncultured and useless. They detested the parlementaires because they thought them haughty and class conscious, and perhaps still more because these officials were fast accumulating wealth, largely at their own expense. They also bitterly criticised successive governments because the burden of taxation fell mainly on their shoulders. But, more than any other social class, they were deeply attached to the political, moral, and religious traditions of the nation. They might speak slightingly of ministers, but they never questioned the authority of the king. They put their confidence in the king for the simple reason that he had restored order and peace in the kingdom.

The people. At the bottom of the scale, below the bourgeoisie, came the people. In the seventeenth century the word was ambiguous, failing to distinguish between the *populus* and the *plebs* of the Romans. The word could be applied to the shop assistants and lackeys, or to the thousands of rogues who were milling around outside the Hôtel de Bourgogne and, according to their contemporaries, never stopped talking, whistling, and shouting. In order to escape from this embarrassing ambiguity, terms like 'le menu peuple' or 'le petit peuple' were employed. Charles Sorel referred to these classes quite simply as rabble ('cette racaille'). Their reading was confined to the little books that were being noisily offered on the Pont-Neuf for a sol. They crowded into the theatres. Though tragedy was beyond them, they enjoyed themselves at the farces and at Bruscambille's *Prologues*.[30]

Changes in Richelieu's time

It was not only the political life of the kingdom which was affected by Richelieu's accession to the highest office. The cardinal also had precise ideas about society, and these he intended to put into practice. He wished to restore the respect for social hierarchy. In his view, society was constituted by classes and bodies with clear divisions between them. For him, political order was impossible if the obscure, ignorant, and docile masses were not directed by an élite that had a vocation for giving orders.

This élite consisted, first of all, of the old nobility. For, though Richelieu was determined to break the anarchic resistance of the great families, he liked the nobility. He felt he belonged to it and was proud of it. The significance of this attitude must be seen against the fact that the nobility had fallen into complete disrepute in the preceding century. Richelieu paid no heed to the ignorance and brutishness of many of its members. He put his confidence into the nobility as a whole, its sense of honour and its courage in war. He asked it to be a good servant to the state.

The class of royal officers he did not like at all. He detested the system by which offices could be bought and which gave them so much importance, for he knew that they conferred upon their holders almost total independence from royal authority. He also knew that behind big words like 'fundamental laws', 'the ancient liberties of the French', 'justice' and 'respect for rights', these people were in fact defending their own interests and money.

At the same time, however, Richelieu called upon men of humble origins to help him in his task of organising the kingdom. It was mainly from them that he drew his intendants. He knew that he could expect all he needed from such personnel: it was highly cultured, had studied law, was trained in the Roman tradition and had acquired intellectual discipline.

Thus, a new society was coming into being. It was based on service to the state, military or civil, on intellectual attainment, and on birth. There has probably been no other period in French history during which the distinction between the élite and the masses was so clearly marked. Writers spoke with lofty disdain of 'cet animal à tant de têtes qu'on appelle peuple', of that 'animal stupide' that has 'pour toutes connaissances que les arts mécaniques'. Social position, moral worth, and intellectual ability seemed to them inseparable. Abbé d'Aubignac wrote the following lines which, though they may strike us as extravagant, sum up exactly the general outlook of this society:

'Dans ce royaume, les personnes ou de naissance, ou nourries parmi les Grands, ne s'entretiennent que de sentiments généreux, et ne se portent qu'à de hauts desseins, ou par les mouvements de la vertu, ou par les emportements de l'ambition.'[31]

The increasing social importance of the financiers

After Richelieu's death the position accorded to the financiers significantly modified the balance of French society. Of course the various social groups continued to coexist, and it might have seemed that they retained their respective importance. In fact, however, it was the financiers who set the tone, especially after the Fronde.

Whatever the pamphleteers might say, it was no longer true that the financiers all had their origins among the lackeys. Many of them were cultured and had a taste for literature and the other arts.[32] Foucquet was a true patron of the arts and was emulated by others of his kind. If one looks merely at the Protestant financiers there was Nicolas Rambouillet who was a knowledgeable collector. The Tallemant family had two of its members in the Académie Française. La Sablière's poetry was much appreciated by high society. His wife, Mme de la Sablière, knew Greek and Latin, mathematics and astronomy, and was La Fontaine's patron and friend. The women in Mlle de Scudéry's set bore the names of financiers. There were the Cornuels, the Legendres, the Robineaus, all of them families known for the place they occupied in the business world and for their very large fortunes.

The take-over of French society by the financiers encountered violent opposition, coming from many quarters. The old aristocracy, discredited as well as economically diminished by the Fronde, witnessed with indignation the rise of the financial upstarts. The feelings of the parliamentarians were mixed. Several of them had entered into partnerships with businessmen. A polemical piece published during the Fronde condemned them for it, listed those involved, and detailed the operations in which they were working hand-in-glove with the tax farmers. But most of the parliamentarians had avoided this kind of opprobrium. Though they had given up fighting the régime that was run by the financiers, they continued to oppose it behind the scenes. It was thus because he could rely on the support of a large body of public opinion, and especially on the Duchesse de Chevreuse, that Colbert managed to engineer the downfall of Foucquet. As the French saw it, the financiers were 'les sangsues de l'Etat'.

The evolution of society under Louis XIV

The régime set up by Louis XIV made interference by social groups impossible and did away with their political pretensions. It is true that the nobility was showered with honours, but this was conditional upon its being content with haunting the ante-chambers at Versailles and begging for posts and pensions. Parlement had lost the right of protest and was reduced to recording the king's wishes. Official posts remained hereditary but no longer conferred any power upon their holders.

However, once the death of Colbert had opened the era of endless wars, the great harmony that had been achieved for a while began to disappear. While the mass of Frenchmen – provincial noblemen, the bourgeoisie, and the people – were going through difficult times or experiencing actual hardship, the class of financiers, businessmen, and suppliers to the army once again began to concentrate the wealth of the nation in its own hands.

On the other hand, the policies initiated by Colbert were beginning to reveal some of their long-term effects. The French discovered ways to prosperity which their ancestors had not known about. Everybody went in for 'business'.[33] There were great ladies at court who made money by establishing contacts between highly placed civil servants and men in the world of business, and made a veritable profession of it. Good bourgeois women unashamedly ran gaming houses. At the end of the reign French society might seem to have retained its traditional structure. In fact, it had undergone a complete transformation.

3

Literature and politics

Before Richelieu

The literature of the beginning of the seventeenth century was much more directly related to political life than it is today. The function now fulfilled by the daily and weekly press was then performed by writers, more particularly by the poets. It was they who celebrated births and marriages in the royal family, and who gave the public moving accounts of royal sicknesses and deaths. The most considerable poets of the reign of Henry IV, Desportes, Bertaut, Du Perron and Malherbe, did precisely that. Part of their work was the result of orders from the court. They were called 'les poètes du Louvre'. It was quite proper that such writing should be rewarded with cash payments and pensions.[1]

This form of official, royally-inspired literature brought with it the high degree of exaggeration that we find in the odes, epithalamia, and funeral verses of the period. At a time when social privilege was in the process of reasserting itself without however corresponding to any spontaneous feeling or respect among the people, when it had in fact to be imposed by force, it was natural for the poets to adopt a tone of frenzied exaggeration. Kings were depicted as gods on earth, and the great families as demi-gods. The smallest success of the royal armies was likened to the greatest exploits in history. Such official poetry did not express, nor did it seek to express, seriously held convictions. It exalted the virtues of royal favourites only to decry their vices after their death. Again, when the royal army, badly commanded by Luynes, failed to take Montauban, Malherbe turned defeat into actual triumph. But he knew all about the real value of Luynes; an epigram he wrote for his friends proves it.[2] Nor was he alone in pushing hyperbole to the point of absurdity. Théophile de Viau, for instance, spoke of the skirmish at Ponts-de-Cé as if it had been a great battle.[3]

The government did not neglect the poets: it used them. But it cannot be said that it encouraged them. Formerly, during the reign of the Valois, the kings of France had imitated the princes of the Italian Renaissance and had adopted the role of enlightened and generous protectors of the humanities. This the French had not forgotten. They recalled the opulent benefits that had been bestowed upon Desportes and Bertaut. But since the beginning of the reign of Henry IV these generous habits had ceased. The king took no interest in the humanities; the revival of the state and its economic restoration were to him much more important considerations. When they were honest, the poets complained about this. They held the king's attitude responsible for the poor state in which literature found itself at that time. In a confidential note Cardinal Du Perron wrote: 'Le roi n'entend rien en la musique, ni en la poésie, et c'est pour cela que de son temps il n'y a personne qui y excelle.'[4]

Marie de Médicis later appeared to be returning to the generous policy of the previous century. But the chaos that surrounded the royal government and the pillaging of the treasury prevented the regular payment of such pensions as had been granted. In any case the revival of French literature was not merely a matter of distributing money. It was a difficult task, and when Richelieu took over the government he addressed himself to it from the start.

Richelieu's contribution

The cardinal had a personal interest in the humanities which does not seem to have been entirely due to political motives. He himself would gladly have written tragedies. But he was too preoccupied with other tasks, though he did manage at least to think up and draft what we would now call scenarios that were fairly full. For a number of years he gathered around himself five authors: Rotrou, L'Estoile, Corneille, Boisrobert and Colletet. He wanted them to write tragedies together. It is likely that he provided them with the plot, and each one of them was given the task of writing one act. It seems from what one contemporary has said that Richelieu himself went into considerable detail about how the feelings of his characters were to be portrayed, and that there was little left for the poets to do except the task of versification.[5]

Nevertheless, it must be admitted that the humanities were for Richelieu mainly a political instrument. Here, too, he followed the doctrine of the state that had preceded him, but which he pursued more energetically than any other politician of his period. The proponents of the theory of the state had duly noted that while politics is a matter of analysing and evaluating different forces in society, literature must be looked upon as one of these forces and consequently utilised. They talked about 'manutention des esprits'. They considered preaching, i.e. propaganda, a more potent force in government than the sword. The Italian Campanella talked about *la guerra literale*. Literature became a weapon in the wars of Europe.[6]

Richelieu took these ideas very far indeed. He established the equivalent of our press offices. He had criers selling books for a sol or eighteen deniers in the streets and squares. He made Père Joseph director of the *Mercure Français*. He introduced the weekly *Gazette*, whose editor, Théophraste Renaudot, was one of his trusted intimates. Indeed he himself wrote articles for it.

But he aimed higher. He wanted to use the best writers of his time to serve the best interests of the state. He appeared to have the highest regard for them and treated them with shows of courtesy that flattered them. He had a bright poet in his entourage, Abbé Boisrobert, whose unofficial job it was to keep open the links between Richelieu and the literary world.[7] He also regularly used the services of Chapelain, whose solid qualities he justly recognised. There were many more who were often to be seen in his company; for example Des Marests de Saint-Sorlin and D'Aubignac. They kept him informed of life in the literary world. Boisrobert in particular was useful in this respect, and he could thus come to the aid of writers by providing jobs and pensions. An old biographer of his quotes the names of twenty-six authors to whom he had granted pensions. We are assured that he annually spent 40,000 livres on pensions and grants.

Richelieu was aware of the prestige the best writers of the period were winning for the nation. It was for this reason that he aided many of them even when they were not working for him. But there is no doubt that the writers who worked to his orders and to support his policies, i.e. the publicists, were those who received the biggest rewards. This happened in the case of Hay du Chastelet, of Silhon and of Jean Sirmond, all of them forgotten today yet among the first members of the Académie Française. They had earned their honours through the services they had rendered the cardinal-minister.

Although he encouraged writers, gave them specific tasks and rewarded them for their services, Richelieu kept an eye on what went into the bookshops and, if necessary, struck hard. When he took over the government there was already in existence a body of decrees, statutes and regulations. In 1620 all these had actually been collected and printed in book form. They had their origins in the previous century and were the result of the determination of the monarchy to halt the progress of the Protestant heresy. Letters from Francis I had, in 1539, laid down the regulations for bookshops and printers. Since 1542, the entry of book parcels into Paris had been under strict control. An ordinance of the reign of Charles IX prohibited the printing of any book without the permission of the chancellery.

The statesmen who had directed the affairs of the kingdom after Henry IV's death had taken these draconian regulations even further. During Concini's régime as well as that of Luynes, the then all-powerful leaders of the Catholic hierarchy sought to exercise control over the bookshops. During the States General of 1614 they had asked that publishers should be prevented from printing anything that did not have the approval of theologians and 'the authority of the bishop of the diocese'. As for foreign books, they asked that their content be communicated to the bishop, and that his permission should have to be obtained before they were put on sale. For their own part, the governments of the crown were quick to suppress any show of independence. Two brothers named Siti were burnt at the stake in 1618 for having circulated a satirical piece against the Duc de Luynes.[8] Letters patent of 1618 set up the Chamber of Publishers, determined their number, the rules for their recruitment, how their syndic was to be elected and what his powers were to be and those of his deputies. The assistant provost-marshal of Paris, his civilian deputy, and parlement were empowered to order the burning of books capable of disturbing public order. Documents dated 1619 show that parcels of books arriving in Paris were still being regularly inspected, and that such inspection was the responsibility of the syndic, his deputies, and the customs officers.[9]

It must be stressed, however, that these severe regulations were aimed only at works attacking the favourite of the moment and those damaging to the official religion. There was total freedom when it came to works that were ribald or obscene, and this was indulged to the point of scandal. They appeared without authorisation but under the imprint of respectable publishing houses, and they were openly sold. Between 1600 and 1623 books like *Muses gaillardes* and *Parnasse satyrique* were legion. Reprints showed how successful they were and how freely they could be sold. In 1623 the Jesuits managed to instigate proceedings against Théophile de Viau. But everyone knew that the *Parnasse satyrique* was a pretext, and that the irreligious sentiments of the poet were the real reason behind the persecution to which he was subjected.[10]

Richelieu dealt with the important question of control over publishing in a way that was rather different from that of his predecessors. There was no need for him to create the machinery for control, for that already existed and worked well. But he submitted it to the civil authority rather than, as before, to that of particular interests. In 1624 a regulation was issued according to which books were henceforth to be examined by four censors who would be chosen by the king from among the doctors of theology. One must be careful not to mistake the implications of this. The furious protests of the faculty of theology help to bring them out. The new regulations meant that the faculty had lost the right to examine books which, so it said, had belonged to it since time immemorial. The four censors, despite the fact that they were theologians, were not to be chosen by the faculty but by the civil authority. It was easy to see that their advice would be consonant with the intentions of the government.

When he was harassed by pamphleteers – first by those supporting the Spanish faction, then by those supporting the queen mother – Richelieu took a certain number of measures. In 1627 a decree of the Conseil prohibited the writing, discussion and disputation of propositions dealing with the power and sovereign authority of the crown, on pain of punishment for sedition and disturbance of public order. The printing of speeches concerning 'les affaires d'Etat, ou la personne du roi, des gouverneurs et des magistrats' without the permission of the chancellery was to be held to be a crime of lèse majesté. Richelieu had a memorandum issued about the legislation concerning satirical writings, in order to prove that whoever published and sold them must pay for them with his life. That terrible man Isaac Laffemas was made responsible for the execution of these measures as the need arose.

However, this government, authoritarian as it was, was not wedded to orthodoxy. Through the simple fact that it clearly separated the transcendent from the temporal, and because it attributed to the state only temporal aims, the doctrine proclaimed its indifference in matters of religious dogma, philosophical opinions, and moral conformism. For his part, Richelieu tolerated an astonishing degree of freedom of thought. Among his own immediate circle Comte de Bautru and Abbé Boisrobert were notorious for their atheism. The scandal of Théophile de Viau's trial had no equal throughout the entire duration of his government.

Although the French had been put out by the loss of their old, independent habits, they did not, therefore, turn their backs on politics. There is no doubt that they were unhappy about a régime that prevented them from talking too openly, and which made heavy calls upon their purses. But their interest had been aroused and politics became for them a subject of constant concern and reflection. That is why French classical literature, at this early period, was preoccupied with politics. The authors made their position clear, whether they approved of the cardinal or cursed him, and they invoked great principles to justify their attitude. It did not occur to them to think that literature ought to confine itself to the description of the passions of love, or that it ought only to express the tender feelings of emotions, or that its function was exclusively to seek elegance of expression. Corneille's tragedies were political because the whole of French literature was at that time preoccupied with the state and its relation to men. Pierre du Ryer, a contemporary of Corneille who also wrote tragedies, gave political problems even more prominence in his plots than the author of *Horace* and *Cinna*.[11] Chapelain was not afraid to admit that he preferred reasoning about the government of the state to devoting himself to the kind of poetry 'laquelle n'apporte que le plaisir'. Balzac called the poets 'les premiers précepteurs du genre humain'. He admired them because they had taught men 'les premiers principes de la politique et de la morale'.

Writers had thus quite naturally taken sides. Many of them sincerely applauded the work of the minister, and they proved it by singing his praises even after his death. Chapelain, Des Marests de Saint-Sorlin, and in particular Scudéry were among these. Others were indignant, in silence. Mainard and Malleville, who were close to men persecuted by Richelieu or faithful to the memory of Montmorency, were secretly hostile. Balzac compared the cardinal to Busiris and Tiberius.[12] Corneille contented himself with speaking neither well nor ill of him.

Writers during the period of Mazarin

Richelieu's successor did not have the same greatness of vision. It took him a long time to understand the importance of public opinion and the services writers could render. He was mean. It was 1649 before he began to employ literary men. He used Gabriel Naudé, La Mothe le Vayer, Costar and Cyrano de Bergerac. Later on, by means of pensions, he obtained the services of Silhon, Ménage and Claude Quillet. It is important to note that, apart from Silhon and Ménage and perhaps also Claude Quillet, who was little more than an agreeable freethinker, his writers had a well-established reputation as atheists. This is not surprising when it is recalled that the Fronde pretended to be the defender of tradition, of the respect for rights, of ancient liberties, and that it was Christian in inspiration. The defenders of the state, therefore, had quite naturally to be Machiavellian and consequently atheists.

But because he had been late in gathering writers around himself, because he had done it meanly, and because in any case his unpopularity was too great, Mazarin had not managed – as Richelieu had – to prevent other politicians from obtaining useful support from literary men.

The most active in that direction was Coadjutor de Retz. Since 1638 he had managed to enlist the help of Saint-Amant, La Lane, and Montplaisir. Later on these were joined by Chapelain, Gomberville, Ménage, Abbé d'Aubignac and Sarasin. When the disorders began, he had at his disposal the most redoubtable writers of his time: Patru, Scarron and, above all, Marigny. They applied themselves to the task of demonstrating that the coadjutor had but one aim, the public good.[13]

Prince Condé, his brother Conty and his sister Mme de Longueville also had their court of writers. Until the defeat of the Fronde they had with them in Paris and at Chantilly La Calprenède, and Georges and Madeleine de Scudéry. At one stage Sarasin left the service of de Retz for that of his enemies, the Condés. This whole group can only be treated as Frondeurs as long as it is understood that it had nothing in common with the Paris Fronde, and that far from defending a tradition of liberty and legality, it did the opposite by praising the aristocratic spirit, speaking not a word of blame against the insolent fortunes of the financiers, and confining their strictures on Mazarin to his being a weakling and a liar.

When the unrest was over the writers remained disunited. Some went over to the Premier Président Pomponne de Bellièvre. They represented those who remained faithful to the memory of the Paris Fronde, to those who still believed in the ancient liberties and public morality. There were many of them, and they were important. The most unyielding among them were Patru, Furetière and the two brothers Boileau. But they knew that they enjoyed the sympathy of their elders, of Chapelain, old Gombauld and Gomberville. Their verses disparagingly expatiated upon authors who preferred to praise the financiers rather than the heroes, who sold their favours to the highest bidder, and who turned themselves into the slaves of all the favourites. In the nineteenth century they would have been republicans.

But others turned towards the financiers. Foucquet had become the generous patron of the arts. He performed with great ability the task Mazarin was neglecting. From 1656 he began to court all the writers of any standing. Pellisson was his private secretary, a pleasant man who knew how to say things that flattered and won devotion. Thus Ménage went over to Foucquet after having spent many years with de Retz, La Fontaine received a pension for some verses he periodically addressed to him, Corneille who had left the theatre returned to it in order to please him and Scarron talked familiarly of Foucquet as 'le patron'.[14]

The government of Louis XIV: the first phase

The personal rule of Louis XIV soon brought these divisions to an end. The writers, in common with the rest of the country, were dazzled by the brilliance of the great monarch. They celebrated the young hero who was giving France new provinces. They praised the 'grandes et merveilleuses qualités' which were to be found together in the king's person. It did not take them long to proclaim that the century of Louis the Great was 'l'une des périodes merveilleuses de l'Histoire' and that it was a worthy successor of the famous centuries of Pericles and Augustus.[15]

The king demonstrated a constant interest in the arts. He expected them to yield still further prestige for the monarchy. Under his influence the various art forms visibly inclined towards the stately and magnificent, even to the point of excess. Of all the examples of dramatic art it was opera, i.e. the grand spectacle, which appealed to him, much more so than tragedy. It was obvious that, in the works of Molière, the ballet-comedies interested him most. The same taste for grandeur which appears in the colonnade of the Louvre can be found in the *fêtes* of the court and in the décor of the works performed there. La Fontaine has written without admiration of those orchestras whose dozen harpsichords and hundred oboes were all the rage, of those corps of dancers whose multitude dazzled the eyes, of those ballets that had become veritable army parades.[16] But La Fontaine belonged to the old generation. The new generation loved it all.

The king saw only one way to implement his grand design: organisation. He wanted a simple but clear-cut framework. When he took over the government Paris had three playhouses. He thought this too many. In 1673 the old Théâtre du Marais was closed by order of the king. Then, in 1680, Molière's players were merged with those of the Hôtel de Bourgogne, again by royal command. There remained only one group of French actors, one of Italian actors and that of the Opéra. This satisfied the king. He did not ask himself whether this perfect organisation was not an obstacle to the free development of talent.

Colbert used all his power to the same end. He had become superintendent of the king's buildings, and that office made him into what would now be called a minister for culture. He had asked Chapelain to help him with matters relating to the humanities. In March 1663 a list was drawn up of men to whom payments were to be made. The generosity of the king was to bring him devoted service, but it also promoted the development of genius. Above all it was to take away from the writers all temptation to seek the patronage of someone else. The same payments were made year after year, until the state of French finances had been so seriously affected by the continuation of the war with Holland that Colbert was forced to cut or abolish altogether this kind of expenditure.[17]

The same desire for organisation led to the creation of a body of academies. At first there were three: the Academy of Sciences, the reorganised Academy of Sculpture and Painting, and the Little Academy, the latter being given the task of working closely with Colbert on inscriptions and other ways of increasing the prestige of the crown. Added to the old Académie Française, which Colbert wanted to awaken from its slumbers, these academies were to form one vast body that was already being called the General Academy before it was in actual existence. Soon more academies were created: the Academy of Architecture in 1671, and the Academy of Music in 1672.

For Colbert, the creation of these academies was not a matter of providing agreeable conversation among a few distinguished intellects. The minister conceived of these academies as working teams. He consulted the Academy of Sciences on the technical problems of his administration. The Academy of Architecture was ordered to provide reports on matters of its competence. If they were to fulfil their tasks, the academies had to be strictly subordinated to royal authority. Colbert reduced their autonomy as much as he could. In 1663 he abolished elections to the Academy of Sculpture and Painting. It lost its elders and its elected head. The Academy of Sciences received no regulations: decisions affecting it were left to the arbitrary power of the court. The Académie Française retained a measure of autonomy until 1672. Chapelain was keeping it well in hand, and he had Colbert's complete confidence. In that year, however, the mode of election was changed to allow the government to control it entirely.

Once the Fronde was over, the whole press did not suddenly cease to exist altogether. Paris had been outraged by Théophraste Renaudot and his official *Gazette*. But the taste for news had been acquired. From 1650 onwards Loret, a Norman, gave out each week a gazette in rhymed doggerel verse. He wrote about political events and the war. But he also announced fashionable weddings, deaths, and important receptions. His *Muse historique* soon received a secret subsidy from Foucquet.[18] His enterprise flourished, although he had rivals. After his death there were even successors who remained faithful to the formula of the *Muse historique*.

In 1672 a man of letters, Donneau de Visé, created a new kind of periodical.[19] His *Mercure galant* took for its subject-matter 'les nouvelles des ruelles les plus galantes'. It contained pieces in verse and prose. It also gave its opinion on the literary scene. In 1677, after a long pause, it reappeared as the *Nouveau Mercure galant*, with Thomas Corneille as Donneau de Visé's associate.

Another periodical began publication in 1665. On the invitation of Colbert, Counsellor Sallo created the *Journal des Savants*.[20] Chapelain assisted him, together with a team of men of letters. The *Journal des Savants* quickly made itself a large number of enemies and Sallo withdrew from it. The journal then failed and appeared only at irregular intervals.

In the process of restoring order the royal government understandably decided to reintroduce control over publishing, as Richelieu had done earlier. The French liked epigrams, songs and political satire. While it was impossible to prevent someone with a grudge from writing satirical verse and reading it to his friends, it was possible, indeed essential, to prevent its being printed.

At the time two important works were being written. There was, first, the large collection of verse which received the title *Livre abominable*, and which with extreme violence attacked the queen mother, Colbert and the Jesuits. The second, *Mémoires pour servir à l'histoire D[u] M[aquereau] R[oyal]*, was aimed mainly at Colbert and seems to have originated from the same centre of opposition.

There was a time, after 1665, when a number of satirical writings were in circulation. Some had been printed in Germany, others in Holland and Belgium, and there were some which had probably been published in Paris or Rouen. They were emulating the *Histoire amoureuse des Gaules* by Bussy-Rabutin, written in 1660, but which its author had not meant for circulation. However, these satires were intended to provide scandal. They told of amorous intrigues at the court of France, the loves of Madame and, a few years later, of Mademoiselle and Lauzun.

In 1667 the government created a new post. Besides the civil lieutenant of Paris there was to be a lieutenant general of police, and the first occupant of the new post was La Reynie, a state counsellor known for his toughness.[21] Paris learnt very soon what this appointment meant. Subligny, a well-known gazette writer and a friend of Molière, had his journal suppressed. La Reynie drafted a decree concerning the management of publishing houses and bookshops, and a campaign was begun to stop the printing and sale of writings thought to be seditious. In 1670, La Reynie submitted a report to Colbert. He was proposing that the minister, by means of the severest measures, should suppress those who were ill-intentioned enough to distribute in the kingdom and abroad satire in manuscript form.

The government of Louis XIV: the second phase

Until the death of Colbert the French could at least feel that, although authority behaved harshly, it was not in vain that they were called upon to make sacrifices and submit to rigorous discipline. Scholars talked much about liberty, whose benefits they themselves enjoyed. But after the death of that great minister it became clear that the régime was changing. The élan of the first years of the reign was replaced by a climate of repression which allowed only displays of conformity. From the pulpit preachers condemned the theatre and inveighed against the novelists. Abbé Du Bos wrote in 1696: 'Si Dieu ne nous assiste, on mettra bientôt la moitié de la ville en couvents, et la moitié des bibliothèques en livres de dévotion.'[22] Literature, if it was to be accepted, had to conform to the spirit that the court wanted to promote in the country.

In such conditions publishing could only decline. People were heard complaining, in 1696, that the public was not buying books. Twelve years later the position had become tragic. In the printing houses of Paris there was serious unemployment. Only books on theology and religion continued to sell. A publisher's catalogue of 1709 contains 135 titles of literary works, 93 philosophical works, but 347 treatises of theology.[23]

The government tried to establish very strict control over French publishing houses. A decree of the Conseil of 6 December 1666 had limited the number of authorised printers. The chancellery, in 1683, demanded that this decree be punctiliously observed. The intendants were ordered to make an inventory of publishers and printers in each town, including their size and opinions.

The old law requiring permission before printing had never in the past functioned properly. Now a corps of royal censors was brought into being to examine books. They were capable of hanging on to a manuscript for three or four years and, in the words of Bayle, they refused their approval 'à tout ce qui sentait une âme élevée au dessus de la servitude et des opinions populaires'. Bayle was not exaggerating when he wrote that the Inquisition was fast establishing itself in France. After all, had not the Inquisition been the highest ideal of the religious faction since the beginning of the century?

The authorities did not merely strike hard at irreligion. They persecuted the best Christians if they did not happen to think like those in power. When Boileau wanted to publish *l'Equivoque*, he encountered a series of prohibitions. For four years he tried to get around them. In January 1711 he was told that they were absolute and definitive. At a time when France was in the hands of the Jesuits, a Christian like Boileau looked like a poète maudit. Two months later he died in despair.

Censorship was just as pitiless towards plays.[24] Until 1697 freedom had in fact been great. In that year, however, the religious faction demanded the creation of examining commissioners. From 1701 onwards actors had to send all new plays to the lieutenant general of police. In later years plays were submitted to a salaried censor for prior approval. To avoid trouble he would cross out everything that might be construed as allusive. Campistron had been imprudent enough to put into his *Phraate* a woman of some ability who had captured the heart of a weak king, as a result of which the author was for a time threatened with the Bastille because the authorities suspected an allusion to Mme de Maintenon. The same Campistron had one day thought of making Saint-Réal's *Don Carlos* into a play. He was told that there was no point in trying it and that the play would not be allowed past the censor. The idea that a king of Spain could murder his son went against the respect due to the great of this world. Campistron was reduced to finding some vaguely similar plot in the history of Rome. He was allowed to write *Andronic*.

This régime of stifling conformism met with general resistance. The central government had to have recourse to spies, to overhearing conversations in public places. It made a large number of raids to discover clandestine printers. It punished in an atrocious manner publishers and hawkers who disobeyed the regulations. Many of them were sent to the galleys. Others crowded the prisons. In 1694 two hawkers were hanged for having sold *l'Ombre de Scarron*. The unfortunate Chavigny de la Bretonnière, who had described in crude language the corruption of some bishops and was a refugee in Holland, was lured into an ambush, seized by the French police, and thrown into a cage at the Mont-Saint-Michel where he died, crazed and half-devoured by rats.[25]

Despite the effort deployed by the French government, a kind of public opinion did make itself felt. There were groups that met in public places to discuss news of the war, of politics at the courts, of the intentions of the cabinets of Europe. Among them were lawyers, businessmen and traders who wanted to know what was happening abroad. They were called nouvellistes. Their meetings were business-like and held at regular intervals, with a president and a clerk. In fact they were the forerunners of the political clubs and the government had to put up with them.[26]

Nor was it able to impede the growing influence of the press. The official *Gazette* was so completely beyond the pale that the public demanded something better. Handwritten gazettes proliferated. Sometimes the police would discover a hideout and arrest the writers. But these were soon replaced by others.

There was one perfectly legal way that was regularly used to discover the news. Foreign gazettes entered France freely and were sold openly. It was an odd weakness in the royal government, which can be explained by the financial profits Louvois first drew from that trade, and from which his successors continued to benefit. These gazettes came mainly from Holland, but they were written in French by French refugees and they were full of news sent from Paris. The government knew this but allowed it to go on. It merely saw to it that ill-intentioned persons were prevented from sending abroad 'des avis contraires au service du roi'.[27]

Although it was indulgent about foreign gazettes, the government acted with extreme severity when it came to learned publications. Literary journals were beginning to appear in Holland, the first having been founded in 1684 by Pierre Bayle as *Nouvelles de la République des Lettres*. It was impossible to obtain permission for its entry into France, despite the intervention on its behalf by Mme de Montespan and the Duc de Montauzier. The *Bibliothèque universelle et historique* brought out by Jean Le Clerc suffered the same fate, although it was extremely moderate. During this period, from 1701 onwards, the Jesuits published the *Journal de Trévoux* which soon became renowned for its prejudices.

Forbidden books came across the same barriers at the frontiers as periodicals. In 1682 Christian Huygens wrote to Abbé Gallois: 'Vous n'ignorez pas les défenses et exactes recherches que l'on fait sur vos frontières en matière de livres, jusqu'à fouiller dans les valises des voyageurs.' On the frontiers of Picardy all book parcels from Holland and Belgium were inspected at the Péronne crossing. The ports, especially Rouen, La Rochelle and Bordeaux, were closely watched.

It goes without saying that some books got through. Along the Picardy border smugglers were engaged on a regular traffic. Boxes of books were hidden in the holds of ships in the ports. But the police kept such illicit imports down to a minimum. In 1682 Abbé Gallois stated that it was impossible to obtain Spinoza's *Tractatus* and *Opera posthuma* in Paris. It was as if some Great Wall of China were stretching around the kingdom, isolating it from Europe, and ensuring the triumph of orthodoxy and the stifling of the spirit.

4

Social and literary life

The beginning of the century

During the reign of the Valois, Renaissance culture had brought about at the court of France and in Parisian society the most exquisite forms of refinement. By the time Henry IV had restored peace very little remained of its elegant and delicate taste. But, for all that, the king wanted to add a touch of brilliance to his court. *Fêtes*, tournaments, masked balls, court ballets were organised with great frequency. These were sumptuous occasions. The women were near collapse under the weight of their precious materials and jewels. In 1595 a chronicler noted that the most beautiful ladies 'étaient si fort chargées de perles et de pierreries qu'elles ne se pouvaient remuer'.[1] They used to wear them up to the tips of their shoes and pattens.

But this display of wealth had something uncouth about it and scarcely corresponded to the exquisite taste of the old court. Henry IV was without culture and did not bring to the arts the same disinterested devotion as his predecessors. Those who had known the courts of Henry II and Henry III were bound to find that of Henry IV vulgar.

The nobility that frequented the Louvre was unable to rid itself of the habits it had acquired in the military camps. These troopers were quite capable of exchanging insults, threatening each other with their swords, or speaking without due respect to a lady. The king sometimes had to intervene to call them to order. This he would do with firmness and good nature, like a leader and soldier speaking to his companions in arms.

This odd atmosphere helps one to understand the forms then taken by poetry. The greatness of the royal authority was celebrated in a tone of gigantic and baroque exaggeration. One can see that the poet was told to influence people's way of seeing the crown, to imbue them with a religious respect for it, which was all the more necessary since the monarchy was not yet firmly established. In the realm of lyrical poetry, the Valois had their long reign dominated by the subtle splendours of the emulators of Petrarch. This kind of poetry disappeared altogether. When a poet of the court of Henry IV addressed the royal mistresses he made specific demands, talked of conquests, threatened to break with one that dared remain insensible. If he celebrated the beauty of these ladies he used the most extravagant metaphors, and no excess seemed excessive.[2]

Finally, there was a vogue at this court for the most vulgar form of satire. Poets would write this on the order of some great nobleman who protected and paid them. They would lampoon men and women of the court whom their master had told them to tear to pieces. Most of the court was very amused by these writings, and the king himself would laugh at them. But there were occasions when poets were beaten up by their victims. That obscene satirist Sigognes was renowned for the beatings he had received. Berthelot was actually assassinated.

There were some great noblemen who allegedly kept up the old traditions of politeness and refined courtesy. Perhaps they pushed too far in the opposite direction, away from the general vulgarity, by way of reaction. In particular, there was the Duc de Bellegarde who had been one of Henry III's favourites, and Marshal Bassompierre. Later on, chroniclers of the period said that this old form of gallantry was stiff, ceremonious, and exaggerated. When Bassompierre was released from the Bastille after a long period of captivity, his old-world manners aroused hilarity. 'La civilité et le respect' he showed the ladies belonged to the beginning of the century and seemed cruelly outdated.

During the Valois period centres of intellectual and artistic life had sprung up in the private houses of some of the aristocracy. During the unrest their activities had been interrupted. But they had not been forgotten. It was still with admiration that people spoke of the circles of Mme de Villeroy and of Marshal de Retz's wife, and of the brilliance they conferred upon the period of Henry III. But the habit of having writers meet in the presence of an aristocratic lady grew again only slowly. Names can be cited, but they amount to little.

Queen Marguerite returned to the traditions of the preceding century.[3] She had come back to Paris in 1605 and had built a magnificent house on the Quai Malaquais, opposite the Louvre. There she brought together a small court of men of letters, novelists and poets. The group was inspired by the spirit of the Renaissance. It particularly prized the philosophy of Plato and the poetry of Petrarch, and it is likely that the poets of the circle of Queen Marguerite considered the 'poètes du Louvre', as the public called them, a collection of barbarians. But the tastes and habits of this circle conformed too much to the spirit of the preceding period for it to be taken as a sign of a real revival of social life.

Apart from Queen Marguerite's circle, only Bassompierre and Comte de Cramail took an active interest in the literary scene. Bassompierre was a great reader and he used to take notes. Arnauld d'Andilly wrote that his house was the meeting place of men of the highest merit. He went on to state that people there used to talk about all kinds of subjects, 'non seulement agréablement, mais utilement'.[4] Comte de Cramail, a friend of Bassompierre and like him later imprisoned in the Bastille, was the protector of Mathurin Régnier. He wrote verse and was mixed up with the controversy about Balzac's *Lettres*.

Marie de Médicis had neither the desire nor the means to promote the life of the arts. But she loved sumptuous *fêtes* and she had very many of them. Some splendid ones were reported at the time of the peace of Loudun in 1616. The following year chroniclers talked with admiration of 'assemblées' at which games, banquets and plays with music were performed. Court ballets very much retained their vogue.

As the king grew older it became clear that the cultivation of the mind meant nothing to him, and that even the life of fashionable society bored him. He amused himself with three or four servants 'à des exercices vils et de néant'. He did not read. He did not like dressing up. He hated conversation. He also stammered. It is not surprising that with such a disposition he hated the world.

Richelieu

Richelieu did what the king had not thought of doing. He

wanted to give French society tone and taste. His direct intervention in this respect was considerable. But he may have had even more influence on manners through the climate he created, the sense of proper behaviour and of rationality that he fostered, and the stigma he attached to all forms of vulgarity and extravagance. It is for that reason that a historian may consider together the government of Richelieu and the work accomplished at the Hôtel de Rambouillet.[5] But the marquise was very jealous of her independence, and her husband remained aloof from the policies pursued by Richelieu. The minister could, however, only be glad of the spirit that reigned in this most highly esteemed salon.

Segrais, in excellently chosen language, has summed up the basic features of the work of Mme de Rambouillet: 'C'est elle qui a corrigé les méchantes coûtumes qu'il y avait avant elle, et elle a enseigné la politesse à tous ceux de son temps qui l'ont fréquentée.'[6] She was Italian by origin and had spent the first part of her life in Rome. When she came to France after her marriage in 1600, she was no doubt struck by the roughness and barrack-room manners of the nobility. At any rate, by about 1615 she was no longer able to visit the Louvre for the simple but convincing reason that seven successive pregnancies had seriously affected her health. She had to give up her fashionable but tiring social life and to welcome her friends in her own home.

She built a beautiful house to her own specifications in the rue Saint-Thomas du Louvre. She turned it into a meeting place for a few men and women of high society and some bright intellectuals. After 1620 one began to hear admiring talk about the Hôtel de Rambouillet which continued to increase over the twenty years that followed. Among writers, there was Malherbe, already old but a constant visitor at the Hôtel, and who celebrated the incomparable Arthénice in his verses. Then there were Chapelain, Conrart and – rather later, during a period when he had left his hermitage in the Charente for a time – Balzac, around 1638.

But these names could lead to misunderstanding. Indeed they have done so with a number of historians. They had induced the belief that the Hôtel de Rambouillet was a kind of academy and that it was the cradle of French classical literature. Now it is true that Mme de Rambouillet liked Malherbe and did not care for Théophile, and that she agreed with the purists. If French classicism were no more than propriety in thought and expression one would have the right to say that it had its centre at the Hôtel de Rambouillet. Yet it is no less true that this small group, which loved the pleasures of high society more than anything else, saw in the humanities little more than a way of adding a touch of wit and delicacy to its lives. It was mainly amusement that Mme de Rambouillet wanted from poetry. She had won Voiture for her salon, who was a real poet. But he was also a kind and helpful man. In order to entertain the marquise he was prepared to turn poetry into an amusement. Chapelain, Conrart and Balzac were indeed frequent visitors at the Hôtel de Rambouillet, but they did not set the tone there. That was the rôle reserved for Voiture, and his verse reflects most faithfully the taste that reigned in the salon.

Voiture, for sheer fun, revived the rondeau. Soon all the Paris salons had their wit who tried to imitate Voiture's rondeaux. Then the fashion died out. This was at the beginning of 1638. Abbé Cotin made riddles modish; after that Paris society, including the Hôtel de Rambouillet, went in for metamorphoses.[7]

This aristocratic society, which remained very attached to the past, loved everything that managed to recall the lives of the old knights. They prized the *Amadis*, the old romances, and the old language. For the same reason they liked the poetry of Marot and, far from observing religiously the rules established by the purists, the habitués of the Hôtel de Rambouillet amused themselves by writing in the language of the old French poets. They often took the names of the heroes of the old epics and used to talk much about valiant knights, and magicians.

These facts allow us to understand how strong the romantic spirit was at this time. Many historians contrast the romantic with the classical. We note, instead, that in the salon frequented by Malherbe, in which Chapelain, Conrart and Balzac liked to spend much of their time, the romantic ideal was very powerful, to the point where it was perhaps more than a simple game, and that it was a token of the attachment the aristocracy still had for the ways of thought and life of former times.

The most obvious rôle of the Hôtel de Rambouillet, and of the salons that imitated it was, therefore, not that of subjecting writers to a doctrine. It was rather to link, more closely than during the preceding period, the world of literature with the world of fashionable society. Because they met in the salons, high society discovered a taste for things of the spirit, and men of letters acquired more elegant forms of behaviour. When one recalls the general brutishness of the nobility at the time of Henry IV, the change was enormous; nor did the writers, for their part, resemble those bluff, highly-coloured poets with a tendency to smuttiness of the previous era.

A type of man was beginning to emerge who reflected these changes in manners and taste. He was the honnête homme.[8] His main virtue – in a sense his only virtue – was urbanity. Whether he belonged to the aristocracy or to the world of letters he had, above all, to respect the requirements of good manners. He was not allowed to affirm his opinions too insistently, or defend them with blind fury. He would play his part in a conversation in which everyone had the right to speak but not to shock. He did not forget the splendid example set by the Valois court. He knew that at the court of Henry III, 'la plus magnifique et pompeuse' that had ever existed, true politeness was practised, and the most pure urbanity, and that false grandeur and baseness were alien to it.

The Marquise de Rambouillet attached the greatest importance to this form of politeness. Even her king, however, did not possess it. Whatever Louis XIII did, a chronicler relates, seemed to her 'contre la bienséance'. She played a vital part in the propagation of these new ideas.

It would not have occurred to the social élite to look for the justification of the ideal of the honnête homme in the writings of the old philosophers. The great value of this new kind of salon was precisely that it allowed society to profit from the intellectual climate created by the writers. Faret's *L'honnête homme ou l'art de plaire à la cour* (1630) was the manual of the new society. In it Faret took up the ideas put forward mainly by Baldassare Castiglione and by Guazzo in Italy during the preceding century. The honnête homme whose characteristics he sketched was also a man who knew his Cicero and Seneca. He had a sensitive awareness of the requirements of good manners, which caused him to shun extremes and cultivate the middle path. His rule was easy and unconstrained dignity. Honesty he prized to such a degree that he saw no difference between a good man and an honnête homme.

The notion that the humanities and urbanity are inseparable, that a writer must be an honnête homme in his bearing and his language, underlay without doubt the founding of the Académie Française by Richelieu.[9] The institution was not the result of a sudden whim. It grew naturally from the general way ideas and manners were moving. Mlle de Gournay used to have writers meet at her home. In 1619 there was talk of a 'vertueuse assemblée de doctes' which could very well be the group of disciples of the ageing Malherbe. Camus, in 1625,[10] talks about a 'grande et fameuse académie qui se commence à Paris' but which historians are unable to identify. Finally, towards 1629, a new group came into being. It was composed of seven men who met at the home of Conrart, one of the king's secretaries. They had no thought of transforming their informal meetings into regular sessions. But Richelieu heard about them, and saw the use he could make of them. He let it be known that he wanted to start an academy and that he intended to provide the nucleus himself. They had no alternative but to submit. The first meeting of the Académie Française was on 13 March 1634.

Above all, the academy was to furnish the cardinal with a number of writers who would, with docility, carry out the tasks he allotted to them. Some had to look over his speeches, others his theological writings. Then there were the polemicists, many of them counsellors of state, who provided the French reply to attacks from abroad. But it would be unfair to ignore the fact that Richelieu also had higher aims. He wanted the academy to work for the greater perfection of the French language. No doubt this was prompted by reasons of prestige, and connected with the aspirations towards European hegemony that were then the driving force behind the policies of the crown. But this prestige was not sham. When French became the language of Europe it became the language of 'honnêtes gens'.

Indeed, there is an obvious relationship between the changes taking place in French society at that time and the creation of the classical French language through the efforts of the academy. It was to be a language which based itself on neither the language of the scholar or scientist, nor on that of the artisan and 'mécanique'. It was above all to make for clarity, sharpness and exactitude and, since it was meant for persons of good education, it had to do without words that were unusual, special, or cranky. Moreover, it had to avoid 'fausses grandeurs' and vulgarity. This language of the 'honnêtes gens' Richelieu asked the academy to codify and propagate.

He presented the academy with a programme. First it was to 'régler les termes et les phrases' of the language 'par un ample dictionnaire' and by 'une grammaire fort exacte'. Then it was to draw up 'une rhétorique et une poétique' to provide rules 'à ceux qui voudraient écrire en vers et en prose'. Richelieu also hoped that it would examine the works of contemporary writers, indeed with their agreement.[11] It would thus become the arbiter of good taste. It was not the cardinal's fault that the academicians showed themselves incapable of fulfilling within a reasonable time the first of their tasks, i.e. the compilation of the dictionary.

Once the aims behind the establishment of the academy have been understood, the reason for the choice of the first members will be understood too. If one accepts the usual idea, and believes that the academy had collected under one roof the writers who had fallen for the classical doctrine, the choices made by Richelieu would scarcely be explicable. It is true that Chapelain and Conrart were among its prominent members. But so was Saint-Amant and, a little later, Tristan. That extravagant man Scudéry was among its most zealous workers. If one looks at all these men and their works it is difficult to discover a literary doctrine they might have shared.

But they were all 'honnêtes gens'. They were all possessed of decency, in their lives as well as in their works. They were all good Frenchmen, wanting to serve the policies of the cardinal within the limits of their ability. There was nothing stilted about their seriousness; Saint-Amant wrote his first burlesque poems during the lifetime of Richelieu. But the burlesque was, according to the opinion of that period, the 'divertissement des honnêtes gens'.

Social life at the time of Mazarin

It was the emergence of a generally agreed doctrine concerning good manners, politeness and honnêtété which gave the seventeenth century its distinctive stamp. No more was there to be seen, in either manners or conversation, that mixture of exaggerated grandeur and vulgarity, the kind of extravagance that had dominated the first years of the century. Even so, however, the already discussed significant changes in the relations between the different social groups that occurred after the death of Richelieu necessarily had repercussions on the upper strata of society, and consequently on the world of literature at the time of Mazarin.

In this field as in so many others the new minister had little in common with the great man he had succeeded. Mme de Motteville passed the following severe judgment upon him: 'Outre son avarice, il méprisait les honnêtes femmes, les belles-lettres et tout ce qui peut contribuer à la politesse des hommes'.[12] Yet he did try to give some kind of lustre of his own to his government. He introduced Paris to the sumptuous spectacles of Italy.[13] He had the renowned Torelli brought from that country, and on 14 December 1645 the *Finta Pazza* was to be seen in all its splendour in the Petit Bourbon playhouse. At the same time Mazarin induced Leonora Baroni to come from Italy, where she was then the most celebrated singer and had perhaps once been his mistress. Other performances were to follow. There were Cavalli's *Egisto* in February 1646 and Luigi Rossi's *Orfeo* in March 1647. Then Corneille was asked to compose a grand spectacle, *Andromède*, which was produced by Torelli.

Mazarin wanted to win over public opinion, but he did not quite succeed. He managed to elicit admiration for the use he made of machines, the *trasformazioni*. But Italian music merely bored the Paris bourgeoisie. The religious faction was showing indignation at the waste of money these shows entailed in their eyes. *Andromède* could not be put on until 1650. In 1654 the *Nozze di Peleo e di Teti* was produced with a vast array of machinery.

It was social change before, during and after the Fronde,

rather than the personal intervention of Mazarin, which brought about changes in the forms of behaviour of the upper strata of society. They became freer in their ways, and their concept of elegance was less rigid. It was now fashionable in the salons to poke fun at 'la vieille cour', i.e. the court of Louis XIII. The queen mother did what she could to prevent these changes. Being Spanish, she attached importance to titles, and to the consideration that should go with them. According to the Marquis de La Fare, she knew from what family everyone came and what his accomplishments were, knew how to be at once proud and polite, and put up happily with the kind of gallantry and politeness everyone had thought so important in her day.[14] Moreover, she could see no harm in the Spanish concept of 'belle galanterie', and believed that it was the best defence against licentiousness.

But the trend towards freer ways was too strong. This was the time when masked balls came into fashion. At such functions people talked to whom they fancied, and sat or stood where they fancied without worrying about things like precedence. Even their dances were changing; they were moving away from the regular and strict patterns to which they had kept in the past.

These freer ways were not necessarily vulgar. On the contrary, among the sections of society which set the tone, there was a very evident desire for elegance and refinement. This was particularly so, before and after the Fronde, with a group of young noblemen and rich parlementaires known among Parisians as the Messieurs du Marais.[15] All of them were openly free-thinkers who were not afraid of scandal. But many of them were also men of excellent taste who were living according to a morality of their own. We are told of one of them that he had an excellent and subtle mind, that he knew the most beautiful poetry in Latin, Italian and French, and that he indulged in the kind of witty and sophisticated banter that the ancients used to call patrician. Mme de Motteville, pious as she was, admitted about another of these free-thinkers that he was both witty and an honnête homme.[16]

This new ethos became even more evident in the changing society after peace returned to France. Men and women, who were generally very free in the principles to which they held, had a very real desire for sophisticated elegance and, as they used to say, delicacy. They had a quick and ironical wit. They had no pedantry about them, and attached the greatest importance to 'cacher discrètement' the knowledge they possessed. This was also the time when the idea of the perfect-man-of-the-world was born. He was still called honnête homme, but this now meant something different from its implications during Richelieu's period. The term now foreshadowed very clearly the Epicurian fastidiousness that one was to meet at the cours galantes at the beginning of the next century.

Social life was thus developing, with the encouragement from those at the top. Until he went into exile, and when military operations did not demand his full attention, the Prince de Condé organised what really amounted to a court. It was said in Paris that his house was 'le temple de la galanterie et des beaux esprits'. Chroniclers have described the fêtes that were constantly held at Chantilly and in which the arts played their part. People would swap sonnets and elegies, bouts-rimées and riddles. Condé himself loved literature. He read Gomberville's novels and was very fond of Voiture and Sarasin. He might even put some homely piece of verse together himself.[17]

The surintendant Foucquet, for his part, truly held court among the splendours of Vaux and Saint-Mandé. There, too, writers and artists met men and women of high society. A large number of pieces of verse and some anthologies that were composed there allow the reader to get a picture of the taste and tone which prevailed among these people. Foucquet had made the Marquise du Plessis-Bellière into a kind of official hostess. She formed the Etat incarnadin and fixed its rules. The Incarnadins enjoyed pleasant talk and abundantly indulged a taste for elegant patter. They placed much value upon well-turned missives and love letters. Their favourite games were composing verbal portraits, comic songs and verses to set rhymes.[18]

A number of Parisian women were imitating these examples and held their own salons. Many of them were given by the wives of financiers, as for example that of Mme Pelissari. Mme Tallemant, a daughter of the famous Montauron, was involved in the literary in-fighting and academic intrigues of her time. Many others, though less well known, tried to imitate these ladies. Historians do not always seem to be aware that Somaize, in his *Dictionnaire des Précieuses* (1660), does not list those who were 'précieuses' in the proper sense of the term, but those very ladies who, at that time, were holding their salons and gathering around themselves social personalities and witty men of letters. As a result, this famous *Dictionnaire* is a useful document about the vogue for salons, and about a large number of those which were opened at that time, but is quite false, to the point of caricature, as a picture of the précieux movement.

The history of literature has reserved a special place for the memory of one of the salons. Mlle de Scudéry was not of high birth. Nor was she rich. But her personality and the reputation of her books drew the attention of her contemporaries to what they called the *Samedis de Sapho*.[19]

They began in 1653, and they lasted less than ten years. They were in no way aristocratic gatherings, and if there were occasions on which some member of the great nobility did climb the dark little staircase that led to Mlle de Scudéry's flat one could be sure he did not belong to the Société des Samedis. The latter was dominated by writers. There were Chapelain and Conrart, some society poets (poètes galants) Isarn and Raincy,[20] and Sarasin was there at one stage. But it was Pellisson who was the 'Apollon du Samedi'.

From the beginning – and they did not wait for the *Précieuses ridicules* – there were people who poked fun at these Saturday meetings. After all, Mlle de Scudéry's gatherings represented so obviously the spirit of the new salons that they could not fail to bring upon themselves the mockery of writers who preferred to remain within the old tradition. The *Carte du Tendre* (1654) elicited hilarity. To quote Mlle de Scudéry herself, there were some who imagined 'qu'on ne parlait jamais chez Sapho que des règles de la poésie, que de questions curieuses et que de philosophie'.[21]

She was certainly right to protest. Far from being pedants, men like Pellisson et Sarasin went at times even to undesirable lengths to introduce into their verse charm and playfulness. Old Conrart himself turned frivolous in order to be with the fashion. They composed madrigals, improvised verse, amorous tales and épitres in colloquial verse. They concocted verses about the story of a turtle-dove, and about the metamorphosis of the acacia or the horse-chestnut. On the death of Mlle de Scudéry's chameleon they wrote him an epitaph in verse. These products of playfulness were collected in a register, the *Gazette du Tendre*. The most famous episode in that story was the *Journée des Madrigaux* of December 1653.

It is within this climate that what historians call 'préciosité' was born.[22] It is a term that has been given a large variety of meanings, many of them vague, and even the most wary run the risk of misunderstanding it. There are those who have seen in préciosité a kind of timeless phenomenon; they find it through the centuries from Chrétien de Troyes to Giraudoux. It appears that they have never heard of maniérisme, which is a notion familiar to German historians for example, and that can be applied with much greater justification to the kind of material some people want to bring under the concept of préciosité.

Others have described préciosité as a phenomenon covering the whole of the French seventeenth century. They have thus, in the face of the most convincing evidence, thrown together under the same heading works as diverse as the baroque excesses of Nervèze or Laugier de Porchères, the somewhat affected refinement of Mlle de Scudéry, and even a few features of the language of Racine which amount to no more than reflections of the langue galante of his period.

The history of French society in the period after the Fronde provides the evidence for a proper assessment. If one wants to get away from vague and pretentious generalisations the word préciosité can only have one meaning. It designates certain attitudes and forms of language that were fashionable at the end of the period of unrest within the new society whose characteristics were very different from those it replaced. This is true to the extent that a study of préciosité is necessarily a study of an aspect of social life. The history of literature reflects only part of that aspect.

It is, of course, true that, in those days of increasing and unashamed pleasure-seeking, the précieuses showed no sympathy for vulgar licentiousness. But they did put the search for personal happiness above all other moral values. For that reason they had some hard things to say about marriage as it was conceived at that time. But they did not go so far as to recommend that men and women just live together. On the other hand they dared to talk about love outside marriage. They thought it ought to remain pure, unaffected by sensual emotions. It may be assumed that what was really behind this attitude was a distrust of the passions and, in contrast, the affirmation of the values of lucidity and freedom even in love.

What also struck the public was their claim to be using a more refined vocabulary. They despised expressions that were 'faibles, communes et bourgeoises'; they favoured 'de nobles, de particulières et de vigoureuses' expressions.[23] They took this doctrine very far and endeavoured to find the 'bons mots' and 'expressions extraordinaires'.

They were not afraid of introducing innovations into the language. They invented new words and endowed old words with new meanings. They talked about 'tendres amis', an expression which strikes us today as normal but which in their day caused a scandal. They dared to say that a woman had the right to 'parer son esprit'.[24] Since they were all society women they disliked popular and vulgar language. In this respect they merely pushed the demands of 'purisme' to their extreme limits. Before there were any précieuses the ladies of high society had already been condemning words which give 'une méchante idée'. The précieuses were at one in wanting to rid society of 'l'impureté des mots aussi bien que des choses' and to bring conversation to a high level of 'spiritualité'.

When all these characteristics are put side by side, the real meaning of préciosité emerges. The précieuses and high society as it was after the Fronde were not quite the same thing. But the précieuses differed from it only because they took to extremes the tendencies that were clearly present in that society: the desire for refined elegance, a very keen sense of the autonomy of the individual which should emancipate him from social pressures as well as from the demands of the instincts, the need for lucidity and freedom. One can understand why these principles and the language in which they were enunciated, elicited the hostility of those who remained attached to the old ideas and who hated the France of

Foucquet and the financiers. 1654 saw the beginning of their campaign of ridicule against the précieuses. They treated the growth of the salon movement as a conspiracy 'contre l'Etat des lettres et la république du savoir'. They expressed their indignation at seeing these women upsetting not only traditional French moral values but also those of the French language. They inveighed against the 'méchantes façons de parler' which Mlle de Scudéry put in her books, and the 'expressions grotesques et monstrueuses' of the précieux writers. It was in this spirit that Molière wrote his *Précieuses ridicules*. He had many friends among the defenders of traditional values and, like them, he belonged to the Parisian bourgeoisie. As a play it is a caricature of genius, but students of history have been wrong in taking it as an exact description of its subject. People seem determined to go on thinking, despite all proof to the contrary, that at the Hôtel de Rambouillet (wrongly assimilated to the mass of précieux salons) chairs were called 'commodités de la conversation' and a mirror a 'conseiller des grâces'.

Society and literature under Louis XIV

Although during the first twenty years of the personal rule of Louis XIV it was the king's court which was the centre of attention for the French – its sumptuousness and the splendour of its *fêtes* saw to that – other centres of social and literary life did continue to exist in Paris as well. There were many Parisian women who held salons; indeed, one is tempted to say that they were innumerable. It may be noted that the Hôtel de Rambouillet had ceased playing any part; since 1645 the Marquise was only at home to a few intimate friends, and she died in 1665. The most important salon at this time was that of Mme du Plessis-Guénégaud. Among its regular visitors were La Rochefoucauld, Mme de Lafayette and Mme de Sévigné. Boileau and Racine were also to be seen there.[25] Another great lady, the Duchesse de Richelieu,[26] gathered around herself 'ce qu'il y avait de meilleur à Paris'. The enemies of Boileau and Racine were shortly to be found in her salon. The Duc and Duchesse de Nevers were also very interested in literary matters, and the Duchesse de Bouillon, who was Nevers' sister-in-law, took charge of his salon together with the Vendômes, his nephews. The financiers were no longer in the position they held under Mazarin. But there were some who played host to poets and provided them with discreet help.

The existence of these salons presupposes that within the French aristocracy there were many men of considerable culture. A number of them are known through the part they played in the lives of the great names in French literature. Marshal Gramont, who was on the most intimate terms with the king, was keenly interested in music and science. The Duc de Montauzier had translated the satires of Persius. The Duc de Vivonne, Mme de Montespan's brother, was an alert and highly critical reader of contemporary works and a very witty man. It was said of him in his day that 'on dirait qu'il est pétri d'un autre limon que nous'.[27] The Comte de Fiesque liked Marot, Chapelle and La Fontaine. Mathieu Marais said of him that 'il avait le goût simple et naturel'. One could go on to name Tréville, Créquy and Nantouillet. Above all one must name the great Condé. When he returned to France, covered with honours but most of the time kept out of state affairs, he was at last able to give his full attention to things of the spirit. He became the protector of Racine and Boileau, and spoke out openly in defence of *Tartuffe*.

The ways of the régime after the death of Colbert necessarily brought about changes in the conditions of social life. The court had become a sad and pious place, and therefore had lost its former brilliance and focal social position to what historians have justly called the cours galantes.[28] They really were princely courts, presided over by personalities like the Duchesse du Maine, Monsieur le Duc, the Prince de Conty, the Vendômes and the exiled Stuarts. They brought together men and women of high society and writers, in their mansions at Sceaux, Saint-Maur, L'Isle-Adam, Anet or Saint-Germain. One must not confuse the kind of company that met at the Grand-Prieur de Vendôme's Temple or at the Duc d'Orléans' Palais-Royal with the cours galantes. But the latter are important because of the part they played in the intellectual life of the period. There were still many salons, too. Mme Deshoulières was hostess to a sizeable number of writers. Among the financiers' wives who held salons were Mme de Hervart, Mme de Pélissari and Mme d'Ussé.

It is odd to see how closely the salons and cours galantes continued to follow the traditions established by the Marquise de Rambouillet and by Voiture. They were still composing madrigals, bout-rimés, rondeaux and épitres 'en vieux langage'. Their members, as during Voiture's time, took pseudonyms from the *Amadis* and the medieval novels of chivalry.

But although the tastes and games of these aristocrats remained within the old tradition, it cannot be said that they were all firmly in the grip of the beliefs and ways of life of the past. One can discern the most diverse attitudes among the men and women who haunted the cours galantes. One day, at Sceaux, they put on a tragedy with a religious subject and the devout Destouches was made welcome by the Duchesse du Maine. At the Temple, on the other hand, nobody took the trouble to hide his lack of religious faith. In fact, whatever the personal convictions of these people might have been, the morality they professed was a kind of epicureanism. They thought that the supreme good was to be found in sophisticated pleasure, and that their lives should not be touched by vulgarity or its prejudices and ambitions. They were to live in a world apart, more free, more intelligent, more sensitive than the rest.

The university

The court and salons set the tone for French society and consequently for French literature. But there was another centre of intellectual life that was powerful, supported by a strong tradition, and whose position allowed it to play a vital rôle: the university.[29]

At the beginning of the seventeenth century it had great difficulty in overcoming the crisis it had undergone during the wars of religion; in fact, it did not really succeed. Contemporary texts provide compelling evidence for this. In 1598 de Thou remarked on its decadence and put it down to the 'confusions passées'. Many colleges had been turned into army quarters during the siege. Buildings were shabby and teachers unobtainable. Indiscipline was rife. The global reforms introduced by the royal government had been of no avail. The fixing of precise regulations, the proper organisation of studies, the drawing up of syllabuses for each year, and the alluring pronouncements upon the status of the teachers had brought no appreciable results. Disorder continued. In 1615 a considerable number of colleges were short of professors, and the residences lacked students. Many pages of the *Francion* that might otherwise puzzle the reader are illuminated and confirmed by contemporary documents. In 1632 a writer noted that the universities had received such a shock in the preceding century that 'depuis elles n'ont pu se relever ni se remettre en leur première splendeur'.

But the origin of this decadence cannot be attributed entirely to the period of unrest. The university seemed ill-equipped to come to terms with the spirit of the new century, and there is no doubt that this was the real reason for its decadence. While society was undergoing an obvious transformation the university remained obstinately attached to its traditions. It seemed to many Frenchmen that its professors were no more than 'pédants' and 'philologues', who were entirely preoccupied with the variants of a Greek text. It was coming to be assumed that one had to choose between the university and the world. It was said that the pedants were lost in their admiration of antiquity, that they could only commune with the ancients. 'Parmi les hommes d'affaires', that is among the men who were engaged upon the activities of the modern world, they were said to be silent. In his *Portrait des esprits* (1625), Barclay distinguished between men of letters who were 'civilisés', who abhorred 'la vilité et la bassesse incurieuse des moeurs des écoliers', and those who only lived 'dans les blocailles de l'antiquité éteinte'. Many contemporaries believed that the writer ought to live with his own time, to speak the language 'de nos princes et de la cour', to 'converser dans le monde'. Unlike the members of the university, who thought that the Greeks and Romans ought to set the tone for them, they maintained that the great families of France had that right. Virgil, in their eyes, was superior to Homer because he had 'conversé parmi les Grands', for he had known Augustus and Maecenas.

Richelieu, of course, agreed with all this. It squared very well with his own policy, and his ideas for an aristocratic society in which everyone knew his place. It has already been noted that he also had more practical reasons for wanting changes in the mentality of the university. He did not like the teaching programmes of the colleges. In his *Testament politique* he expressed the view that schools of commerce would be more useful than colleges of the humanities. At the time of his death he was proposing a new university that would promote research in the natural sciences, the teaching of mathematics and physics, and which would gather together 'tous les ordres de connaissance'.

Throughout the course of the century the university was unable to regain the splendid reputation it had known at the time of men like Budé and Dorat. Around 1645 the recruitment of professors was still a difficult matter and men had to be taken on who had no proper qualifications. For a while they thought of educating, at the university's expense, 'des enfants de bonne espérance' who would later become professors or tutors; but this project was still-born. The university remained outside the mainstream of the arts during the entire century. Only the faculty of theology acquired some sort of notoriety under the reign of Louis XIV, and this did not help the university's prestige at all.

This decadence on the part of the traditional university was of considerable importance for the development of French literature. Of course, cultured Frenchmen were still well-versed in Latin literature in the seventeenth century. It was by translating Latin texts, writing Latin dissertations and verse that they learned to master their own language. Whatever the situation in which they found themselves, and for every moral dilemma, they were able to quote some apt phrase from Cicero or Tacitus, or a verse from Virgil or Lucan. Whether they were watching a tragedy or reading an ode or an épitre in French, they remembered Seneca's tragedies and the odes and epistles of Horace. But this Latin education which one admires today should not be overestimated. It amounted to little when compared with what Greek and Latin education had provided in the preceding century. It could still offer an adornment for the spirit and some enlightenment. But it no longer dominated the intellectual life of the French.[30]

This should help us to understand why French classical literature links up with the Greco-Roman tradition, while retaining at the same time a large measure of freedom and being, in fact, quite modern. Corneille, for instance, could take the subjects of his tragedies from Livy and Seneca. He could obey some fairly general injunctions of Aristotle that had been transmitted through the writings of humanist critics. His plays are nevertheless modern and French in their essence. French society as it evolved under Richelieu was too vigorous, too sure of itself, and too much orientated towards the future for it to follow slavishly in the footsteps of ancient literature as the university would have wished.

The traditional bourgeoisie did, however, constitute a highly cultured social group that had close links with the university and was very much its product. As a class it had no contact with the court or aristocratic society. It detested the financiers who shocked it because of the way they displayed their wealth and because most of them were vulgar. It was jealous of the parlementaires and the officers of the sovereign courts whose fortunes were frequently enormous and whom marriage often linked with the aristocracy. The limits of this class are hazy, but if within it there were families of very different levels of prosperity they certainly shared the same cultural and moral traditions. They were the doctors and lawyers, university teachers and what a contemporary called 'la foule du Palais' – attorneys and their clerks, young men who had finished their studies and had managed to be taken on by some great family as a secretary or maître d'hôtel or a major-domo.

Writers belonging to the world of the court usually spoke of these bourgeois with great disdain. A moralist, writing in 1653 about the various social categories, placed what he called the 'chicane' into the same group as the 'commerce' and the 'mécaniques', i.e. under the general heading 'le vulgaire'. He put it close to the 'pédants' and very far away from the highest class into which he placed those who were close to the queen, that is ministers, academicians and the court.[31]

This was very unjust. The middle and petty bourgeoisie that had been educated in the colleges of the university was without any doubt the most educated class. It certainly was the most solidly cultured class and the surest instrument for the preservation of the moral traditions of the nation. But everything it stood for was in contradiction to the tastes, ways of thought, sentiments and manner of living of the court and aristocratic society. Already at the time of Henry IV this bourgeoisie did not like the displays of luxury and the way fashions kept changing; it despised the court ballets, and L'Estoile who so well represented the tastes of his class talked of these ballets with obvious hostility. Letters written by the Dean of the Faculty of Medicine, Guy Patin, and by Jean Chapelain provide most useful evidence for the way this class saw its period.

It so happens that when one analyses from what social class a large number of French writers originated, one discovers that they were bourgeois by birth and education. Chapelain was the son of a notary. Colletet was an impecunious lawyer. Claude de L'Estoile belonged to the legal world. The father of Malleville was secretary to the Duc de Retz, and Balzac's father was secretary to the Duc d'Epernon. It is obvious that this class played a rôle in the intellectual life of the French seventeenth century which is quite out of proportion to the scant respect shown to it by the upper strata of society.

Part II

French Thought in the Seventeenth Century

5

Religion, society, and literature

Religion dominated the life of the French in the seventeenth century, and even those who refused to accept the dogmas of a Church had to define their attitudes and outlook in relation to religion. The study of the evolution of beliefs thus necessarily has a place in the history of literature. But an account of this evolution and of its literary counterpart cannot be properly understood unless it is carefully placed into the context of the political and social life of the period.

The Catholic movement during the first half of the century

While under Henry IV the authority of the crown was gradually imposing itself upon France, the religious faction irreducibly remained as the heir of the League, as a real party, with its private aims, organisation, and resources; in fact its hold upon the kingdom was tending to increase. The Catholic hierarchy could believe that it had won the long war in which the French had fought each other, and it was determined to exploit its victory to the full. It demanded that it alone should be entitled to sit in judgment upon men of the Church, to administer hospitals, supervise the printing and selling of books, make and unmake marriages, annul or alter the terms of wills. It thus set itself up in opposition to the civil authority and the magistrature, without reservations or qualification. It could do this because it knew that the king was above all anxious to preserve peace, and that he was consequently prepared to make concessions. Moreover, men of the ultramontane party occupied some of the most important positions in the state, and in the upper levels of society former supporters of the League were numerous.

It might have seemed that religious questions had lost their political implications. There was much talk of spirituality, the inner life, and mysticism. Religious orders were being created, most of which were dedicated to a contemplative life. But it so happened that the leaders of this movement, which seemed to be totally spiritual, had formerly belonged to the League faction. The founder of the Ursulines was the sister of bishops who had belonged to the League. Behind the foundation of the Oratoire was the son of the clerk of the Sainte-Union, together with the son of one of the Séguier ladies. There was a famous confessor, who was a descendant of an official of the Duc de Savoie, who had been mixed up in Marshal de Biron's plot. Madame Acarie, who played a vital part in the religious renaissance, brought to France the cult of St Theresa and the order of the Carmelites; she was the wife of one of the founders of the League. One cannot fail to see the close links that existed between the Catholic renaissance in its spiritual forms and the growth of the religious faction with its programme of domination, its determination to subordinate the objectives of French politics to the interests of the Vatican and of Spain, and its claim to have the right to enter into even the private lives of Frenchmen in order to subject them to the exigencies, if not precisely of the scriptures, at least of the hierarchy.

To understand the mentality of the nation at that time, one must distinguish between this faction and the mass of the French people. The nation, as a whole, was Catholic. It was so with a firmness bordering on the fanatical because it held the Huguenots responsible for the catastrophe which had all but ruined the kingdom. But the Catholicism of the bourgeoisie had its roots in moral traditions that had nothing to do with the Catholicism of Rome and Madrid.[1] The French bourgeois believed in the sacraments, the cult of the saints, and private worship. But they did not think that these constituted the basic elements of Christianity. They loved their priests but not the 'monks', by which they meant Capuchin friars and Jesuits whom they took to be pawns of Spain. They believed in the need for a common faith that would be recognised by all Christians. But they were not prepared to accept with blind and stupid docility any imposed dogma. They managed to reconcile the faith of Catholicism with a very acute need for freedom of thought.

It was people with this kind of mentality who provided the solid foundation for the nation's effort towards recovery. Most of the parlements, the royal officers, the entire 'robe' as they were called, the whole of the enlightened bourgeoisie remained faithful to the national tradition. Pierre Pithou, who was procurator-general of the Paris Parlement, published a book on *Les Libertés de l'Eglise gallicane* in 1594. He denied the pope the right to meddle in the affairs of the kingdom. It was only in the spiritual field that he accorded him authority, but even here he took care to recall that the power of the pope was not absolute since he was bound by the canon law, decrees, and traditions of national churches. Pithou's work contained the doctrine that was common to all who refused to accept the claims put forward by the religious faction. Senior magistrates, whose authority counted for much among enlightened Frenchmen, emphasised the basis upon which the French monarchy had been built. They maintained that the kings of France had legitimately shouldered the responsibilities of the emperors and had therefore inherited their functions. At the time when the university was being reformed the illustrious de Thou clearly stated that, since the emperors had possessed the right to determine the way ecclesiastical institutions were organised and run, the kings of France (as emperors in their kingdom) were by tradition responsible for ecclesiastical discipline and the education of the young. The king of France therefore proceeded to reform the colleges without bothering about the fact that they were pontifical institutions.

The very strong pressure exercised by Roman Catholicism at the end of the sixteenth century and at the beginning of the seventeenth naturally brought with it an increase in religious literature. The number of religious works published during that period was considerable: four hundred have been counted between 1580 and 1610. It is typical that three hundred and eighty of these were translations from Spanish, Italian, or Flemish. We are therefore witnessing a real invasion of foreign spiritual ideas. Moreover, these ideas emanated from precisely those countries that had supported the efforts of the League. Cardinal Bérulle, who in the period that followed was the most interesting of the Catholic writers, must be seen against this background.[2] His *Discours de l'Etat et des Grandeurs de Jésus* (1623) was immensely successful and left its mark on the religious literature of the century.

Most historians of religious literature seem to think that Bérulle's work stands outside the main currents of history but, in fact, it can only be explained in terms of its historical context. Bérulle had begun by being a regular member of Mme Acarie's salon, and her connections with the League were obvious. He had been to Spain. The last period of his life was entirely devoted to political activities. His aim was to gain the support of the queen mother for the ultramontane faction while Marie de Médicis was still able to dominate fully the thinking of her son. Richelieu was his main enemy. He did whatever he could to bar Richelieu's path to power. He died in 1629, just in time to be spared the combined experiences of Richelieu's victory, the queen mother's flight abroad, and the decapitation of Marillac who had been his collaborator.

But even if his thought has to be seen against its political background it has none the less great merits of its own. It is touching to see the resolution with which he tended to reject whatever was temporal and human, and to accept only the infinite, eternal, and absolute. His philosophy amounted to a tragic view of the human condition. Bérulle, like the existentialists of today, liked to bring out the misery of our existence. He talked about the stupidity of infancy, the similarity between sleep and death, and between life and a long pilgrimage 'en misère, en ignorance, en péché'. At the end of it all: death. But not death as the ancients understood it, as the cessation of life. Bérulle conceived it rather as a principle of destruction that man carries within him from birth and which is the supreme law of human existence.

This tragic conception of the human condition led him to believe in the prime importance of gaining redemption through Christ. The religious thought of Bérulle is therefore in the tradition of the religions of salvation of antiquity. It maintains that what we can expect from God is not necessarily the illumination of the intellect. Lost in the darkness of life and destined to die all a man can do is to hold out his hands to a redeemer.

After Bérulle's death other religious writers took up his doctrine and drew inspiration from it. The venerable M. Olier and Père Jean Eudes were among these. In particular, however, there was Père Condren, for whom all philosophy amounted to a few simple statements: God is all; man is nothing or no more than misleading appearance.

Not all Catholic writers were prepared to consider all created existence as condemned beyond appeal. Those who were not drew on the authority of François de Sales.[3] His *Introduction à la vie dévote* (1609) put forward a view of life which equated human wisdom with the demands of religion. Life, he held, was only meaningful if the aspirations of the finite and created were compatible with the thought of the infinite and eternal. The doctrine led to the conclusion that the ideal Christian life did not demand the sacrifice of feelings and activities normal in a man of the world, so long as they did not betray the maxims of authentic Christianity.

Human society, and in particular French society in the seventeenth century, was thus deemed morally acceptable. Christians could play their part in it with a good conscience. They could live at the court, take part in its activities, and seek positions and honours at it. They could covet the title of honnête homme, and be rewarded with it for having lived in accordance with the virtues the title implied.

This doctrine is to be found throughout the vast literature François de Sales inspired. It is, for example, behind Père Le Moyne's *Dévotion aisée* (1652) which Pascal condemned with such violence in the *Lettres Provinciales*. Though taken rather far, it is also to be found in Des Marests de Saint-Sorlin's *Les Délices de l'esprit* of 1658. In this most systematically audacious work, Des Marests even justified the desire to acquire reputation on the grounds that the immortal soul wanted a good deed or a good piece of work to share in its immortality. He extolled the pleasures man can derive from science and virtue. He went so far as to justify the desire for wealth, i.e. a great career, because the thought of power is good. It is through the thought of power that man freely wills to rise above the vulgar material world, develops refinement of taste, and discovers ever more sophisticated pleasures through the use of his freedom.

When Richelieu took over the government the prestige of the Catholic hierarchy stood high. The cardinal had no wish to reduce it. On the contrary, he took pains to indicate the important place it had a right to occupy in the country, and only sought to prevent its intervention in the running of the government. In any case, if he had tried to humiliate the hierarchy he would have found an obstacle in Louis XIII. The king was very pious, and tended to be submissive when faced with the religious faction. The young queen, in so far as she had any influence, had similar inclinations. One can thus explain the extraordinary progress made by Catholicism during this period. The most striking example of this was no doubt the creation of new religious families, particularly the Oratoire and the priests of Saint-Sulpice, who, together with the Jesuits, undertook to transform France into a country that was entirely Catholic in ways of thought and of life. What was characteristic of this movement was its intention to enter into the innermost being of Frenchmen to ensure that they completely conformed to the prescriptions of their religion. It was a matter of making sure that they were married in church, that their children were baptised, that they scrupulously observed the laws on fasting and abstinence, that they did not swear, that they did not get drunk, and that they did not say evil things. Clearly, this was quite a programme. In 1629 the Duc de Ventadour formed a secret society to see that it was carried through without weakness. Orthodox historians praise the charitable works carried out by this society. But the Compagnie du Saint-Sacrement (as it was called) caused anxiety among the uninitiated because it was shrouded in secrecy, because its procedures tended to be indiscreet, and because of the spy-network it had developed. It looks as if this anxiety was not without foundation since the parlements had to intervene in its activities, and Mazarin finally dissolved the Compagnie.

At least it may be said that the policy of the religious faction showed certain results. The traditional Catholicism of the enlightened classes was in gradual retreat before a kind of Catholicism that was more interested in ceremonial, ritual, and pilgrimages. A letter from Guy Patin to his son illuminates these changes in climate.[4] It is not only the populace which is 'bigotte' but the bourgeoisie, too; even the upper class has been affected, *plures etiam supremi generis occupavit.* Paris has become 'l'abrégé de la superstition', and decent people and real Christians have no alternative but to keep quiet. Guy Patin was in no way a free-thinker. He was a Christian, but he was unable to recognise the old religion in the kind of Catholicism that the religious faction was in the process of creating.

The progress of this exceptionally intense religious movement was bound to lead to disagreements and internal conflicts. By 1640 French Catholicism had to reckon with Jansenism.

The centre of this movement was Port-Royal, an abbey for women to the south of Paris.[5] Like many others, it had been 'reformed' in 1608, i.e. the rules of the order were being observed in their full rigour. This reform had been the work of the young abbess Angélique Arnauld. She belonged to one of the bourgeois dynastics of Paris. The prestige of the Arnauld family in cultured circles and among the well bred was considerable.

For many years the spiritual direction of Port-Royal had been in the hands of François de Sales. It was later taken over by a friend of Bérulle. In 1633 another friend of Bérulle, Abbé de Saint-Cyran, became the nuns' confessor. He was a cleric without any desire to teach a new and personal form of Christianity. But he had studied at Louvain, and had there been the companion of a Belgian bishop, Cornelius Jansens or Jansenius, whose friend he had remained. Like Jansenius, the Abbé felt that Roman Catholicism had lost something of the spirit and virtues of primitive Christianity, and that it should return to that supreme teacher St Augustine in order to bring back some of the basic truths that were in danger of becoming lost. Men had to be reminded that they could do nothing without divine grace, that the world is in a state of sin, and that only a small number of predestined people escape damnation. Moreover Saint-Cyran did not like the Jesuits. They did not seem to him to have anything to do with authentic Christianity.

Given the social context of his time, it is not difficult to see the general significance his doctrine must have had. Stating that the spirit of Christianity was absent from contemporary Catholicism was tantamount to calling into question the entire set of values upon which Catholic Europe had been rebuilt at the end of the wars of religion: the glorification of papal power, the rôle of the Vatican at the princely courts, the sumptuousness of its ceremonial in which the preoccupation with prestige was only too obvious. To say that the world was in a state of sin meant that Christ himself had not been able to redeem it as a whole but merely a handful of predestined mortals. It also implied that the political order was bad, that it was radically so, that it was based on evil, on the desire for riches and vainglory.

It was a doctrine that was very likely to worry Richelieu. At the same time the Augustinian doctrine set itself up in opposition to the Company of Jesus, for a variety of reasons. In a sense, the Company had identified itself with modern Catholicism, the very Catholicism that Augustinianism wanted to take back to its purer origins. It also worked with the conviction that, given the monarchic constitution of Europe, its main task was to make sure of the support of the princes, the aristocracy, and of the ruling classes. It asked, for a start, for the passive submission of the faithful, and obedience to the rules of the Church and the prescriptions of the hierarchy. To ensure the submission of the masses, it planned pilgrimages, ceremonies, demonstrations of piety, and all kinds of sacramental observances.

Not least, the Society of Jesus had accepted humanism. While it is true that it had rid it of whatever might be dangerous to the Catholic order, and that the God of the philosophers had been made quite indistinguishable by the theologians of the Company from the God of the Old Testament, Catholic humanism as it was presented to the Christian masses and to the pupils of their colleges by the Jesuits could only be an object for scandal for the Augustinians.

It was in 1638 that the Augustinian movement first came to the attention of the public. Richelieu had been watching with apprehension the growing influence of Saint-Cyran in the religious world. He also knew of the imprudent statements the holy man had made against his policies. Richelieu thought it wise to put him into Vincennes prison. Jansenius was dead, but in 1640 the enormous bulk of his *Augustinus* appeared at Louvain in which he expounded his system. The following year it was published in Paris. A papal bull promptly condemned it and, on the order of Richelieu, Isaac Habert, the Paris theologian, fulminated against it. Jansenius was reproached for minimising the importance of the sacrament of penitence and, in general, the efficacy of sacraments. His doctrine that the essence of Christianity lies in the love of God was treated as criminal.

From that moment the opposition of the Augustinians to the Catholicism of the court, the episcopate, the Jesuits, and the upper classes never ceased. In 1642 Antoine Arnauld, who was a disciple of Saint-Cyran, published a *Théologie morale des Jésuites extraite fidèlement de leurs livres*, and a treatise on *La fréquente communion* in which he emphasised the aberrations to which a badly-understood sacramental life could lead. The Jesuits replied with an *Apologie* by Père Caussin (1644), a monumental work by the erudite Père Petau, and polemics from the pens of Père Pinthereau and Père Annat.

The religious world was divided. Antoine Arnauld received the support of some members of the university and of many Parisian priests. The Jesuits, and the French episcopate which supported them, took steps to obtain a condemnation of the Jansenists from Rome. But the movement received increasing and more active sympathy from other quarters. For example, many persons at the court expressed their support for it, some eminent parlementaires showed their approval and it was noticeable that a number of young doctors of the faculty of theology had leanings towards it.

It was on the morrow of the siege of Paris that the enemies of the Augustinian movement began their agitation which eventually brought about the condemnation of the movement. They still had a majority at the Sorbonne. On 1 September 1649 the syndic proposed the condemnation of seven propositions which summed up the doctrine of the *Augustinus*. These involved only matters of pure, dogmatic theology, the problems of the fall, of grace, and of rewards. But it was not difficult to see in the action of the syndic the first stage of a campaign designed to ruin the Augustinian movement.[6]

The second stage came in the following year (1650). A collective letter from eighty-five bishops was sent to Pope Innocent X in which he was asked to condemn five of the propositions the syndic of the Sorbonne had brought up for consideration by his colleagues in the preceding year. Rome took its time over the reply. Finally, in a bull of 31 May 1653, the five propositions were indeed condemned.[7]

The opponents of Jansenism were determined to work for its complete destruction. The Assembly of the Clergy asked the pope for a new expression of censure which would make it clear that the five propositions were actually contained in the *Augustinus*, and that they were being condemned in terms of the meaning given to them by Jansenius. The assembly received satisfaction through a bull of October 1656. At its session of March 1657 it decided to send copies of this latest bull to all members of the clergy and all those who had a Church benefice; the recipients were to sign a declaration signifying their humble and complete submission.

The royal government did not at first act with great speed to obtain these signatures. At the end of 1660, however, the king intervened in person. The decisions taken by the Church assembly in 1661 were firm. The Conseil de Conscience signified its support. Anyone in receipt of Church money who refused to sign or was evasive lost his living.

There were men of good will who tried to find ways of compromise. The vicars-general of Paris issued an instruction in June 1661 which allowed the signing of the submission without the renunciation of Augustinianism. But this instruction was condemned by a papal brief, by the Conseil du Roi, and by the Assembly of Bishops. Another instruction was then issued which demanded submission pure and simple.

Thereafter the history of Jansenism became ever more patently part of political history, and it is within that context that it is best studied. For all that, it was also closely linked with the intellectual and literary history of the period, to the point of being inseparable from it.

In 1638, Antoine Le Maître, a Paris lawyer and an Arnauld on his mother's side, had decided to retire from worldly affairs. He had gone to live at Les Granges next to the abbey of Port-Royal. He was followed there by his two brothers, one of whom was Le Maître de Sacy. Thus it became known in society circles that there existed a group of people living apart from the world who were distinguished by their virtue, piety, and knowledge. Richelieu distrusted pious people, and he dissolved Port-Royal. But at his death its members returned. In 1643 there were four of them. By 1646 there were twelve. Theologians knew Antoine Arnauld best. But it was Antoine Le Maître and Le Maître de

Sacy who were most admired in society circles. In 1649 they were joined at Les Granges by Pierre Nicole and Claude Lancelot.

These were men who knew their literature and philosophy, and who were not shut up within the confines of theological controversy. They had founded the Petites Ecoles for their friends' children and had thus been led to thinking about methodology, language, and literature. These preoccupations led to a number of publications. There was the *Grammaire générale et raisonnée* (1660) by Lancelot and Antoine Arnauld. The *Epigrammatum delectus*, with a very important preface by Lancelot had appeared in 1659. Le Maître de Sacy published a translation of the *Fables* by Phaedrus which was frequently reprinted. Above all, there was the *Logique* of Port-Royal which served as a primer in logic for many generations of Frenchmen. A little later these same men induced Brienne to publish La Fontaine and Racine and, in 1669, a *Recueil de poésies chrétiennes et diverses*. This was followed by the publication of Nicole's *Essais de morale* (1671–8).

It would certainly be difficult to connect all these works with the theology of Jansenius and the five propositions. Nevertheless they had for their contemporaries a very specific meaning. There was a close correspondence between these sober, methodical, and profoundly serious works and the habits of mind of the French bourgeoisie. The latter was aware of this. It became usual to connect the Company of Jesus with the ways of society literature, with its sparkle, urbanity, and modishness, and to connect with Jansenism whatever was great and serious in literature.

Hence the authority of these Messieurs (as they were then called) in some sections of Parisian upper-class society and among the best of the French writers. The Duchesse de Longueville protected Port-Royal most splendidly, Mme de Sablé ended her life close to the nuns of Port-Royal and Mme de Lafayette prized the *Pensées* of Pascal above all else. La Fontaine worked for the Messieurs of Port-Royal. After quarrelling with them, Racine reconciled himself with his old teachers. Boileau could only bear Jesuits who in their heart sympathised with the Jansenists. Mme de Sevigné was mad about Arnauld and Nicole. But what really demonstrated the influence Port-Royal exerted on the intellectual life of the French was that Bossuet agreed with the Messieurs of Port-Royal on the meaning and duties of Christianity, although he remained hostile to the theology of Jansenius throughout his life.

Pascal

Pascal is the writer most closely identified with Port-Royal. He belonged by birth to the class of royal officials that constituted the most vigorous and dedicated part of the nation. His father had been president of the Cour des Aides in Montferrand, but he had sold his office in 1631 to live in Paris so that he might take his place in the scientific circles of the capital. He was considered one of the best mathematicians of Paris and was frequently to be seen at the academy of Père Mersenne. His son Blaise was allowed there with him, and it is from these men of science that the young man received his intellectual training.

The Pascals were not originally a pious family. They were Catholics like the rest of the cultured bourgeoisie, i.e. they knew exactly where religion ended and temporal activities began. It took a number of coincidences from 1646 onwards to bring the family into contact with Port-Royal, and to keep it there. In 1652 Jacqueline Pascal shut herself up in the abbey; the following year she took her vows. Her brother kept up a cordial relationship with the Messieurs, yet without ever becoming one of them.

That is how he came to be involved in the Jansenist polemics and to write the *Provinciales*. In January 1656 it had become clear that the majority of the Sorbonne Assembly would vote for the expulsion and condemnation of Antoine Arnauld. The latter prepared his *Apologie* which, however, seemed inadequate to his friends. Pascal, who was present at the reading of the document, offered to write another reply to the opponents of Arnauld: this became the first *Provinciale*. Its success was overwhelming. Thus encouraged, Pascal went on to write the other *Lettres*, eighteen of them. He stopped only with the agreement of his friends, and in order not to compromise the hope of some kind of settlement.

Critics who talk about the *Provinciales* without placing them into their social setting and the conjunction of events that caused them to be written are bound to make nonsense of them. Indeed, the position adopted by Pascal on the problems of morality is not peculiar to him.[8] It is the position of the enlightened bourgeoisie to which he belonged by both birth and education. Like the whole of his class, he had the loftiest ideas about the moral law and its exigencies, and he tended to identify religion with the moral law. He had a deep dislike for any religious doctrine that pushed the moral law into the background in favour of ritual, ceremonial procedures, and ready-made prayers. What he liked in the Messieurs of Port-Royal was not so much their position on the theory of grace, free will, and predestination. It was, rather, that they were bourgeois Frenchmen like him; that they understood Christianity the way he did. They believed, as he did, in the efficacy of the sacraments and in the propriety of the various acts of worship. But they believed in these things, as he did, with the proviso that the sacraments and acts of worship were treated as supports of moral behaviour and were not made to take the place of such behaviour or exonerate one from living in accordance with its principles.

It was also because he belonged to the French bourgeoisie that Pascal thought of the moral law as a body of obligations valid for everyone. He rightly saw that his opponents did not share that view. They believed in the existence of particular laws for particular classes, some for the nobility, others for the bourgeoisie, some for those who knew their way about the world, others for those who did not. For the theologians of modern inspiration, duels were entirely justifiable in the case of noblemen for whom the point of honour was a sacred concept. For the bourgeois, duels would be inexcusable and, in fact, nonsense. In the eyes of a Jesuit moralist it was quite proper that a man should be able to elude an obligation with the assistance of a bright theologian while, on the other hand, another Christian who was less clever and unable to afford the services of a confessor of his own would be compelled to fulfil his. Such propositions horrified Pascal because he was a French bourgeois.

This was the real point of opposition between Pascal and the casuists. His detractors have misrepresented the meaning of the

Provinciales. They have said that he had attributed opinions to the Jesuits which they had never put forward: Chateaubriand treated him as a gifted calumniator. These are scandalously false accusations. It is known today that Pascal neither invented nor altered the texts he quoted.[9] It has also been said that he seemed to attribute only to the Jesuits doctrines that were shared by all theologians. But Pascal was not fighting the Society of Jesus. He was fighting a certain conception of religion which offended the traditions of French Catholicism. It is also wrong to think that the *Provinciales* are an attack against moral laxity and nothing else. The reproach Pascal addressed to the Jesuits was not that they were teaching that kind of morality, but that they supported both sides of the argument, severe maxims and the others, because what seemed to matter to them was that they preserve their power, retain their hold on peoples' consciences, flatter so that they might seduce and dominate.

The immediate and immense success of the *Provinciales* can only be explained in these terms. They expressed, with strength, passion, and genius, the deepest feelings of an entire class of French society. It was not necessary to believe in predestination and grace, or to adhere to Jansenist opinions to admire the *Petites Lettres*. It was enough to believe in the moral traditions of the French bourgeoisie, its way of seeing Christianity, and to share its old suspicions of Rome and Madrid. Pascal had merely expressed aloud, albeit with tremendous force, the thoughts of innumerable Frenchmen who lacked the courage or ability to give them voice.

Shortly after finishing the *Provinciales*, Pascal began to work on a demonstration of the Christian faith. After 1658 he devoted all the time to it that his poor health permitted. When he died this work was still in the planning stage, and even the main lines of the argument – whatever some may have said – had still not been definitely decided. Some years after his death his family, with the agreement of some of the Messieurs of Port-Royal, published the fragments under the title *Pensées*.

Among the notes he had scattered about the papers one main idea emerges. It is that Pascal had made his choice between the religious philosophy of humanism and that which Bérulle had put forward in his treatises at the beginning of the century. He was completely and passionately on the side of those whose conception of Christianity implied the condemnation of the philosophical view of human virtue and of a social order which pretended to be the highest expression of human reason.

Pascal thus had the courage to adopt a position which was diametrically opposed to the philosophical doctrines favoured by his contemporaries. Most of the latter, believers and non-believers alike, held that the universe reveals a supreme intelligence which is the source of its beauty. Pascal replied that our God is a hidden God. They said that there was eternal and absolute justice, and that it was the foundation of human society and its laws. Pascal derided this notion of justice, for justice varies from nation to nation. They based their beliefs on reason and its presence in man, in his spiritual nature, and took it to be an emanation of divine reason, capable of attaining certain knowledge of the true. But, for Pascal, 'cette belle raison corrompue a tout corrompu'. What is called 'principes éternels' is for him no more than habits of the mind.

With the profound intuition of genius, Pascal had understood that his century, despite its profoundly religious appearance, was imbued with maxims that left no room for the Christian spirit. Most enlightened Frenchmen were Catholics. But their Catholicism was a kind of Christian rationalism. It was a reasonable religion which became more so with each successive generation. It was a religion which had its roots in philosophy rather than in the bible, and its God was the God of Cicero and Seneca rather than the God of Abraham, Isaac, and Jacob. Its sense of sin was being lost. It knew less and less of miracles and prophecies, and hardly believed in the efficacy of prayer.

The Christianity whose demonstration Pascal had undertaken had nothing in common with this kind of reasonable religion. He based himself on a religious philosophy he had found ready-made, that of Augustinianism, i.e. the philosophy of Bérulle and of the writers who were inspired by him. He was as convinced as they that the universe is in the grip of sin, that human reason is incapable of discovering the divine order in nature just as it is unable to understand the eternal laws of justice and injustice. This was Pascal's point of departure from which, desperate though it may seem, he undertook to bring man back to real Christianity.

He made it difficult for himself. Most apologists before him had used methods of demonstration that were more comfortable, more likely to satisfy reason. They demonstrated the existence of God and that of the soul through the beauty of the universe and the presence within us of the moral law. Grotius, who had been the most famous of these apologists, had provided the model for them by leading the reader, by stages, first to a form of philosophical idealism, and then to the truth of Christianity. This is precisely what Pascal refused to do.

It would be too easy to explain this refusal through Pascal's natural pessimism. Nor would it be entirely true to say that Jansenism provided the reason for it, because Pascal's philosophy scandalised the theologians of Port-Royal, the great Arnauld as much as Nicole. They used his genius, but they were far from approving his theses. Pascal had harsh things to say about reason because he had been and still often was in the company of scientists who, like him, devoted their lives chiefly to mathematics and the physical sciences. He knew that many of them, probably most of them, refused to accept arguments wholly based on reason. Some were thus led all the way to atheism. Others stopped at scepticism. Many accepted the truths of religion, but only through an act of submission on the part of their intelligence. Pascal knew that reason cannot lead a man to faith.

But just because he was a scientist and knew how scientists thought Pascal believed in proof by fact, and he believed that he could find support for his theses in such proof. He was convinced that there was no point in invoking the spiritual nature of man and the presence within him of some kind of reason that was allegedly a reflection of divine reason. What would convince the scientists, he thought, was a true and concrete description of the human condition. He would not proceed by metaphysical deduction but by the analysis of facts, the facts of history, of the miracles, of the prophecies.

It is this basic position, the desire to make concrete reality his starting point, which explains the steps of Pascal's argument. There is the concrete reality of man as he is, thrown on this earth without his wish, surrounded by darkness, and whose reaction to the starry heavens is simply terror. Then there is the concrete reality of man that is summed up by terms like lies, dissimulation, hypocrisy. There is also, however, his desire for God, and frustrated hope, and agony. All these are observed facts, certain facts. Only Christianity gives an account of all these, and by that very fact its truth is demonstrated.

History provides even better proof. It acts as a kind of witness. The prophecies and miracles of the old and new testaments show that Christ was God. The apostles who witnessed the life of Christ, the martyrs whose blood constituted its own kind of testimony, all confirm the truths for which the Bible and gospel would in any case be sufficient proof.

In adopting this position Pascal could assume that his demonstration of the truth of Christianity was well in tune with the general outlook in scientific circles, with their evolution towards the positive methods that based themselves on exact knowledge and the analysis of facts. But the attitudes of the rest of society were changing in a different direction. They were groping for a kind of humanism which had faith in human reason and in nature. It is not an accident that the eighteenth century was the century of Voltaire and not of Pascal.

Catholicism at the time of Louis XIV: Bossuet and Fénelon

At the death of Mazarin the prestige of Catholicism was immense but its political activities remained under the control of the civil authority. In fact, the claims of the ultramontanes were very closely watched. There was, for example, the case in which Louis XIV felt that the papal government had offended him in some obviously petty affair, as a result of which he reacted with a violence that no Protestant prince would have allowed himself and demanded the most humiliating excuses from the Holy See. No imprudent theologian at the Sorbonne could get away with a thesis favourable to papal authority without incurring the sanction of parlement.[10] The choice of bishops was made with vigilant care so as to prevent some ultramontane from joining the episcopate. The Compagnie du Saint-Sacrement remained dissolved. Colbert was convinced that France had too many priests and monks. In 1666 he thought of putting back the age at which one could take religious vows. It is likely that he would have been glad to bring about a schism in France, on the lines of that in England.

But, during that period, the religious faction continued its work with the aid of the queen mother and very highly placed supporters. In 1662 a young lawyer called Claude Le Petit was burnt alive after having had his hand cut off. He had been convicted of having written some verse which, though not even impious, had been lacking in respect for the Virgin Mary. He had been given away by a priest. Parlement condemned him to death.[11]

The religious faction could be happy. One of its writers was congratulating himself on the fact that heresy had been stamped out, that the art of elegant swearing had gone out of fashion, and that godlessness was being rooted out and its adherents punished. This atmosphere brings out all the meaning of Molière's *Tartuffe* and *Don Juan*. It enables one to understand why an honest and Christian man like Boileau should have felt himself threatened because he had spoken slightingly of some highly placed members of the Catholic hierarchy.

Between 1680 and 1685 the forces that had managed to contain the religious faction disappeared. Colbert died: and as the king grew older he became more conscientious about his choice of friends and showed himself more docile in the face of those who tried to influence him; this was particularly so with Mme de Maintenon. He became pious. Already in 1679 he admitted to 'weaknesses', thought the scriptures 'le plus beau des livres' and made ready to effect the conversion of the Protestants.[12] The most powerful man at court was now the king's confessor. For a long time that post had been occupied by Père La Chaise, a likeable and moderate man. After 1709 it was taken over by the terrible Père Le Tellier who was loathed because of his fanaticism, and who was forever pushing the king into brutal measures against the Protestants, the Jansenists, and against all those who were not submissive to the demands of the faction.

Most of the king's ministers were pious men. Le Peletier said his vespers every day; Pontchartrain had a room at the Oratoire; Torcy knew all the psalms by heart. Whatever the problem, Beauvillier had 'les yeux fixés sur l'intérêt de l'Eglise', and nearly always on the interests of the pope. Over a number of years the Duc de Chevreuse was the intimate confidant of the king, a devout man who repeated to the Prince everything Fénelon told him.

So far as the zealots were concerned the most important goal was the return to Roman orthodoxy of those who had left it. At no time in the century had they accepted the Edict of Nantes. But it had been royal policy not to interfere with it despite purchased conversions and bullying. In 1685, however, when the religious faction had dominated the affairs of the kingdom, it imposed the revocation of the Edict. The episcopate was elated, and Bossuet happy that the Protestants were dispersed and that God had at last agreed to 'purger la France de ces monstres'. But the horrors accompanying the revocation and the ensuing devastation enlightened receptive Frenchmen, who learned the high price of orthodox régimes. They only had to compare the power of England and Holland, where tolerance was practised, with the decline of France and the decadence of Italy and Spain.

Louis XIV's Jesuit confessors also persuaded him that it was essential to destroy Jansenism, and his soldiers tore down the abbey at Port-Royal. If Louis XIV thought that he had thus finished with Jansenism it was only because he failed to recognise that many Frenchmen, although indifferent to the problem of grace, saw in Jansenism the centre of resistance to despotism and the articulation of their hostility to the Catholic hierarchy.

The French also blamed the religious faction for the war policies followed since 1680, thinking the taste for prestige insufficient explanation. The main cause of French mistakes seemed, clearly, the fact that England had been made the chief enemy, and the religious causes for this were all too obvious. Louis XIV's aim was to restore the Catholic Stuarts to the English throne, and so Catholicism to Great Britain. For him and his political advisers the war was a kind of crusade against the heretical powers. Racine, after he had become Mme de Maintenon's poet, aptly described the basic philosophy of the régime when he praised Louis XIV for being the only king, in a world in which there were so many, who had armed himself to fight God's battle and the only one who fought for the rights of heaven.[13]

While the influence of the religious faction weighed heavily upon the policies pursued by the kingdom, its stranglehold on the lives of Frenchmen had become almost intolerable. The law permitted the intervention of the police in family matters, harrying those who appeared lazy or licentious and even those who were neither of these things but were 'en péril évident' of becoming so. In each case the police had authority to imprison people without trial.

The religious party had also, for a long time, considered plays to be one of the 'pompes de Satan'. The king, though he had loved them so much in the past, stopped going to them around 1686. Courtiers no longer dared go to the theatre for fear of incurring royal displeasure. In 1694, Bossuet came down heavily on a poor monk who had with immense timidity imprudently tried to justify the theatre. It would have taken very little for plays to have been banned altogether.

This illustrious prelate was in fact the strongest personality in the religious faction, and, like it, was not content that France was a Catholic country but wanted it to become what the Compagnie du Saint-Sacrement had wanted it to be since 1630. It is little use trying to understand him in the abstract and outside history; only the development of French society from 1655 to the end of the century can help explain him.

Like Pascal, Bossuet belonged to the bourgeoisie. But he came from a family that had allowed itself to be attracted by the extreme elements of the religious faction. His father had close ties with the Compagnie du Saint-Sacrement. He himself was devoted to this secret society, not least because it had smoothed his way in the career he had chosen. He became bishop of Condom, tutor to the Dauphin and, in 1681, bishop of Meaux, near Paris and the court.

He had all the appearances of a man who was moderate, conciliatory, with breadth of vision. He endeavoured to get on with everyone in authority, with the royal government as well as with that of the Nuncio. He even managed to be considered by the Protestants and Jansenists as a man with whom one could reach an understanding. In society he was treated with esteem : Mme de Lafayette loved to talk about how pleasing his character was and Mme de Montespan took him into her most intimate circle. He was said to be 'l'homme du monde le plus gracieux et le plus obligeant'. The archbishop of Paris used almost identical words, saying that he was 'le plus doux du monde' and that he was 'd'aucun parti'.[14]

His sermons had brought him a great reputation. Some historians have maintained that his sermons and funeral orations had not aroused universal admiration during his lifetime, and that his contemporaries had preferred those of Bourdaloue and Fléchier. The chroniclers of the period prove the reverse. In 1657 it was already understood that Abbé Bossuet 'prêchait divinement'.[15] Bayle, writing in 1675, called him the Coryphaeus of the preachers. The reason why, in later years, his contemporaries mentioned his eloquence less often was that after 1670, i.e. very early, he was only rarely in the pulpit. He had other occupations which took his time.

His oratory admirably exhibits the picture French society had of the world at that time, as well as what might be termed its metaphysics. It was a grandiose picture, still showing clear traces of the baroque era. The universe was like a stage on which tragedies were played out that were full of incidents and catastrophes. The actors could only be obscure individuals. But the spectacle assumed pathetic proportions when the actors had names like Cromwell, Henriette d'Angleterre, or Condé. Above the stage hovered Providence, a mysterious power that caused the actors to move about without their being able to discover why or where. It alone determined whether their enterprises prospered or failed; their own foresight, calculations, and strength counted for nothing. Bossuet's contemporaries found in his funeral orations a magnificent expression of their own thoughts on God, the universe, and the human condition.

He had also brought himself to the attention of the public through a quite different activity. In 1655 he had published the *Réfutation* of a Protestant catechism, and since then he attached the greatest importance to the conversion of the members of the Reformed Church. His views on this were expressed in his *Exposition de la foi catholique* (1671), a remarkably skilful and moderate book. In fact it was so moderate that it worried some members of the hierarchy, and the Protestants, for their part, felt that the real differences between the Christian confessions had been avoided rather than resolved. But its skill, which helped to bring about the conversion of a number of highly placed Protestants, including Marshal Turenne, seemed to justify it in the eyes of many Catholics.

That is how Bossuet appeared before 1680. Thereafter, however, he showed what he was really made of, and his real intentions became clear. The king having become devout, and Mme de Maintenon having made herself the intermediary between the religious faction and the king, Bossuet began to support with all his authority the evolution of the monarchy towards a régime of stifling orthodoxy. It was then that he adopted towards the intellectual problems of his time what one of his biographers has called his attitude of imperious immobility. Bossuet thought nothing of calling in the police to silence all who failed to agree with him. He had Richard Simon's *Histoire critique* seized and the meetings of scholars at the home of Abbé Launoy prohibited. He condemned the scientist Ellies du Pin. He took steps to have the *Méditations Chrétiennes* of Malebranche seized in Paris. He was hoping for a France in which everyone would think and live as the religious faction thought he should. In 1694, when that timid apology for the theatre by Père Caffaro appeared, he lambasted the cleric and had him suspended from his duties.[16] He was one of those who at that time desired the disappearance of all playhouses from the lands of the most Christian king.

Bossuet proceeded to demonstrate a rare ability to highlight the irreconcilable differences between Churches and doctrines. His *Histoire des variations des Eglises protestantes* (1688) opened many eyes, including those of many Protestants. Thanks to Bossuet, they were able to recognise the essential aspect of the Reformation, i.e. the right to 'varier' in the sincere quest for truth. Enlightened men, of whom there was a growing number, were horrified at the despotic doctrine in his *Politique tirée de l'Ecriture Sainte*, and they were increasingly attracted to the view, soon to be taken up by Montesquieu, that it is liberty which promotes the strength of nations. In the realm of history and particularly in theology Bossuet's interference ruined the work which Catholic scholars had accomplished over more than a half-century in trying to reconcile respect for dogma with freedom in research. He made them realise that the conflict between these two was irresolvable, and they concluded that they had to choose between faith and free enquiry in the historical sciences.

However, Bossuet retained a considerable following in an

important section of French society, both before and after his death. He personified for them some of the essential traditions of the nation: a sense of order, respect for law, the suspicion of exceptions and privileges, and a certain preference for the concrete. Whatever did not fit well into the framework of positive reason was for him chimerical and dangerous. The French bourgeoisie as a whole could see its reflection in this kind of approach. Little did it realise that what it admired in him was mainly its own inadequacies.

Fénelon was different. He was an aristocrat by birth and upbringing. Throughout his life these origins remained in evidence, and when he later on showed himself to be sincerely concerned about the miseries of the people he did it in a way characteristic of a member of his class. Apart from this he was sensitive and artistic. He was a complex man, changeable, and indefinable and inclined to melancholia. He dreamt of Greek landscapes and the beauty of ancient history.

Fénelon's family had the closest possible ties with the Compagnie du Saint-Sacrement. He himself was a priest and was soon in charge of the house of the Nouvelles Catholiques. This was in fact a detention centre in which the religious faction had young Protestant women locked up, and even children, in order to convince them of the desirability of a rapid conversion. The treatment meted out to these wretched girls was calculated to be a most efficient instrument for fast conversions.[17] After the Revocation of the Edict of Nantes, Abbé Fénelon was sent to Saintonge to try out his talents for effecting conversions there. He fulfilled his task without undue violence, but with a zeal that took some odd forms.

From a date that is not known with certainty he became a close follower of Bossuet. He showed for the bishop such a frenzied admiration that some contemporaries were shocked by it. At the same time he managed to enter the society of a number of duchesses who were close friends of Mme de Maintenon. In 1689 he was appointed tutor to the Duc de Bourgogne, the grandson of Louis XIV. His friends expected him to become archbishop of Paris and even, one day, to direct the affairs of the kingdom.

There was thus nothing in those years that could have led

one to foresee the events which were soon to arrest that dazzling career. In October 1688 Fénelon met Mme Guyon. Without any desire to found a sect, this woman was preaching a kind of spiritual mysticism. Fénelon treated all this at first with reserve; but then he did allow himself to be convinced, after which there was no holding him. He introduced Mme Guyon to his friends. Important people became worried. In 1694–5 meetings were held at the seminary at Issy to appraise Mme Guyon's doctrine. The strong personality of Bossuet dominated these. But Fénelon succeeded in finding a series of formulae that gave the illusion of agreement among the prelates.

The Issy meeting did however give rise to a quarrel which assumed disgraceful proportions. Bossuet decided to take the bit between his teeth. He discovered another Luther in Fénelon and dared accuse him in one of his books of having had sinful relations with Mme Guyon. He alerted the King of France and the Holy See. Fénelon defended himself with much elegance and wit as well as with tireless tenacity; it has been calculated that he wrote what would have been the equivalent of 2,500 pages of print.

It seemed as if Bossuet had the last word. In 1699 the Holy See decided to condemn twenty-three propositions extracted from Fénelon's *Maximes des Saints*. But all this violence had only succeeded in scandalising public opinion. The public had been struck by the vigorous denials with which Fénelon had met the accusations of his opponents more than once. There was talk of the fanaticism of the bishop of Meaux. His writings were thought 'fatigants'. Chiefly, however, decent people had the courage to think and say that this quarrel was ridiculous, and that the 'sciences solides' and good sense alike could not care less about these spiritual discussions.

However, if one can overlook the sickening aspects of this quarrel, one can see that it was concerned with an important problem. Bossuet looked at spiritual matters from the point of view of prudence and reason. He was after all a traditional bourgeois, and was thus distrustful of illusory solutions and the dubious promptings of personal feelings. He could not believe in anything that could not be clearly ascertained; it had to work and be tangible. In other words, Bossuet wanted the lives of Christians to be faithful to their duties as Christians. Fénelon, on the other hand, with his aristocratic cast of mind and his poetic make-up needed more freedom for the soul, more spontaneity, less awareness of the rewards of piety,

Fénelon had provided a philosophical justification for this attitude to spiritual matters. He believed that there was present in man a simple, infinite, immutable spark that is God himself. That was for him the only philosophy worthy of its name; it was the eternal philosophy of Plato and St Augustine. He reproached Bossuet, as well as the entire Jansenist school, with having abandoned this pure doctrine and with having reduced the moral life to the level of vanity, i.e. the satisfaction of private interests. The basic differences between these two metaphysical systems comes out very clearly in the debate on the virtue of hope which led to a violent clash between Bossuet and Fénelon.

These differences had political consequences.[18] The philosophy of Fénelon was based on the belief in the primacy of the universal. In politics, he was thus led to subordinate totally and without qualification the interests of states and princes to those of humanity as a whole or, rather, to the demands of the moral law. He said most explicitly that man belongs less to himself than to his family, less to his family than to his country, and less to his country than to humanity.

He therefore had to condemn the policies of Louis XIV. He did not shrink from doing so and had the courage to send the king a fearful letter in which he passed judgment on French policies in the light of eternal justice. His *Télémaque* was written in the same spirit. It expounded the maxims of a Christian policy. Perhaps he was not thinking of the king when he wrote the book. But when it appeared the public was bound to see in it innumerable allusions to recent events.

For these reasons Fénelon has seemed to some to be a forerunner of the Enlightenment of the next century. This is of course nonsense, but it is easy to see how it arose. The public was unaware of the relations Fénelon had with Père Tellier and the Jesuits. Nor did it know that the prelate had urged the persecution of the Jansenists and that the bull *Unigenitus* was the answer to his prayers. On the other hand, the maxims of *Télémaque* squared very well with a number of beliefs of the philosophes. They were directed towards a peace policy and the interests of the greatest number. What the French welcomed in Fénelon was that he was a philosopher at the service of humanity.

Bossuet and Fénelon dominated the religious history of France in the second half of the seventeenth century, but not so overwhelmingly that one can forget all the other names. Bourdaloue, Mascaron, Fléchier, Massillon were all admired by the Frenchmen of their time, and they have even today an honourable place in the history of French literature.

From 1670, Bourdaloue had an immense success in Paris with his sermons.[19] During Lent 1671 ladies sent their lackeys to reserve them seats at the church twenty-four hours before the sermon of the Reverend Father. His brand of eloquence corresponded very well with the taste of the period. It was in line with the analyses of the emotions that found so much favour in those days, and it contained striking descriptions of the manners of the time. Apart from that it was firm; as Mme de Sévigné put it, Père Bourdaloue 'frappait comme un sourd'. His contemporaries also remarked on 'son zèle amer' and his 'emportements'. Louis XIV was led to say that he did not care for such an unmethodical approach in his churches.

Mascaron's oratory was quite different.[20] Listening to him one was aware of his close affinities with fashionable society. His language was calculated to seduce. But, so far as his doctrine was concerned, his demands were rigorous, and he talked about human virtue as did the Augustinians.

Fléchier was also much seen in fashionable and literary circles.[21] For that reason he was welcomed into the Académie Française. One can understand this when one observes the care he took to make his sermons elegant and harmonious.

At the very end of the century the court was entranced by a young man from the Oratoire, Père Massillon.[22] His sermons enable us to get the feel of how taste had evolved. French society was now asking less for an orator who appealed to its reason than for a kind of oratorical skill that could stir the emotions and bring tears to the eyes. Massillon's sermons fulfilled these needs.

Other movements: humanism and religion

Catholicism thus dominated the life of the French nation throughout the entire seventeenth century. It was the inspiration behind royal policies. It put its stamp on the whole population, regulating its beliefs and habits. There were very many Frenchmen who did not accept the demands of the religious faction, but not even they called into question the dogmas of the Church, or the sacraments, or the status of the hierarchy. That is why so many historians are surprised at the explosion of unbelief which marked the early years of the next century.

The reason for this explosion is to be found in the fact that the political and social dominance of Catholicism merely hid, but did not manage to suppress, currents of thought that had been very powerful since the sixteenth century. The most important of these was humanism.

In those days humanism was not the vague attitude of mind that is fashionable today. It stood for a body of extremely well-defined values. It traced its origins to some great names, in particular to the man the French continued to call 'le divin Erasme'. When Grotius came to live in Paris at the height of his fame he was welcomed as the representative of the noblest and most revered of the spiritual traditions.

The vast majority of humanists were profoundly religious. But not in the manner of Bérulle. They did not derive their inspiration from St Augustine but from the Stoics. The God they were talking about was not a hidden God but infinite reason. This reason manifested its wisdom and goodness in the work of creation. Grotius wrote that 'Un entendement règle le monde, qui ne peut être que l'entendement divin'. Following Justus Lipsius he asked men to see the work of that divine reason in the progress of the arts as much as in the activities of ants and bees.

It is this God of reason who endowed man with intelligence. The humanists could not believe that this intelligence was in any sense obscured by the fall. But they did believe in the existence of sin. They could not have denied it and still remained Christians. They did, however, reduce the significance of the concept to a minimum. They assimilated it to weakness and ignorance, but not to corruption. They could see human nature only as intact and spontaneously directed towards the good. It was thus not so much to save us that God became man but to bring us enlightenment. Reason is not humbled by faith. It is illuminated by it, discovers new truths through it, is taught new virtues.

The difference between humanism and the Augustinians can be seen particularly clearly when it comes to determining the morality of pagans. This might seem a point of secondary interest. But to men who had been brought up on Cicero and Seneca, and who were accustomed to seeing in Cato the most sublime kind of human being, it was a question of capital importance. According to the Augustinians, the great men of antiquity had known neither truth nor virtue. As Bérulle put it, they could only accede to 'des ombres de nos vérités, et des présages de nos mystères'. Even Cato's virtue amounted to no more than an illusion of vanity. It can be imagined that to many university professors, and many Frenchmen who could not forget the lessons they had learnt in the colleges, affirmations of that type must have appeared blasphemous.

It can occasion little surprise that some of the more exacting minds, minds that were aware of the incompatibility of certain doctrines, opted for pagan wisdom and secretly broke with Christianity. They may be divided into two types. There were the Deists, who were probably numerous. And there were others, no doubt small in number, who went all the way to Atheism.

We possess a most valuable account of the Deists at the beginning of the century. The *Quatrains du déiste*, condemned by the apologists, had long been lost, but they[23] have been found and published in our time. They are the work of a college teacher whose name still eludes us. With little elegance but much force they point to the impossibility of reconciling the philosophical concept of God with Christian dogma. They thus take up the arguments of Celsus and Porphyry. In fact they do this with such precision that one may assume the unknown teacher took his arguments straight from these ancient writers. The author maintains that God, i.e. supreme wisdom, cannot possibly regret having created man, or curse the creatures he himself has brought into existence. The story of the fall is incompatible with his goodness. And how can one believe that infinite forgiveness and infinite justice could condemn the majority of mortals to eternal torture?

The Deists were thus no longer Christians. But they remained imbued with the religious spirit. They did not even dislike particular religions, or despise forms of worship, or take up arms against the hierarchy. They thought that a visible religion was necessary together with a ritual, clergy, and even a certain number of dogmas that were freely interpreted by everyone within the secrecy of his own conscience. This was not hypocrisy on their part. They were profoundly convinced that the universal religion must be embodied in particular religious confessions. Conscience must remain free, but actions must fit into the framework of the laws of the city. Here, too, the Deists of the seventeenth century followed the tradition of Celsus, of Julian the Apostate, of Themistius, and the ancient philosophers who had tried to arrest the progress of Christianity. And, like them, they deduced from this religious philosophy the dogma of tolerance.

Far from considering themselves irreligious, the Deists came to think of themselves as the most religious of men because only for them was the religion of the supreme being completely pure. The religion of the masses they called superstition. It was superstition or, as they said in those days, 'bigotterie' which had covered Europe with ruins, and it was still creating disorder within states. It was based on ignorance, prejudice, and fanatical passions. The striking similarity between the vocabularies of the *Quatrains du déiste* and Bacon's twelfth essay *On Superstition* leads one to think that Deism was at that time a religion common to the enlightened minds throughout Europe, and that there were links between the Deists of France and England.

Deism, however, was not able to satisfy all men. Its moderation and its ambiguous attitude towards the various religions must have looked maddeningly flabby to those who liked their answers clear-cut and were inclined towards more radical solutions. There were consequently also Atheists.

There were two kinds of Atheism, which belonged to two different social classes. On the one hand, there were the young noblemen who took their cue from men like Théophile de Viau around 1620; the gentlemen of the court of Gaston, Duc d'Orléans, about 1630–40; or the licentious youths, at the time of the Fronde, whom Parisians knew as the Messieurs du Marais. On the other hand, there were learned bourgeois who knew the philosophical systems of the past, who had studied not only Lucretius but also Pomponazzi and the Paduans, and who sometimes journeyed to Italy to attend Cremonini's courses at Padua. The differences between these two atheistic groups were of course not clear-cut. The nobility had some cultured free-thinkers, and the bourgeoisie had some solidly educated debauchees. Nevertheless, it is undeniable that these two forms of Atheism had very different origins. For the first group free-thinking was above all a way of non-conformity, a reaction against the atmosphere of piousness and pharisaism which had taken possession of France. Far from wanting to avoid scandal they courted it. The other group consisted of philosophers. Their conduct was calculated not to attract the attention of the religious authorities. Those among them who sought to propagate their ideas did so with the utmost discretion, by way of manuscripts that no one thought of publishing.

The naturalism of the Padua school had a greater influence upon these philosophers than even Lucretius.[24] They believed that the universe was eternal and infinite, that it could be compared to a living organism in which all the parts are interrelated and in which the formation and destruction of particular beings are merely accidental to the life of the organism as a whole. Neither the notion of a Creator nor that of a spiritual soul could have meaning in a doctrine which taught that creativity and organisation were immanent in matter. The novels of Cyrano de Bergerac in their secret form and the *Theophrastus redivivus*, which is known to have existed in manuscript in 1659, prove that the materialism of the Paduans was one of the intellectual origins of Atheism during that part of the seventeenth century.[25]

This form of Atheism was not only a metaphysical system but also a political doctrine. The Atheists were Machiavellians. Machiavelli had not simply proffered advice to heads of state. He had also put forward a theory about the origin of society and power. Power is a result of the desire for power; it is not the result of the action of God or pure reason. It rests on force. It is exerted on the minds of men through trickery, religious trickery in particular. All the great leaders of men, be they Romulus, Clovis, or Mohammed, founded their empires on religious illusions that were deliberately and systematically fostered. Whatever the religion, the clergy is never more than the instrument of that policy.

In the eyes of their contemporaries, Machiavelli's doctrine must have seemed to be the political aspect of Atheism. True, the Atheists claimed that they confined themselves entirely to facts and that mysteries of all kinds were outside their province. It is also true that, after having spoken their minds about Romulus or Mohammed, the most noted Atheists – La Mothe le Vayer and Naudé, for example – took care to add that their accounts served to show only more clearly the greatness of 'notre sainte religion'. But Machiavellism placed religion so effectively outside the study of society that it in fact ignored it; or rather, its rejection of it was so unambiguous that it was in truth a system 'sans Dieu', and consequently atheistic. In this radicalism it incurred the displeasure not only of the religious faction but also of the humanists. The latter had learnt from Erasmus that they must subordinate politics to morality. They believed in an eternal law, and particular laws were only valid in their eyes if they conformed to the requirements of absolute justice, i.e. God. The Machiavellians did not believe in morality. They only believed in politics. For them the law was just because it was the law.

Atheism at the time of Richelieu and Mazarin could find a home only in closed philosophical and political circles. It can be taken for granted that for a number of decades after 1660 there were ever fewer Atheists. However, another doctrine was beginning to penetrate into France. Some copies of the *Tractatus* had managed to get into Paris. From about 1670 France had her Spinozists, and the philosophy of Spinoza was then considered to be a systematic form of Atheism.

In the literary world there were some who did not succumb to the spirit of orthodoxy, and who went as far as to deny the spirituality of the soul or even the existence of God. Des Barreaux, Jean Dehénault, and Saint-Pavin were real free-thinkers, whose poetry covertly, but also at times overtly, revealed their rejection of Christian truths and of the dogmas of idealism. Chapelle and Dassoucy were notorious Atheists. Mme

Deshoulières, who was a friend of Chapelle and Dehénault, was reputed not to have believed in the immortality of the soul.[26]

As public opinion became alienated from the world of its rulers in which the religious faction laid down the law, and as more and more Frenchmen came to detest the régime which stifled them and made mistakes into the bargain, the number of Atheists increased sharply in the upper classes of society. The Duc d'Orléans was an Atheist, so were his daughters and counsellors. At the Temple, the Prior's circle was rabid in its Atheism. The salons soon followed suit. To be admitted to them as a person in the fashion, we are told, one had to make a profession of Atheism. The Princess Palatine, in 1699, said that at the court and in Paris one could no longer find a young man who did not want to be an Atheist.[27] Such accounts demonstrate the revolution that occurred in the minds of Frenchmen at the end of the seventeenth century, and they show the magnitude of the error of historians who thought that this revolution did not occur until the following century.

Among the philosophical movements that were opposed to the complete domination of France by Catholic orthodoxy, Epicureanism certainly occupied the first place. It did not merely offer a materialistic metaphysics in which men were no more than ephemeral manifestations of eternal nature. It also provided a conception of life in which pleasure (*volupté*, in the sense in which the ancients understood the term) was the only acceptable absolute moral value.

Epicureanism did not only stand in opposition to religious beliefs. It also combated the doctrines of stoicism which was the dominant philosophy among the humanists – or at least most of the humanists – during the first forty years of the century. The stoics held that man was defined by the presence within him of reason, which was the image and reflection of divine reason, and that as a consequence everyone must regulate his conduct in terms of universal criteria. It followed that everything within us that is sense, that reflects the action of our body upon our soul, could only be considered as a source of error and disorder.

But the first signs of a new form of Epicureanism appeared around 1620. Théophile de Viau, Boisrobert, and Des Barreaux were not common debauchees. Their rejection of religious beliefs and even of idealistic doctrines was based upon their conception of nature. Théophile in particular expressed his views on nature and the place man, in his opinion, occupied within its eternal and blind world.[28] He was persuaded of the powerlessness of our reason, and of the irresistible force of the passions. These Epicureans of 1620 already foreshadowed the consequences of their philosophy for the relations between the individual and the social order. Society, they thought, was wedded to the search for vain honours and wealth. According to their view, the wise man must steer clear of this false order and must believe in only one value in his relations with others: friendship.

At that time Epicureanism was still a doctrine without authority. This situation changed after 1630. First, the change took place among scholars and philosophers. This was essentially the work of Gassendi. At the beginning of 1634 he brought out his *Apologie d'Epicure*. He then began work on a major book, *De Vita et Moribus Epicuri*. This was not published until 1647. But it may be taken for granted that he taught the Epicurean doctrine in the circle of the Dupuy brothers. This accounts for the *Discours de morale sur Epicure* written in 1645–6 by the poet Sarasin who belonged to that circle.[29]

In fact the *Discours* was singularly prudent. It made the Epicurean idea of pleasure look very austere. It emphasised the characteristics which distinguish it from what we normally mean by pleasure. But the essence of Epicureanism is there. The supreme good is said not to reside in virtue but in a kind of internal joy that has its foundation in the peace, harmony, and freedom of the soul.

While Gassendi, and Sarasin under his influence, provided the public with a philosophical justification of Epicureanism, others provided it with the spectacle of lives lived in accordance with the Epicurean doctrine of pleasure. The most notable of these was Vauquelin des Yveteaux,[30] once tutor to the Duc de Vendôme and then to the eldest son of Henry IV; but the religious faction kept him away from the court after the death of the king. He spent the rest of his life in retirement, which he devoted to the search for sophisticated pleasures. According to his numerous admirers, he was the Epicurus of his time and the glory of his age. He summed up the rule of his life in a sonnet. There were some who condemned these verses with indignation. Others saw in them the maxims of real wisdom.

Contemporaries would also point to Des Barreaux.[31] He was not afraid to shock pious souls with the things he said. Nor is it impossible that he was a licentious man. But what is more important is that he was a philosopher and that he knew what he was preaching. He had been a disciple of Théophile de Viau and a pupil at Padua of the philosopher Cremonini. In 1641 he went to visit Descartes in Holland and was later, in Paris, made welcome by the Dupuy brothers and their friends. To judge by his verse, his Epicureanism amounted mainly to a great disdain for reason, and an acute sense of the vanity of all the values most men esteem. His conclusion was that we have no other way of escaping from despair than to throw ourselves 'dans le sein des plaisirs'.

But it is Saint-Evremond who best represents the Epicureanism of the years that separate the government of Richelieu from the personal rule of Louis XIV.[32] It has been the custom to study him with Bayle and Fontenelle because he happened to live on to the beginning of the following century. But he was already keenly interested in the humanities in 1638, and by 1640 he was an assiduous visitor to the home of Gassendi. He belonged to a world that remembered Montaigne, that admired Théophile de Viau, and in which the *Satyricon* of Petronius was considered to be the most exquisite work of Latin literature.

He was therefore an Epicurean. But not like Gassendi. Gassendi equated pleasure with indolence, i.e. the absence of pain. But Saint-Evremond went so far as to teach the active pursuit of pleasure. He thought that wisdom consisted in putting into that pursuit sophistication, balance, and prudence. His letter *Sur les plaisirs* which he wrote to his friend the Comte d'Olonne in 1657, as well as the pages he devoted to Petronius which were written between 1653 and 1660, prove that he had already at that stage worked out his definitive system of morality.[33]

Once Louis XIV took the kingdom personally in hand there could be little hope for Epicureanism. This was not because the court lived an austere existence during the first twenty years of the king's reign. The fêtes and pleasures at the court, which the king prized most highly, hardly testify to this. But Epicureanism was inseparable from an attitude of aloofness from political life. The Epicurean was a man who cultivated with care his own personal life, and was therefore prepared to allow anyone but himself to indulge in the pursuit of military glory, titles, offices, and fortunes. The government of Louis XIV could not be expected to approve of that kind of philosophy.

The Epicurean tradition was nevertheless continued by a few. But after 1680, when the reign made for conformity and the gloomiest kind of piety, when the cours galantes were becoming the real centres of fashionable social and intellectual life and beginning to play the rôle Versailles was no longer capable of filling, Epicureanism became the most generally accepted philosophy.

In the eyes of the public, this stage of Epicureanism was personified by Abbé Chaulieu. He had been a pupil of Chapelle who had himself been influenced by the teaching of Gassendi. It was thus the Epicureanism of 1640 which was being given a new lease of life by Chaulieu. But he had also known the Epicureans of 1660, and through Mme Deshoulières and Jean Dehénault he had links with the Epicureanism of Des Barreaux as well.

Abbé Chaulieu taught that wisdom lies in following nature, that thought is a dangerous guide, that the supreme being has given us sweet and true feelings, and that the mind is good for nothing except for corrupting these feelings.

Chaulieu's influence was great. He was the trusted friend of the Vendômes and in the favour of Monsieur le Duc, Prince de Conty, and in fact all who were sickened by the spirit of conformity that reigned at Versailles. Through these men and women Epicureanism became the moral doctrine of those who counted in society during the last years of the reign. And it was at Sceaux, at Anet, at the Temple, and at Vaux-le-Vicomte that the young Voltaire was introduced to the tradition.

6

Science and philosophy

The scientific societies

It was twenty years before scholars and scientists succeeded in organising themselves after the end of the religious wars. But by 1620 there were several societies in Paris in which they met regularly.

By far the most important of these societies met at the house that had belonged to de Thou and was then the home of Pierre and Jacques Dupuy. It was known as the Académie putéane. It met daily, towards the end of the afternoon.[1] Its members were philosophers, scholars, and scientists. Among its literary members were Chapelain, Ménage, and Perrot d'Ablancourt, while Balzac kept himself informed of its activities far away in his Charente. Among the other societies in Paris that of de Mesmes is noteworthy, but that of Père Nicolas Bourbon is also worth mentioning. He used to meet his friends in his small cell at the Oratoire. In 1635 another cleric, Père Mersenne, formed an academy 'toute mathématique' which included the greatest names in mathematics, Roberval, Désargues, and Mydorge. Etienne Pascal also belonged to this little group of eminent mathematicians.[2]

A kind of republic of letters was coming into existence. These academies kept each other informed of their work, and not only of their own work but also of that of groups of scholars throughout Europe, from Italy to Holland and Germany. A vast correspondence provided the means for this exchange of information. In this connection the erudite Peiresc's name particularly comes to mind, who from his retreat in Provence provided scholars with information in the most admirably agreeable and skilful prose.

What particularly impresses one in the work of these scientific societies – disregarding for the moment the mathematical academy of Père Mersenne – is that the same men were interested in all the sciences, in the progress of astronomy as well as in the problems of philology and morality. At the Académie putéane they discussed the variants of a Greek text, but they also talked about the customs of oriental peoples and the recent eclipse. It can be assumed that each member of the society did not bring the same interest to all the disciplines. But all its members had some interest in all these questions.[3]

At the same time a common mentality was evolved, a common conception of science, its conditions, and its methods. The members of the societies had broken with the Aristotelianism of the schoolmen. If there were some who remained faithful to Aristotle, it was because they saw in him the enemy of metaphysical fantasies, the man who, above all, wanted to be a scientist. All of them were agreed that the mind gets lost the moment it constructs systems. They rejected deductions based on *a priori* premises, and ambitious argumentation. They believed only in organised experience.

This conception of science appeared clearly when they spoke of man. They satisfied their desire to investigate human nature by analysing the accounts of historians and travellers, and not by looking into metaphysical theories about man. The illusory character of contemporary metaphysical doctrines seemed clear to them. They could not accept the metaphysicians' view that man possesses a spiritual reason, that this reason is always the same wherever there are men, and that it illuminates all men in the same way. The scientists, for their part, held that none of these metaphysical statements can be true, and that there is no proposition to which all men subscribe. Nor is there an exception in the cases of the existence of God and the immortality of the soul. Whatever the metaphysicians might have said, the scientists did not think that there was any rational evidence for either of these beliefs.

It must not, however, be concluded that the members of the Académie putéane were Atheists to a man. Some Atheists there were among them, particularly La Mothe le Vayer and Gabriel Naudé. But they were certainly few, and they did not betray it in their writings. 'Scepticism' was the name they gave to the attitude they had in common with the other scientists. This did not mean that they did not hold any truth to be certain. They merely wanted to convey that the mind can only attain concrete truths, and that the affirmations of metaphysics can be neither proved nor disproved.

Three men may be said to have personified the spirit of the new science. Gassendi was the most important.[4] He had come from Provence in 1628. The Dupuy brothers had welcomed him and he occupied an eminent position in their circle. The Tétrade was the name given to the group of intimate friends that was founded by Gassendi within the Académie putéane with La Mothe le Vayer, Gabriel Naudé, and Diodati. In 1643 Gassendi became a professor at the Collège Royal and his influence began to spread. Chapelle, Cyrano de Bergerac, and Saint-Evremond became his fervent admirers and disciples. Guy Patin became his friend.

He was a priest, a canon, and official theologian at the cathedral in Digne, and one may be fairly certain that he remained throughout his life sincerely submissive to the Church, its dogmas and prescriptions. He read his breviary regularly until his last moments. He spent his whole life fighting all manifestations of the metaphysical approach, but he must have thought that faith allows us to enter regions that are closed to natural ways of knowledge.

Gassendi spent many years on the *Syntagma philosophicum* which expounds the whole of his thought. Published after his death, its doctrine follows the Epicurean tradition of the ancients. Basing himself on Epicurus and Lucretius he attacked the rationalism of his century which itself had obvious connections with traditional Stoicism. The influence of his doctrine was immense. It is a very strange mistake to link, as is done all too often, seventeenth-century thought and literature with Cartesianism. The Frenchman of 1640 and 1650 thinks in terms of Gassendi's philosophy, whether he be physicist or psychologist, interested in morals or politics. He is prudent, methodical, and entirely taken up with the lessons taught by experience. He is afraid of ambitious rationalist constructions and systems. He distrusts big words and their seductive influence on the uninstructed. It was the philosophy of Gassendi which inspired Chapelain, the authoritative theoretician of classicist doctrine.

It was also Gassendi who was the inspiration behind the

doctrine of Vaugelas on language. For on no occasion does the author of the *Remarques* think of invoking reason to approve or condemn a given expression. He confines himself to usage. He can even be found to approve an idiom after having himself pointed to its irrationality. He wrote that 'Il n'y a qu'un maître des langues, qui en est le roi et le tyran, c'est l'usage'. He was thus a faithful disciple of Gassendi.

The same outlook can be found in La Mothe le Vayer and Gabriel Naudé. The first published nine *Dialogues faits à l'imitation des Anciens* in 1630–1, which are a manual of sceptical thought; then, in 1643, *Opuscules*, which were inspired by Pyrrho. Naudé, in 1639, brought out his *Considérations politiques sur les coups d'Etat*, whose misleading title covers a treatise on political philosophy that is in tune with Gassendi's approach. Both writers in fact put forward their views with a rigour Gassendi had deliberately shunned. Rather than fly off into metaphysical speculation, they kept to facts, which in their case meant historical evidence and that provided by travellers. So far as the grand principles of rationalism went La Mothe le Vayer contented himself with pointing to the contradictions they involved, showing that, in terms of hard fact, we know of no single value in history which has received the universal assent of all men at all times. Nor did Naudé go to metaphysics to find out about the notions of absolute justice and political power. He looked at the facts and noted that power is simply force, that taking power amounts to staging a coup d'état, and that the solid foundation of social order is based upon the pretensions of kings and priests.

Cartesianism

Gassendi's doctrine reigned supreme in intellectual circles until about 1660. During that period another philosophy came into being, which gradually supplanted it. That was the philosophy of Descartes.[5]

It became very clear, as early as 1626, that Descartes was adopting a position that ran counter to that professed in the Dupuy circle. The latter saw the progress of the humanities as coming through the acquisition of factual knowledge. They were philologists. Descartes made a radical break with history and tradition. Where they tried to obtain reasonable conclusions from observed facts, he maintained that the reasonable did not count and that only the absolute was worth having. Again, while the friends of the Académie putéane, and Gassendi most of all, had a deep distrust of metaphysics, Descartes wrote in 1630 that it was his aim to 'démontrer les vérités métaphysiques d'une façon qui est plus évidente que les démonstrations de la géométrie'.

In a sense, Descartes was, therefore, outside the main currents of his time. But not quite as much as one might think. He was in agreement with his enlightened contemporaries when they condemned the philosophical teaching dispensed at the university, which was a mixture of Aristotelianism and scholasticism and quite unable to assimilate the great discoveries that the last half century had yielded in the sciences. Also, his ideas on the physical sciences squared very well with Gassendi's atomism. He wanted to explain physical phenomena in terms of the make-up and motion of extension: the world was for him assimilable to a machine. A Gassendist and a Cartesian therefore had no quarrel about what kind of research was required.

It was different when it came to metaphysics. But even here the views of Descartes were not peculiar to him. They were in line with those of Bérulle and his school. Like Bérulle, Père Gibieuf, and Père de Condren, he accorded the highest place in his universe, and therefore in his metaphysics, to the idea of an infinite being that imparted its wisdom to the mind of man and was more clearly present to man than man himself. Descartes went so far as to write that the human mind has intuitive knowledge of the 'nature intellectuelle', that the latter when considered without limits is God, and that when it is limited belongs either to an angel or to man himself.

Descartes' thought rapidly caught on. This was because he affirmed that it was possible to have a 'science générale' that would throw light on all the various particular sciences. This confidence in the power of the mind must have made quite a contrast with the prudence and indeed timidity of Gassendi. Descartes' *Discours de la Méthode* (1637) provided a method of thought. In 1644 he published the *Principes de philosophie*. Numerous scientific discoveries brought him to the attention of the public. His metaphysical system was to earn him the admiration of the religiously inclined. It seemed to them the best defence against the scepticism that was very clearly the normal result of Gassendi's approach. The Messieurs of Port-Royal who lived in the orbit of Antoine Arnauld were Cartesians.

When Descartes died in Stockholm in 1650 he was known and admired, but his school was not yet supreme. It did, however, advance rapidly thereafter. The return of his body from Sweden in 1667, and the funeral honours given to it in the church of Saint-Etienne du Mont, provided the occasion for the adherents of his doctrine to demonstrate their strength. The academies that came into being around 1660 were Cartesian. A very rich magistrate, Habert de Montmort, had established an academy for physicists. It was reputed secretly to favour the diffusion of Cartesian ideas. The ablest Cartesians, Rohault and Cordemoy, were welcome members of the academy that met at the house of Condé.[6]

Other societies, directed towards the humanities rather than physics, followed suit. In 1663 Abbé d'Aubignac transformed the informal meetings that had been held at his house for a number of years into a regular academy. His education had been Cartesian and he stood for the principles of clear demonstration and rational deduction where the preceding generation had wanted erudition. In 1667 de Lamoignon began to form an academy. Most of its members were Cartesians. In particular, it contained Rohault, Clerselier, Cordemoy, and Abbé Fleury; they were soon to be joined by Boileau.

Cartesianism had begun to conquer the highest positions of French society. Counsellors of parlement, maîtres des requêtes, and royal officers all began to succumb. Great noblemen were gradually conquered: the Duc de Luynes, the Duc de Nevers, and Marshal Vivonne openly patronised Cartesian circles. Even the salons opened their doors to the new philosophy, and the ladies of society proclaimed that they were both learned and Cartesian. This was not merely because they wanted to be in the fashion. Cartesianism had confidence in reason, and consequently in the inspiration of personal taste. Thanks to this, it was no longer necessary to know Greek and Latin to appreciate the delights of a madrigal. Only good sense was required. And Cartesianism taught that women have as much of that as men.

Among clerics, Cartesianism met with hostility from the Jesuits.[7] But it gained ground in the Oratoire, at least with some of its members. This was because they recognised the kinship between some aspects of its doctrine and the main theses of Augustinianism as exemplified in the doctrine of Bérulle, their founder. Those in charge of the Oratoire were, in fact, becoming worried about this, and the clerics involved had to sign an undertaking that they would only teach the sound doctrines of Aristotelianism and remain within healthy traditions.

Both the Church and the government tried to halt the progress of the new philosophy. In 1671 the faculty of theology recalled that only the teaching of Aristotle had been authorised. The royal government repeatedly issued strict orders with the same message. In 1680 it cancelled lectures that were to be given by the Cartesian Régis. In 1691, and again in 1704, professors of philosophy under the jurisdiction of the university of Paris had to give a signed undertaking not to teach the philosophy of Descartes.

These attempts at repression were of no avail. There were Christian philosophers who thought that Cartesianism provided the most effective barrier against religious unbelief. This was true of the theologians of Port-Royal as well as of Bossuet. Bossuet saw the metaphysics of Descartes as an instrument for demonstrating the existence of God and the immortality of the soul. Like Arnauld and Nicole, Bossuet looked upon Cartesianism as a modern expression of the *philosophia perennis*, the philosophy of Plato and St Augustine which could be called the Christian philosophy. He demonstrated his conviction in the religious value of Cartesianism by appointing Cartesians to important posts and surrounding himself with them. Thanks to him two Cartesians, Malézieu and De Court, obtained posts with the Duc du Maine. The court at Sceaux, where his influence was considerable, was entirely Cartesian.

This current of Cartesianism, which did not seek to set itself up in opposition to Christian thought but rather to complement it, explains the philosophy of Malebranche and its popularity in French society at the end of the century.[8]

Malebranche belonged to the Oratoire. That means that he was an Augustinian. We are told that he discovered Cartesianism in 1664 and that he was won over to it. Descartes' doctrine appealed to him for its Augustinian content. It brought out the radical differences between the senses and reason, and came out strongly in favour of reason. Malebranche, it is true, also had points of difference with Descartes, but he always resolved these in conformity with Augustinian doctrine.

Malebranche's philosophy was therefore essentially religious. Nevertheless, and whatever the intentions of its author might have been, it had aspects which gave encouragement to those who were opposed to orthodoxy. His great work *La Recherche de la vérité* (1674–5) was really a treatise on the causes of error. Among these causes he named uncritically accepted traditions. He showed with admirable lucidity to what errors the imagination and the emotions can lead. In a different key and with entirely opposite intentions, he therefore implicitly offered the same criticism of beliefs and orthodoxy that had been put forward by La Mothe le Vayer and Naudé even before 1640. It is not that we are reading into the works of Malebranche lessons unintended by him: but history itself points to the conclusion that *La Recherche de la vérité* exerted its influence mainly in this direction.

But even the metaphysical system of Malebranche postulated principles that went against religious beliefs. One of his basic tenets was that God does not act through the will of individuals. Yet the entire Christian faith depends upon these individual wills. It is by an act of will on the part of an individual that God wanted incarnation and redemption; it is because there are individual wills that He is addressed in prayer; it is for the same reason that there is a belief in miracles. Malebranche was aware of that radical difference, and he deployed infinite subtlety to surmount it. It was inevitable that his works should have results he himself condemned.

The same difficulties appeared within Cartesianism. After 1660 eminent Cartesians, particularly Rohault and Sylvain Régis, expounded Descartes' system with the main emphasis on the mechanistic account of nature. In their case the Cartesian doctrine tended to link up with the philosophy of experience. And it became increasingly Descartes' method which was held to be important, to the detriment of his metaphysics. In this context Fontenelle presents a notable example. He remained faithful to Descartes' method of thought, but entirely closed to his metaphysics.

Thus understood, Cartesianism served as a critical instrument. At the end of the reign of Louis XIV resolute Atheists like Boindin, Mirabaud, and Terrasson[9] were Cartesians and based their Atheism upon Cartesian thought. They took over from Descartes the rejection of final causes. This made physical events into simple products, activities that were the results of 'impulsions', and nature became no more than an 'arrangement matériel', the result 'd'un hasard extrême'. The Jesuits found here plenty of excuses for their old tenacious opposition to Cartesianism, which was in their eyes a system of the universe entirely 'mécanique et géométrique'.

The opposition the Cartesians encountered among the defenders of religion was repeated by those who had remained faithful to the philosophy of experience or, more precisely, the Gassendists. If one carefully examines the atmosphere in the scientific societies of Paris, one notes that the spirit of Gassendi remained much more in evidence than many historians seem to think. It dominated Mme de la Sablière's circle as well as that of Henri Justel.[10] In London, Saint-Evremond was showing himself to be strongly anti-Cartesian and to be faithful to the lessons Gassendi had taught him.

This opposition to Cartesianism centred around two points which are connected with the general development of ideas in the seventeenth century. There were excellent men who were not prepared to share the disdain the new philosophy had for humanism and Greco-Roman culture. Descartes had considered Low-Breton and Latin as being on the same level. His disciples remembered this only too well. Listening to them, one received the impression that the study of nature demanded that one despised antiquity and good scholarship. This annoyed the followers of Gassendi. One of them treated the Cartesians as illiterates. Their complaints cannot have been unjust; we find them repeated by Leibniz.

There was another point on which Cartesianism introduced

disagreeable habits. It accustomed the mind to dogmatism. Gassendi and his friends of the Académie putéane had been careful to resist the temptation of system-building and arriving at peremptory conclusions, to bring out instead with great prudence the various aspects of a problem, to allow their readers to come freely to their own conclusions. The Cartesians admitted only one truth, i.e. that of their system. People were shocked by the tone they tended to adopt. Descartes, said the Chevalier de Méré, is 'un maître de roquets'. This dogmatism was all the more irritating because the unprejudiced were aware of the all too large number of imprudent hypotheses in the Cartesian system. Dr Menjot, a follower of Gassendi, praised Pascal for having poked fun at Descartes' physics, and for having called it 'le roman de la nature'.

It was the custom for a long time to link the doctrine of classicism with Cartesianism. This was a clumsy mistake. But it is still being made. However, it is now known that classicism is not the product of 1660, and that there had been men at the beginning of the century who championed a literary doctrine that was already entirely classical. It is known even more clearly that between 1630 and 1640 there was a ten-year quarrel between a group that was called the Réguliers and those who objected to the growing respect for rules. Moreover, if there are men who are entitled to be called the theoreticians of classicism they are Chapelain, Conrart, Balzac, and, a little less so, La Ménardière and Abbé d'Aubignac. By 1640 the Réguliers had won, which amounts to saying that classicism had won. Cartesianism had nothing to do with it.

Twenty years later, however, Cartesianism began to spread. The circles and societies which were concerned with literary questions came to take an interest in it, and it was then that its influence began to exert itself. But it did not bring with it, as some have thought, a doctrine of order and good sense: that job had been done long ago. What it did contribute was dogmatism and abstract arguments. It condemned in the name of universal reason all the mystery, all that is intangible in the imagination. By the sorriest paradox it seemed to want to exclude from literature all that was original and personal.

The first example of literary Cartesianism was the preface

to the *Epigrammatum delectus* published by the Messieurs of Port-Royal in 1659. Its author was probably Lancelot, who was a Cartesian.[11] He particularly emphasised that real beauty is to be found in truth, and that the source of beauty is to be found in the true. Literary works must therefore stick to reason. There are universal and certain principles to which writers must conform. Beauty is unchanging and eternal. It is constant, certain, and timeless.

It would of course be an oversimplification and consequently unjust to make Cartesianism solely responsible for this kind of mentality. It should be seen as a systematised aspect of a general move by the society of the period towards universal and fixed values. But in giving this new mentality its systematic form, Cartesianism gave it a consistency and sharpness that it would have lacked without it. Alert observers realised this. In his early days Boileau had been a Cartesian. Later, however, he became worried by the turn things had taken. He told his friends that the philosophy of Descartes 'avait coupé la gorge à la poésie', that it 'desséchait' the mind and accustomed it to a 'justesse matérielle' which had nothing in common with what is appropriate in poetry or oratory. At the end of his life Boileau realised that Cartesianism was the philosophy of the Moderns, and consequently the enemy of that grand concept of literature which he had always sought to promote and defend.

Cartesianism also influenced language. In 1662 Antoine Arnauld and Lancelot published a *Grammaire générale et raisonnée*, which was an application of Cartesian method to the science of language. Where Vaugelas had been content to study usage, these two authors wanted language to obey the demands of reason. This strange doctrine led to the exclusion of exceptions, idioms, and old and colourful expressions. This had the inevitable result of impoverishing language, making it dull, abstract, and flat.

Scientific societies at the end of the century

As the religious faction increasingly influenced the policies of the crown, intellectual life began to slow down. Some 'cabinets', as contemporaries called them, continued to be meeting places for scientists, but they were few in number and without much influence.

Between 1670 and 1680 there was still one such 'cabinet' which played an important rôle. It was that of Henri Justel,[12] a rich Protestant bourgeois, who weekly received at his home mathematicians, physicists, and other scholars. Among his guests were Auzout, Huet, Thévenot, and Toynard. Famous foreigners on their way through Paris also found their way to him. Locke, Christian Huygens, the young Leibniz, Puffendorf, Algernon Sidney, and Samuel Pepys are known to have been his guests. There was at these meetings the same emphasis on free inquiry as that which had characterised the Académie putéane. They knew about Spinoza. Fontenelle said of the Justel circle that it was 'un cercle de rebelles qui conspiraient contre l'ignorance et les préjugés dominants'.

It was to be expected that in the atmosphere of oppression that was closing in on France there would be no room for a 'cercle de rebelles'. Henri Justel recognised this. In 1680 he sold his well-stocked library and began to prepare his escape to England.

Other societies continued to meet. Among them one remembers particularly the circle formed in the Faubourg Saint-Jacques by Abbé de Saint-Pierre, Fontenelle, Varignon, and Abbé Vertot. They concerned themselves with history, morals, and politics. In 1692 there was also a real club at the Luxembourg; at this Fontenelle, Charles Perrault, Abbé Dangeau, and Abbé Renaudot used to meet. The main characteristic of these new groups was that they were interested in the study of politics from a scientific point of view, using statistics, and taking account of the rôles of industry, commerce, and business affairs in their analysis of the state.[13]

Fontenelle exemplifies the spirit that reigned at the end of the century better than anyone else. He began to be talked about in 1675. From that year he frequently stayed in Paris, until he finally moved there permanently. He was a frequent visitor at the salons of the précieux, but also at the learned societies of mathematicians, chemists, and travellers. He was a disciple of Descartes at the time when Descartes was in fashion.

Publications of all kinds testify to the variety of his interests, which were also those of the entire period at the end of the century. These included the *Dialogues des morts* (1683) and *Lettres galantes* (1686), but also the *Entretiens sur la pluralité des mondes* (1686) and a *Histoire des Oracles* (1686) which constituted a formidable critique of religious traditions. He was completely free of orthodox beliefs, but prudent. If he thought it desirable, he was quite capable of publishing *Le triomphe de la Religion* (1687) and of invoking the word having been made flesh.

He made his mark in both the literary and scientific worlds. In 1691 he became a member of the Académie des sciences and soon became its permanent secretary. The Duc d'Orléans put him up at the Palais-Royal and there Fontenelle made his home among open-minded people who witnessed with indignation the idiocies of the reign. The right-thinking maintained that his *Histoire des Oracles* was the shame of the nation.

His devotion to Descartes was odd. He certainly had retained nothing of Descartes' metaphysics, and did not believe that human thought can attain to God immediately and without argument. Perhaps he was not an Atheist, but it would be surprising to hear that he had been a firm believer in God the creator. Nature was for him an immense machine, an interplay of forces and, as he used to say, of rope, pulleys, and levers which it was up to the scientists to disentangle and measure. If he disliked Newton's system throughout his life, this was because he saw it as the instrument of the counter-offensive of the metaphysical spirit.[14]

Cartesianism had accustomed him to think of reason as the opposite of vulgar prejudices and old traditions. He did not share the respect of the followers of Gassendi for history, which went to the lengths of respecting error provided it had a long ancestry. This was why he applauded the efforts of some of the senior officers of the administration who tried to maintain a rational notion of the state in difficult circumstances. It is not an accident that he welcomed the stern work done by d'Argenson. Fontenelle managed to distinguish between a tyranny that sought to maintain by force prejudices and abuses, and an authoritarian government that was strong and intended to promote the orderly reign of reason.

His influence spread rapidly. It can be seen particularly in men who were discreetly preparing the intellectual revolution of the following century. Dumarsais was his admirer and avowed disciple.[15] That learned man Boindin used to carry a carnelian with the profiles of Descartes, Bayle, and Fontenelle, and this saying from the scriptures daringly taken from its context: *Tres sunt qui testimonium perhibent de lumine*. The significance of these simple facts has been better understood since we learnt of the importance of clandestine literature in the first half of the eighteenth century and the rôle of Boindin and Dumarsais in it.

Two other writers exerted a considerable influence on the development of ideas. It is significant that both of them lived in exile, that it was abroad that they wrote the works which provided the French in their kingdom with the philosophical lessons for which they were waiting.

Saint-Evremond had been obliged to flee the country in 1661 because the police had discovered a letter from him in which he showed himself to be extremely critical of the peace of the Pyrenees. The King of England saved his life. Apart from a brief stay in Holland, where he visited Spinoza, he henceforth lived in London. In 1689, after he had acquired a European reputation, the French government intimated to him that he could return to France. It was too late. In London he lived a modest and quiet life surrounded by his friends. He preferred to remain with them and he died in 1703.

He was not a man of letters; he published no books. But he liked writing short essays on moral topics, or on history or literature. These essays he circulated. Publishers managed to get hold of them, and, often without his permission, his writings were printed with increasing frequency. It is no exaggeration to say that this exile became for twenty years the intellectual leader of France.

Saint-Evremond remained loyal to the Gassendism of his youth. He disliked Descartes and Cartesian dogmatism. He also disliked the orthodox mentality of the official religion, but he had no wish to substitute for it a kind of orthodoxy of reason. He believed that if it is impossible to subscribe whole-heartedly to the tenets of any one faith, it must be equally so with categorical denials. He was deeply convinced that the human mind is naturally unstable. He said that 'nous passons notre vie à croire et à ne pas croire'. He resigned himself to it.

In any case, it was not so much his religious thought that interested his contemporaries as his short papers in which he developed his views on morals. It has been shown above that, even before 1660, he had expounded a form of Epicureanism which had affinities with that of Gassendi, though it went further and recommended the active search for sophisticated pleasures. From his exile in England he sent letters to his friends in France in which he continued to express the same views. One day, when he was visited in London by the traveller Bernier, the two men came to the conclusion that abstaining from pleasure is a great sin. Before expressing horror at this, one should remember that the Epicureans had the greatest disdain for vulgar sentiments and low desires.

Another exile who exerted a strong influence on cultured Frenchmen at the end of the century was Pierre Bayle.[16] He was Protestant by origin but allowed himself at one time to be persuaded into Catholicism; he returned to the Reformed Church later. He was thus *relaps*, a crime French justice punished with severity. In 1670 he had to flee to Geneva. There he made contact with the most eminent Protestant theologians and, in 1671, he became professor of philosophy at the Protestant academy of Sedan. In 1681 that institution was closed down by royal decree, and Bayle went to Holland. In 1684 he began to publish a literary journal, the *Nouvelles de la République des Lettres*. This quickly made its mark in learned circles throughout Europe. The Royal Society of London let Bayle know of its admiration for his work. In 1695 and 1697 he published the two enormous volumes of his *Dictionnaire historique et critique*. Here, in alphabetical order, were dissertations which impressed by their immense erudition and exceptional penetration.

His thought had close links with that of La Mothe le Vayer and Naudé. He believed in no philosophical system, Cartesian or other. He thought that the first duty of a scholar was that he should exercise his critical spirit, examine problems without any kind of prejudice, beware of make-believe. His *Pensées diverses sur la comète* (1682) illustrate this approach. Like La Mothe le Vayer he showed how much of the old anthropocentric illusion there was in the popular view of things, i.e.

the deeply-rooted illusion that man is at the centre of everything and that natural phenomena can be explained in terms of their relation to man. Again like La Mothe le Vayer, and like Naudé, he explained the errors of the mass of people through the political fictions and desire for power of kings and priests.

He was not opposed to religion, but he wanted his Christianity to be reasonable, enlightened, free of prejudices and fanaticism. In this he echoed the thesis of a powerful contemporary doctrine which was hotly debated among Protestant theologians, and which seemed to give birth to a new conception of Christianity. However, Bayle concluded that the efforts of these 'rational' theologians were based on illusions. Too concerned with the admirable works of divine wisdom, they failed to see the part played by evil and the irrational, i.e. the rôle of sin.

Bayle later lost interest in historical research and devoted himself to the study of the great speculative systems. He exchanged polemics with the theologians of the new school, chiefly with Jean Le Clerc who was its most important and worthwhile member.

In the general development of ideas in the seventeenth century the awareness of the beliefs and customs of distant countries played an important part. Tales of travel abounded, especially after 1640. Many readers preferred them to novels. They provided material for people who were trying to attain to positive knowledge of man, particularly of man in society If one were to believe some of the accounts that have been given of this literature one would run away with the idea that it provided the French mainly with the notion of the noble savage, and that it simply pointed to the contrast between the innocence of man in nature and the corruption of man in society. But neither authors nor readers were as naive as this.

The first, and chief, lesson the French learnt from these travel stories was that men are infinitely diverse and that there is nothing that all men conspicuously have in common. As regards the notion of God in particular, they discovered that there was no unanimity, and that the Brazilians for example were 'sans aucune croyance certaine de Divinité vraie ou fausse'. That is what La Mothe le Vayer and Naudé had said on the basis of the oldest accounts, and later ones published after their death bore them out.

In the second place the travel literature showed that it was possible to have a variety of conceptions about religion It suggested, for example, that the Chinese had a religion without temples, without forms of worship, and without clergy. Among the people of Peru there was one religion for the initiated and another for the people. One can easily imagine to what kinds of thoughts such facts would lead in readers who were tempted by Deism. These travel stories did not say that savages were all naturally good and innocent They often affirmed the opposite. But they taught the French that the peoples of Nouvelle France knew a 'charité naturelle', that the Incas had 'connaissances naturelles' thanks to which they had evolved 'l'idée d'un parfait gouvernement'. They also discovered that the Topinambous had 'un amour cordial et fraternel' for mankind. These facts, noted down by travellers, gradually undermined some of the traditional certainties.

Only one traveller used his observations to provide him with systematic conclusions. That was Baron de Lahontan, a nobleman of Béarn who had been an officer and had lived a long time in Canada He had a natural bent for philosophy, and Leibniz, who knew him at the court of Hanover, thought highly of him. In 1703 he published his *Nouveaux voyages* and *Mémoires de l'Amérique septentrionale*, as well as *Dialogues avec un sauvage américain* and *Lettres.*[17] In these writings he rather sharply attacked European society, or rather all society. Private property seemed to him the sole source of all evil. It had to be done away with, together with hierarchies and Churches. Lahontan summarised his ideal solution for human happiness in one word: anarchy.

Writers who recognised the philosophical interest of these travel tales made use of a peculiar kind of novel-form to expound their ideas, i.e. the novel of imaginary travel. The genre had existed for a long time. It had been used mainly by philosophers, for example by Thomas More, Bacon, and Campanella; Locke had quite recently also tried his hand at it. Now literary men were taking it up.

Denis Veiras' *Histoire des Sévarambes* (1675), *Les aventures de Jacques Sadeur* by Gabriel de Foigny (1676), and the *Histoire de*

Caléjava of Claude Gilbert (1700) have only one thing in common, and that is a traveller cast by the sea on to an unknown continent. There he discovers a civilisation which he at first finds very strange. In the end he discovers its real roots.

By the use of this genre writers thus had the opportunity of expounding their ideas on the perfect society, and of putting forward the most audacious doctrines about politics and religion. By all appearances Denis Veiras was an Atheist, and Gabriel de Foigny was probably a Deist. Veiras replaced the traditional God with the idol of society that was in complete control of all the thoughts and all the actions of its citizens. Gabriel de Foigny, on the contrary, was a kind of peaceful anarchist who dreamed of the disappearance of all hierarchies. His ideal was mankind without rules, where property was unknown, and equality and liberty truly reigned.

No doubt these imaginary constructions did not express tendencies that were widespread in contemporary society. On the other hand they were not inconsequential dreams either. They represented a feeling that was to spread, the feeling that the existing social order was unreasonably imperfect, and that there was a contrast between the existing institutions and those which the human mind is able to conceive and secretly wants to create.

7

Ancients and Moderns

When a society becomes fossilised in its outlook and ways of life it is inevitable that its literature merely keeps to its traditions too. On the other hand one may expect that a society which is undergoing both political and social change will give rise to a kind of literature whose forms and modes of expression are new. When one has realised the extent to which the seventeenth century in France was dominated by a desire for new achievements, one may justifiably assume that its literature possesses characteristics that are original and forms that are new.

There are, it is true, still historians and critics for whom French classical literature is the result of a return to order after the wars and anarchy of the preceding period. From this they draw the conclusion that it can be defined in terms of its links with tradition, which in fact means the literatures of Greece and Rome. But this interpretation of seventeenth-century literature fails to recognise the strength of the wish for renewal, the need for a new creativeness which animated that illustrious period. It fails to recognise the opposing forces, the conflicts of attitudes and contrary forces which gave the masterpieces of the time that magnificent feeling of inner tension, and their value as original creative works.

In the arts it was humanism which represented tradition at the beginning of the century. This was identified with the Greek and Latin literatures which the sixteenth century had discovered and resuscitated. It was a tradition which found its expression in the splendid works of Ronsard and the Pléiade. But even early in the seventeenth century there were writers who felt that it had lost its value, and that the modern world had to create its own forms of thought and beauty. That was the beginning of the opposition between the moderns and the ancients. Many histories of French literature place the start of that famous quarrel around 1675. In fact, however, the differences between the two theses became clear at the turn of the century at the same time, incidentally, as in Italy, where *moderni* and *antiquari* were flexing their muscles for their first battles.

The ancient tradition

In order to understand the significance of the conflict one has to remember that the education dispensed to the French in their colleges was at that time entirely devoted to the study of the languages and literatures of Greece and Rome. The moderns must therefore have been people who rebelled against the education they had received. Conversely, those social groups which remained more attached to the ancient tradition were by nature more sympathetically disposed towards the university.

As has been shown earlier, the university had lost much of its prestige during the period of unrest. Nevertheless, it retained its hold over the educated part of the nation. It was this 'pays latin', as it was called, i.e. the professors of the Montagne Sainte-Geneviève, which fashioned the new generations, and it did not restrict its activities to teaching ancient literature. The professors carefully watched developments in contemporary literature and judged them in terms of the models of Greece and Rome. If one looks at the names of those who presented to the world the works of Alexandre Hardy one notices that they were professors of Paris colleges. The education given by the Jesuits was, in this respect, similar to that of the university, although there were some small differences.

This kind of influence was particularly strongly felt among the parlementaires, the magistrature, and clerics of all kinds. These social groups remained much more closely identified with the humanist tradition than the nobility. An important remark by Balzac assures us that around 1615–20 Ronsard was still idolised by 'le Parlement de Paris, l'Université et les Jésuites'.

The professors of the Montagne Sainte-Geneviève were little known because all their publications were in Latin. However, at this time, many of them were enjoying considerable authority among men of letters, and so did some of the university publishers. This was especially true of Fédéric Morel and Nicolas Richelet, as well as of Nicolas Bourbon who has been mentioned above. The latter was a friend of Vauquelin des Yveteaux and Balzac, and the Académie Française made him a member because it knew of his influence in the 'pays latin'.

We thus have the explanation for the fact that the humanist tradition remained so lively through the first half of the seventeenth century. Under Louis XIII there were still men in Paris who continued to speak with religious reverence of the 'divin Erasme', and who claimed Scaliger, Justus-Lipsius, and Pithou as their intellectual ancestry. They kept themselves informed of the humanist publications of Europe, particularly those of the great school then coming into being in Holland. They could do this all the more easily since the books were written in Latin. So far as literary questions were concerned, the works of Heinsius and Vossius enjoyed undisputed authority among them. This was the mentality that reigned in the Hôtel de Mesmes and in the Dupuy circle.

The influence of the humanists upon the new literature was great. Few French writers could escape it. True, Saint-Amant bragged about not knowing either Greek or Latin.[1] But Théophile de Viau, who was so openly 'modern', wrote Latin with consummate elegance, and we may note that the epitome of society poets, Voiture, knew his classics to perfection. Sarasin was often seen at the Dupuys. Above all, those whom one takes today to be the theoreticians of classicism, Chapelain, Balzac, and Ménage found themselves in the circles they frequented among scholars imbued with Latin and Greek literature. That is how they picked up the habits of the philologists. Balzac wrote Latin verse, suggested corrections to a passage from Terence, and kept in touch with developments in the world of scholarship. Chapelain was quite capable of discussing the variants of a passage from Ovid and the relative merits of the Latin of Saumaise and Heinsius. Ménage had his Latin verse published.

For these reasons the works of criticism published in the first half of the century base themselves upon the teaching and the example of the ancients. Of course, Chapelain, Balzac, La Ménardière, and the others made their own special contribution. But they were agreed on the essentials. They thought that the ancients provided criteria that were without doubt valid, and that it was enough to keep the masterpieces of Greece and Rome in mind for us to pass proper judgment on the works of contemporaries. They did not intend slavishly to follow the ancients. Indeed they took care to affirm the opposite. But Chapelain thought that the experience of the centuries had shown the exemplary value of the ancient models, and Abbé d'Aubignac maintained that the masterpieces of antiquity clearly conformed to the eternal laws of reason. That is why these critics condemned everything in modern literature that strayed from the paths trodden by the ancients.

But French humanists had made their selection among the ancients. They were far from lavishing their admiration on all of them. Pure antiquity meant Virgil, not Lucan or Statius.[2] Similarly, real comedy was not exemplified in Plautus, who was vulgar and popular, but in Terence who had written for the Scipios and Lelius. They were not very sure about Seneca or even Tacitus, because those authors wanted to shock. They acknowledged Cicero as the master of perfect eloquence. French humanists had thus made their choice between 'bonne latinité' and, as they put it, the Lucanists.

There was humanist inspiration behind the Pléiade. Its peremptory dismissal by Boileau has led to the conclusion that the seventeenth century as a whole despised Ronsard. But it has already been seen that this great poet had retained the admiration of the university and the parlementaires. In 1623 Claude Garnier brought out a magnificent edition of his *Oeuvres*. Chapelain ranked him above all the moderns. Between 1620 and 1630 there was a whole group of poets who tried to write in the Ronsard tradition, including Jean de Schélandre, Hodey, and Claude Garnier. Around 1627 the Illustres Bergers, i.e. the most notable poets of the young generation, organised celebrations on the anniversary of Ronsard's birth, with speeches, recitations, and prizes. In the middle of the century Guillaume Colletet was still faithful to the leader of the Pléiade, and he wrote verses to honour him as well as Malherbe. Later still, Pellisson was discovering in Ronsard 'une infinité de choses qui valent bien mieux . . . que la politesse stérile et rampante de ceux qui sont venus depuis'.[3] That is more or less what La Ménardière also wrote. He toasted the 'grand' Ronsard, and reproached his contemporaries for having caused modern poetry to lose its 'sérieux' in favour of the trivialities of galanterie and badinage.

Modernism

Since the beginning of the century there was also, in opposition to humanism and its attachment to tradition, a movement towards something new and modern. Of this the literary opinions of Malherbe, as they have come down to us through his disciple Racan, are absolutely characteristic. He loathed Ronsard, and among the ancients he admired only those poets whom the humanist critics despised. He preferred Statius to all the other Latin poets. He declared his admiration for Seneca the tragedian, Ovid, Juvenal, and Martial. But when he quoted Homer and Virgil it was to 'reprendre' them, i.e. to criticise them. The historians of the nineteenth century naively thought that one should explain these opinions through Malherbe's weakness for paradox. But this is no paradox. Malherbe was a 'modern' and Régnier, who reproached him for rejecting 'toute l'Anticaille', knew that very well.

Around 1620, poets writing for the 'jeunesse de la cour' had been won over to this new outlook. Théophile de Viau, Saint-Amant, and Boisrobert were moderns. So were Charles Sorel, Godeau, and the young poets who, in some of the literary circles, were trying out new forms of poetry. They were writers who affirmed, with greater or less intransigence, their intention to free themselves from the ancient traditions. The *Fragments d'une histoire comique*, published by Théophile de Viau in 1623, contained what might be described as the manifesto of the modern school.[4] It maintained that the so-called imitation of the ancients was mere larcency, stolen ornaments. It wanted to get rid of figures of speech that had become meaningless: no more talk about Apollo and the Muses because nobody believed in them any more. 'Il faut écrire à la moderne', the manifesto said; the meaning must be clear and easy to recognise, the language direct and significant. As for antiquity, the reaction of the author is summed up in three words from one of his poems: 'La sotte antiquité'.

The reaction of his friends was the same. One recalls the speech Boisrobert made about the ancients. He spoke about them with extreme irreverence. Saint-Amant returned to the same subject many times. He kept saying that his lack of Latin did not make him believe that he was worth any less esteem. Homer knew Greek, but that was the language of his nurse.[5] Consequently Homer was, after his fashion, a modern. If one wants to see just how far disrespect towards the ancients could go one should read Sorel's *Le berger extravagant*. The author can see only fraud in poetry that models itself on the ancients. He is not impressed by Homer, Virgil, or of course Ronsard. And he also condemns the use of mythology. His *Banquet des dieux* was a farcical parody of the ancient epics.

Thus there was now a sizeable number of statements which, when added up, amounted to the system of the moderns. First, it maintained that the only aim of art was to give pleasure. This may seem insignificant and vague. But it acquires precise meaning if we put it in its context, and recall that humanism had subordinated art to higher aims which were intellectual and moral. The affirmation of the hedonistic conception of art amounted to the rejection of the high opinion the humanist tradition had of the humanities. It also involved the affirmation of the freedom of the artist from any kind of rules. Art is not connected with traditions and prescriptions. The works of an artist are the free creations of his mind.

Imitation was another principle of the humanist tradition. According to the supporters of the ancients, poets would not be expected to create anything entirely new. It was enough that they imitate an ancient work, and their value was to be judged by the quality of their imitation. The moderns, on the other hand, maintained that the poet must, above all, be original. Théophile said: 'Je ne défère guère aux exemples, et me déplais surtout en l'imitation d'autrui'.[6] He wanted the poet to have the right to 'suivre en tout sa nature'. Saint-Amant echoed these sentiments. He also condemned all imitations: 'Je l'abhorre tellement que même si je lis parfois les oeuvres d'un autre, ce n'est que pour m'empêcher de me rencontrer avec lui dans ses conceptions. Le moindre original d'un Freminet est beaucoup plus prisé que la meilleure copie d'un Michel-Ange.'[7]

The word the moderns constantly used to designate the principle that in their view ought to replace the authority of the ancients was reason. They believed in a single, universal reason, common to all men at all times and throughout the world. Because of this, they did not think that the ancients possessed any advantage over them. By the same token no authority had the right to demand blind docility from them for its decrees. It was the poet's reason which must dictate his verse to him. Thus rationalism and modernism came to the same conclusions, and it comes as no surprise that Théophile was the favourite poet of Descartes, and that there was a lasting friendship between Balzac and the author of the *Discours de la méthode*.

The moderns, taking reason as their starting point, believed in the progress of the human mind. They held that there was no point in fighting against what is now called the march of history. Claude Garnier reproached them for this. He refused to follow them in the belief that 'il se faut ranger au temps'. A curious document allows us to be present, about 1627, at a dialogue between a poet of the old tradition and the modernist Godeau. The latter affirms that it is a law of nature that everything must come to an end and that, though antiquity may be venerable, he thinks that it is still preferable to look for new forms of perfection rather than to stop; we should push forward where antiquity merely pointed the way. Godeau, in a *Discours* on the works of Malherbe, came back to the belief that nature had not conferred solely upon the ancients the ability to achieve perfection in the sciences. It would be wrong to rebel against them, but it would also be wrong to refuse to surpass them.

Modernism and the Baroque

'Baroque' is the term increasingly used by historians to designate the works with modern tendencies that appeared during the first part of the seventeenth century. The term does not, however, mean the same thing to all of them. Some mean by it an absolutist aesthetic theory which manifested itself in seventeenth-century works, but also manifested itself during the Hellenistic era or in some nineteenth-century works. Others reduce the baroque to certain plastic or literary means of expression and fail to distinguish it from maniérisme. In fact it seems more reasonable to use the notion of the baroque in the context of the history of civilisation, and to define the word in terms of ways of thought and feeling and means of expression which emerged at the end of the wars of religion, mainly in the Europe of the Counter Reformation, and which brought out or mirrored a stage in the development of the new society. The baroque writer or artist was a man who had understood what the original elements in the new society were, and it was these elements which he sought to express in his works.[8]

The most important fact about this new society was the re-establishment of privilege. This had been done by force, and was maintained through the pitiless suppression of all shows of independence. The new order rested upon convincing displays of force; it captured people's minds through its audacity; and it sought to justify itself through works that were to impress the imagination.

The arts and letters of the period necessarily found their inspiration in that new order. It was no longer a question of portraying feelings of harmony, as had been the case during the Renaissance, or dreams of happy elegance of a society which was conscious of having gained a new life and to have rediscovered the beauty of ancient civilisation. Instead, they had to impress and humiliate the spirit, to make it feel the might of the privileged.

The low state of culture at that time made their work all the easier. A society cannot lose itself for forty years on end in wars and anarchy without suffering the consequences. The men in charge of the country rose to their positions through the services they had rendered in the military encampments. It was not refinement they had learnt there, and it may be assumed that the art and literature of the ancients were unknown to them or, if not, a matter of indifference. What impressed them was strong sensations, even the extravagant seemed agreeable to them or dazzling. They needed a modern literature.

It is true that the writers who worked for this new society were not completely ignorant of the literatures of Rome and Greece. But what they looked for in those literatures was a vindication of their taste for the outrageous. It was with a sure instinct that they turned to the writers of the Roman decadence, as if they had been aware that, at the end of the great crisis of the preceding century, Europe differed little from the Roman

Empire of the time when the emperors were faced with a world in ruins and attempted to restore order and to maintain it.

Modernism at the beginning of the seventeenth century was therefore baroque. The style of fashionable novelists was baroque. The poets were baroque and differed among themselves only through a greater or smaller degree of extravagance in their imagery. In fact, the new tragedy was baroque. The characteristics of baroque taste can be defined as follows: basically, all it wants is to create effects. It is far less a question of pointing a truth or expressing a feeling than of impressing people or delighting them by some extravagance. The desired effect is achieved in two ways. First, through the 'extremeness', the frenzied exaggeration of some stroke. Thus when Malherbe, to celebrate the victory by a few French squadrons over some enemy cavalry by a river, wants us to believe that this river overflowed because of all the blood and corpses, he expressed himself like a baroque poet, and he used means which at that time seemed entirely normal.

Secondly, the author may try to achieve his results through the extreme ingenuity of the thoughts he expresses. Baroque literature made much use of what was then called 'la pointe'. It did so without any consideration for truth, precisely because it was not concerned with truth but with creating an impression. It was not afraid of playing on the different senses of a given word, for it brought words together for reasons of sonority and not of sense. It did this not only in the novel but also in poetry and the theatre.

Finally, baroque aesthetics looked for diversity. It cared nothing for the unity of a work of literature, be it unity of subject matter, of inspiration, or of tone. In the theatre, for example, it happily lumped together several plots, multiplied coups de théâtre, and juxtaposed tragedy and comedy. And it did all this, not because it was hamfisted, but deliberately, and because it believed that it was a source of beauty.

It was at the end of the sixteenth century that baroque modernism was at its most audacious. This is not surprising when one recalls that it reflected the mentality of French society at the end of the civil wars. But even then there were men who opposed the progress of this kind of modernism. Du Vair was the first to champion true oratory, of the kind practised by Cicero and whose rules had been formulated by Quintilian, as against the extravagant rhetoric then fashionable among preachers and lawyers.[9] Cardinal du Perron protested against the follies of the new literature, 'Nous allons entrer dans une grande barbarie', he wrote. Those who remained attached to the ideals of sobriety and purity felt as if they were on a small island in the midst of an ocean of outrageous nonsense and frenzy. They were men like Honoré d'Urfé, Jean de Lingendes, and Vauquelin des Yveteaux. Their great reputation compensated for their small number. But taste was beginning to change. Colletet provides an important clue to this change when he says that the famous sonnet by Laugier de Porchères, *Sur les yeux de Madame la Duchesse de Beaufort* had lost its vogue. It means that some baroque excesses, or rather some forms of the baroque that were least compatible with a somewhat more exacting taste, were by that time no longer tolerated.[10]

The baroque 'pointe', however, did not disappear quite so quickly. It remained an admired form of expression. About 1625, Abbé de Crosilles and the novelist La Serre, both men of letters, reproached a volume of *Lettres* for offering 'rieu d'intéressant' because it did not contain enough pointes. In 1629 Faret, a disciple of Malherbe, was still praising the 'aiguillon', which was the pointe that often ended the poems of his friend Saint-Amant. But from 1630 onward, the pointe became the object of increasing criticism. It seems that this criticism was particularly violent among a group of writers which included Abbé d'Aubignac, Patru, Perrot d'Ablancourt, and Vion d'Alibray, nearly all of whom played some part in the elaboration of the doctrine of classicism. Vion d'Alibray took exception to the use of pointes in his translation of the *Aminta* in 1632. He had the courage to criticise the famous line in *Pyrame et Thisbé* by Théophile about the dagger which blushes because it had killed its master. He returned to the attack in the foreword of his translation of *Torrismondo* in 1636.

This reaction soon bore fruit. When writing *La Veuve*, published in 1634, Corneille on his own admission took care to avoid pointes. Abbé d'Aubignac wrote around 1636–8: 'La pointe étant fort peu d'usage . . .'. When he published his *Esprit fort* in 1637, Claveret apologised for the pointes that might be found in it. He reminded the reader that they were fashionable when he wrote it, i.e. 1630–1, and admitted that 'le style du temps' had become 'plus sérieux'. At the time of the row about the *Cid*, an author noted that the pointe was becoming increasingly unfashionable. In 1644 Mlle de Scudéry talked about it as a device that was totally out of fashion. A letter from Sarasin of that time says that nobody wanted to listen to them any more and that some, like Mairet, dared no longer use them in public and were disconsolate about it.

That does not mean that the taste for the baroque had entirely disappeared. In poetry it continued rather longer. Men whose tastes had been formed between 1620 and 1630 – particularly Saint-Amant, but also Tristan, Scudéry, and Malleville – remained faithful to métaphorisme, i.e. a baroque phenomenon. About 1640 Père Le Moyne and Germain Habert gave a thousand examples of extravagant metaphors and very specifically baroque ones. In prose the baroque style can be seen in La Serre, Dassoucy, and chiefly in Cyrano. We are today very aware of the merits of Cyrano, of the vigour and originality of his style. But the new criteria of taste condemned all of them utterly. As the contemporaries saw it, Cyrano, La Serre, and Dassoucy were nothing but 'des extravagants'.

Thus, after 1640, the baroque is no more than a sign of fidelity towards an outdated aesthetic. It is therefore a blatant error to suggest that the baroque is synonymous with French civilisation in the seventeenth century, and an aberration to see in French classicism a kind of sub-group of the European baroque when, in fact, it is the very reverse and came into being as a reaction against it. Historians who see in Pascal a baroque prose writer, and in Racine's *Phèdre* a baroque tragedy merely show that they had *a priori* notions of the meaning of the terms 'baroque' and 'classical', and that they go against all the evidence because they want to squeeze the facts into moulds manufactured in advance. It goes without saying that if, as some apparently want it to, the word 'baroque' were made to designate all forms of art and literature to which the seventeenth century gave birth, then classical tragedy would have to be called baroque. But, in that case, words would have lost their meaning.

The doctrine of classicism

After 1630 the baroque was no longer the dominant form of modernism. A new aesthetic doctrine had been formulated and was taking its place. This was no less modern in inspiration, but it was based on different moral and literary values which could reasonably be called classical.

Although it may seem paradoxical, if one allows oneself to be impressed by the disdain showered on him by Malherbe and Boileau, one must go back to Ronsard to trace the origins of classicism. Perhaps not to the Ronsard of the first *Odes* and the magnificently exuberant poems of his youth. But certainly to the mature poet. Until the end of his life Ronsard was constant in his belief that Homer and Virgil provide the exemplars a writer should follow. Ronsard sharpened his doctrine throughout his long career, and in his last years he recommended 'le souverain style', i.e. the style that is grand without being inflated. He had condemned poets who were too daring, like Du Bartas who seemed to want 'écheler les cieux'. The doctrine is implied in what Ronsard praised and condemned He also refused to be wooed by the prestige of the incipient baroque.[11]

Ronsard had his faithful admirers who thought it an honour to continue in his tradition. The two most important were Bertaut and Cardinal du Perron. Although their works show only too clearly that they lacked their master's genius, they at least followed his doctrine. They showed the same disapproval of baroque extravagance and the same liking for the purity of the ancients, the same feeling for nobility and sobriety.

Some went even further. They disapproved of what they called the 'ardeur' of Ronsard, that is his flights of enthusiasm and his linguistic daring. They avoided subjects that were too lofty. They put all their energy into the due perfection of form. They had done with the clever inventions and abrupt forms of earlier poetry. The word which summed up for them the essential quality of a poem was 'douceur'.

The movement had started early. In 1600 Vauquelin des Yveteaux noted that a number of young men wanted to introduce a new language at court and were proud of the douceur in their poems. But they were without genius, and such quality as their work has is the result of patience and labour. In 1606

Vital d'Audiguier objected to those he called 'les correcteurs modernes'. He taxed them with putting 'la douceur du langage' above all other considerations in a work of literature. In 1609 Claude Garnier poked fun at the 'bande moderne' and poets who were no more than cold-blooded rhymsters 'avec leurs plates chansons et leurs froides stances'. Later Jean de Schélandre was to accuse them of being merely 'censeurs des mots et des rimes' and of trying to substitute the pretty for the beautiful.

These different verdicts illuminate each other. They show that a form of modern style was coming into being which was different from the baroque and which, in fact, opposed it. The connections between this and the social history of the period are clear. Once peace was consolidated and social life reorganised, the taste for sophistication reappeared. But this differed from older forms; the social élite did not return to the clever and elegant displays fashionable at the court of the Valois. And it also rejected baroque exuberance. It wanted a literature ruled by good taste, whose language was pure and correct. It wanted douceur. This was the style that was in time to dominate at the court and the salons. It is the style of neither the baroque nor the humanists. It is modern. In fact it is already classicism.

One event had a decisive importance for this evolution. Malherbe had for a long time been a modern closely identified with the baroque. But, after 1615, he showed signs of new interests, of having new ways of being modern. This change quickened during the last seven years of his life. It was then that he gathered around himself – apart from some already older poets like Mainard and Racan – young men like Chapelain, Vaugelas, Balzac, Faret, and Godeau. And it was these young men who, in the years to come, devoted their energies to constructing the doctrine of classicism.

This was indeed the group justly recognised by historians as having been responsible for founding classicism. Classicism was not the work of Boileau, nor even of the great writers of the early period of Louis XIV's personal rule. By the time Molière and Racine were beginning to put their masterpieces on the stage and La Fontaine published his *Fables*, it was already thirty years since men of letters had first formulated the principles and rules and had won the public's respect for the classical style. For they had not merely worked out a doctrine. They had managed to get it accepted. It had taken about ten years, from 1630 to 1640. By the latter date unanimity had been achieved among the writers, and the few who refused to bow to the new ways were considered to be 'extravagants'.

The progress of the doctrine, and its final victory, was due to the work of a number of critics. This fact is sufficiently important to justify closer appraisal by the historian. It was not the renown of some classical work which convinced people of the excellence of the doctrine. The only writer of genius of that period was Corneille, and he did nothing to further its progress. It will indeed be seen that he submitted to the very strict discipline of the doctrine only with badly concealed repugnance. The maxims of the new literature were expounded and defended by theorists. Before taking the shape of magisterial literary works classicism asserted itself in works of criticism.

The most famous of these theorists was certainly Chapelain.[12] He was very much a modern. What displeased him in the works of Ronsard was his 'servile et désagréable imitation des Anciens', and he reproached the poet 'de n'avoir pas songé au temps où il écrivait', and for having put into his poetry a number of things which the people could not understand 'pour qui est faite la poésie'. That was a remarkable statement, and it showed the difference between classicism and humanism. The latter, in the middle of the seventeenth century, continued to maintain that all truth and all beauty were contained in the ancients, and that all the moderns could do was to imitate them. For Chapelain, the most typical of the classical theorists, literature exists for the living or, as he said, 'pour le peuple', and the duty of the writer is to bear in mind the time at which he is writing. The only authentic literature is modern.

But Chapelain's modernism had nothing baroque about it. The characteristics he admired in Ronsard, which caused him to place him above all living poets despite the reservations already noted, have every right to be called classical. What he admired in the leader of the Pléiade was 'une certaine égalité nette et majestueuse', his disdain for ornaments which are reminiscent more 'du sophiste et du déclamateur que d'un esprit véritablement inspiré par les Muses'. That was exactly the interpretation of Ronsard's work already found in Bertaut and Cardinal du Perron. Chapelain thus linked up with these two precursors of classicism, across the narrowness of approach of Malherbe.

Baroque extravagance he therefore condemned. Evenness, balance, and discretion were the qualities he most admired. But despite the firmness of his views he had tolerance. He saw no reason for disapproving of either Saint-Amant or Scudéry or Tristan. His classical orthodoxy did not have the uncompromising narrowness of the succeeding generation. It was the latter that Boileau chose to imitate.

Apart from distinct differences of temperament, Balzac found himself in agreement with Chapelain. He was as modern as Chapelain. He had even been, in his early days, a modern with passionate violence. His *Lettres* of 1624 had been considered as a manifesto of modernism and had aroused the anger of the university and the humanists. He continued to ridicule all his life the minutiae that seemed to preoccupy the philologists. His worst enemy, his bogeyman, was the humanist Guyet.

In fact, however, Balzac gave up his extremism quite early. He was convinced that the Romans were the masters of the moderns. Even before the *Lettres*, his friend Nicolas Bourbon, a humanist, had taught him to appreciate the greatness of Rome. He it was, said Balzac, who 'm'annonça le premier la grandeur et la majesté de Rome, que je ne connaissais point, et qui m'emplit l'imagination'.

Thus, in spite of his earlier strident statements, it was for Balzac no longer a question of breaking with the ancient tradition but of interpreting it. No doubt it did not mean for him what it had meant for Ronsard. It was Latin rather than Greek. It demanded order, balance, gravity, and majesty. Of course, in this Balzac was asking for nothing new. It has been said that he had found these requirements in Rome, among the Bentivoglio and the Strada. What matters in this context, however, is that Balzac was responsible for the fact that French writers subsequently conceived antiquity in a way quite different from that of the humanists, and which in addition made nonsense of modernist criticism.

The doctrine which had been developed by Chapelain, Balzac and some others was thus complete. The towering personality of Boileau concealed that fact for a long time, and the Boileau legend was perpetuated by the colleges in the eighteenth century and the university in the nineteenth century. Today it is clear that it was not Boileau and his *Art poétique* that had imposed classical order upon French literature. This work had been done by a few men of letters during Richelieu's time in the realms of theory and criticism.

The import of their work can now be properly assessed. It would really be oversimple to explain classicism in terms of the return to discipline and to the qualities of good taste and clarity. It owes its existence to the firmness of its position in relation to humanism and baroque modernism.

Antiquity, which provided the humanists with a cult, was retained by the classicists for its most unchallengeable values. They remained faithful to the ancients and strongly opposed those who wanted to break with the past. But their cult for the ancients was selective and limited to essentials. That of the humanists struck them as superstitious. The university was by then largely out of touch with the world of letters. French writers talked with disdain of those whom they called philologists or, more brutally, pedants.

Classicism is therefore distinctly modern. But, as has been seen, it is very different from the baroque. It wants writers to write for their time, but it rejects the extravagant, the excessively ingenious, and exaggeration. It wants the poet to respect reason, truth, and reality. It holds that a work of art must possess unity. Among the Roman writers it only accepts those who obeyed these maxims.

Classical doctrine was thus complete by 1640. However, changes in French society brought with them new preoccupations which, in turn, brought out particular aspects of the doctrine. After Richelieu's death, during the 'bonne Régence' and even more after the Fronde, when they were the real masters of the kingdom, it was the financiers who set the tone. It was no longer a question of accepting or rejecting the rules. On that point unanimity had been achieved. The new question was whether French literature should allow itself to be carried along by the prevailing frivolity, whether in a society of 'coquets' it, too, should become 'coquette'.[13] The financiers loved luxury, elegance, honeyed charm. They lacked the solid Greco-Latin education of the old bourgeoisie. The literature that delighted them consisted of madrigals, pretty sonnets, and impromptu verse. In the theatre they preferred a new form of tragedy, the romanesque and elegant kind provided by Thomas Corneille and Quinault.

The men of the old generation tried to fight these crazes. Chapelain did not try to hide his distaste. He did not like the poets who won their successes in the drawing rooms of the financiers. He was lost in a world in which people went into ecstasies over some elegant sonnet or madrigal, while despising the great art forms. He, in turn, could only despise this literature of 'colifichets'. Abbé d'Aubignac was particularly outspoken about the works inspired by the financiers. Olivier Patru was among those who put up the strongest resistance to them. Some literary newcomers, like Furetière and Gilles Boileau, seconded the efforts of their elders.

It was Malherbe's name that was invoked by the opponents of the culture of the financiers. It was made the symbol of serious, great poetry. The grand lyricism associated with his name, the political and religious subjects he had treated in his odes and paraphrases, the seriousness of his thought and tone, these were the characteristics of the poet they dwelt upon. They also linked this quite naturally with an admiration for his best disciples, Mainard and Racan. It was in this context that Chapelain wrote to Mainard: 'Vous êtes notre maître et le serez toujours'.

It was against this background that, around 1660, the opposition between writers hardened. Not, let it be said again, opposition between proponents and opponents of the rules; even less between classicism and the baroque since, with the exception of a few 'extravagants', there was nobody left to claim kinship with the principles of the baroque. It was the opposition between the defenders of a great tradition, which had been assimilated to that of Malherbe, and the partisans of a 'poésie coquette' that cared little for truth or gravity, but very much for elegant ingenuity and coquetterie.

'*Querelle des anciens et des modernes*'[14]

It goes without saying that the 'poètes coquets' and the

supporters of grander poetry did not have the same attitude towards antiquity, and that the former tried to be much more 'modern' than the latter. However, the question of the relationship between ancient literature and modern society was for a long time kept in the background. But after 1660 a number of works appeared that drew the attention of the public to precisely that problem.

Oddly enough, the question was first obliquely posed. It was about modern epics. In 1662 Abbé de Marolles published a *Traité du poème épique*. He was maintaining that one could admire Homer and Virgil without coming to the conclusion that these authors had to be endlessly imitated He based himself on the old idea of the modern faction that the only rules one should obey are those of 'bon sens' and not the authority of ancient models. On the question of mythology, he came out in favour of the Christian supernatural because of the close relationship there ought to be between literature and the society in which it appears. As regards the subject matter of epics he wrote: 'Je serais même d'avis que le poète n'en choisit pas d'autre que dans la religion qu'il professe'.

In 1664, Louis Le Laboureur, at the head of his poem *Charlemagne*, put forward the same thesis. He thus justified the choice of his subject. He used an argument in his defensive plea which was to have an important place in the controversy. Emancipating oneself from antiquity was, for him, the mark of a good Frenchman, who should glorify the feats of his own nation. In singing the praises of the emperor of the Occident, he felt that he was showing the feelings of an 'également bon chrétien et bon Français'.[15]

The problem of the 'modern' epic had thus been raised. It was debated by two men who frequented the Cartesian circle of Habert de Montmort. It is therefore reasonable to suppose that this 1660 version of modernism had its origins in Cartesianism which was then in full spate. There is also a letter of 1665 addressed to Habert de Montmort by one of the members of the circle. It contains a violent attack on the humanists. It treats them as miserable grammarians and dated sophists. It reproaches them for knowing all the languages except their own, and the history of the past to the detriment of that of their own time. They were wrong to call themselves knowledgeable. For the knowledgeable man knows how to do useful things with a sure touch.[16] It was a remarkable statement, and it throws into high relief the Cartesian inspiration of this kind of modernism.

The moderns were now showing their colours with increasing frequency. In 1667 Louis Le Laboureur published his *Avantages de la langue française sur la langue latine*. He did not content himself with stating that it was absurd to write Latin verse in the middle of the modern world: sensible men were agreed on that. He went much further. He undertook a comparison between the great poets of antiquity and some recent poets. He maintained that ancient poetry had nothing that was superior to the *Temple de la mort* by Philippe Habert and the *Métamorphose des yeux de Philis en astres*, that French tragedy had no reason to fear comparison with that of Greece and Rome, and that Brebeuf was in a dozen places superior to Lucan. He then raised his sights still further and dealt with more general points. Languages, he said, change like human beings, and French is superior because it is alive. If the French language changes, this is not a form of weakness but a sign of vitality. The same theses are to be found in 1670 in a book by Des Marests de Saint-Sorlin, *Comparaison de la langue et de la poésie françaises avec la grecque et la latine*. He praised the modern poets Voiture, Sarasin, Malleville, and the Haberts, for their refinement, their delicacy, and their exquisiteness, and modern novelists for their rich imagination. He also defended the Christian supernatural. In addition he put forward an idea that was to become very important in the controversy: that women, simply guided by their reason, are better judges in literary matters than the most learned university tutors.

So far it had been merely a matter of rather general professions of belief. They had been made without real polemical intent and with the greatest courtesy. The naturally intemperate language of Des Marests de Saint-Sorlin and the peevishness of Boileau transformed these academic discussions into a quarrel in which the insults were soon flying. In 1673 Des Marests placed at the beginning of a new edition of his *Clovis* a few verses against the *Passage du Rhin* by Boileau.[17] In the year that followed, the latter attacked the modern epic in his *Art poétique*. He also included a diatribe against Claude Perrault, for the bad reason that he did not like his family. But the family was very influential in official circles, as well as in literary ones, and at the Académie. War had begun. A meeting of the Académie, on 13 August 1674, turned into a demonstration by the modern faction. Quinault, Charles Perrault, Des Marests and, a few days later, Charpentier affirmed that there existed a modern literature worthy of modern France and its king, Louis the Great. Soon the Académie de peinture joined in. It decided that henceforth the subject for competitions need no longer be taken from mythology but could be chosen from the Bible. It might have seemed that the quarrel was dying down quite quickly. In fact men remained divided and personal antipathies were not appeased. The appearance of peace was shattered in 1687. Charles Perrault read a poem at a session of the Académie on the *Siècle de Louis le Grand*. In it he praised modern literature and spoke with scant respect of the ancients. Boileau, in the middle of the session, voiced his disapproval in no uncertain fashion. The following year, Charles Perrault published the first volume of *Parallèle des Anciens et des Modernes*. Two more volumes followed in 1690 and 1692.

The theses Perrault put forward in these volumes were not a little controversial. He placed the *Iliad* and *Odyssey* below Scudéry's *Alaric* and Père Le Moyne's *Saint-Louis*. He thought Pindar grotesque and Aristotle a schoolboy. Looking at the splendid *Idylles* by Theocritus his only reaction was: 'Vilain temps; vilaines moeurs'. Such extravagant stuff explains Boileau's exasperation. The result was exchanges of unpleasant epigrams and verses between the two men and their friends. Finally, in 1694, Boileau 'fit faire sous main des propositions d'accommodement'. Racine played the part of mediator. On 30 August 1694 Boileau and Charles Perrault embraced each other in the presence of their fellow-members of the Académie.

Much later, in 1714, the quarrel broke out again. By then Boileau and Charles Perrault were dead and new champions had come forward. Houdar de la Motte had published an abridged *Iliad* in French verse at the end of 1713. So far as the moderns were concerned the alleged translation could only illustrate what Homer should have done but could not do because he was only a barbarian. A learned lady, Mme Dacier, decided to avenge the old poet. She published the *Causes de la corruption du goût*. Once again men of letters divided into two camps and, in the words of Montesquieu, they cordially exchanged the most vulgar insults.[18]

Personal enmities had played an unduly great part in this protracted quarrel. What is more serious is that too often debates centred around questions of detail that had been badly defined and were lacking in real importance. It was ludicrous to quarrel about the Christian supernatural. It was scarcely more intelligent to align oneself for or against Homer. But behind these clumsy controversies one discovers basic lines of cleavage which are significant historical facts.

Historians have believed that the quarrel could be explained through the invasion of the world of the humanities by the philosophy of Descartes. At first sight this looks a promising theory. For it is true, as has been shown, that so far as literature went Descartes was a modern. Furthermore, the first signs of the existence of a modern faction, around 1662, are connected with the Habert de Montmort circle, which was Cartesian. Descartes' rationalism was a natural opponent of the idea of literature that saw itself as closely linked with the ancient tradition. But the facts are different, and they contradict this kind of explanation of the quarrel. Boileau, the protagonist of the ancient faction, was a Cartesian. Bossuet's group at Versailles was Cartesian, and one may say without exaggeration that the nucleus of the modern faction was to be found precisely there. On the other hand all the moderns, Des Marests, Charpentier, Huet, and Charles Perrault, were very strongly hostile to Descartes. We must conclude from this that the history of philosophy does not explain the quarrel.

In fact, the history of the modern faction coincides with the history of French society. It was not for nothing that Louis XIV and his government had aroused in the French their national pride. The public felt that it was living in a great period of French history. In its public sessions the Académie liked to celebrate 'l'avantage que Sa Majesté fait remporter à son siècle sur tous les siècles'. Des Marests de Saint-Sorlin constantly returned to the idea, already expounded by Louis Le Laboureur, that the cause of the moderns was related to the greatness of the nation, and that a good Frenchman who was loyal to his king must believe that the century of Louis XIV was as good as that of Pericles and Augustus. He was indignant about men who 'ayant tellement perdu l'amour et le respect qu'ils doivent à leur patrie',[19] were constantly decrying the French language and those who cultivate it. Similarly, Charles Perrault saw in the refinements and increasing luxury and urbanity of French society a splendid flowering of French civilisation rather than a sign of decadence.

That was the reason for the criticism the moderns passed on the greatest names of ancient literature. They did not maintain that Euripides was literally 'bad'. They held that Greek tragedy went hand in hand with an almost barbarous culture, and that meant almost barbarous taste. They therefore said that they were superior to the ancients in manners, order, and all that has to do with experience and thought.

They also liked their period. They liked even its more debatable virtues. They went so far as to prefer the galanterie of the moderns to the emotion of love as it had been represented in Greek and Roman literature. They preferred the epics of Scudéry and Père Le Moyne to those of Homer because the latter depicted a society which was still barbarous in customs and taste.[20]

The doctrine of the moderns was thus understandably that of the public at large. It was supreme in the salons. It had captured the ladies of high society. Most of the time it dominated the Académie, and Bossuet worked very hard to obtain the admission into that company of supporters of the ancients. All the same, he was unable to prevent the moderns for long from regaining their majority.

Still, there were some men who refused to be enticed by the new doctrine. These were the ancients. Among them was a number of great names of the nobility, for example Condé, his nephew Conty, and the Duchesse du Maine. There were also senior magistrates like the Lemoignons and the Daguesseaus. And there was the small group of eminent writers that was formed around 1674 in the orbit of Mme de Montespan and her sister Mme de Thianges with Racine, Boileau and La Fontaine. At the time the courtiers called it derisively the

'Cabale du Sublime'. Mme de Lafayette, La Rochefoucauld and his son Marsillac belonged to it. Bossuet, who was already famous, was its spiritual head. Later, after Mme de Montespan had suffered her eclipse, the Cabale continued with the additional membership of La Bruyère and the young Abbé Fénelon. Observers got into the habit of contrasting the 'gens de Versailles' with the 'beaux esprits de Paris', by which they meant the academies, salons, and the modern faction.

Strongly attached to the past, these men did not share the masses' confidence in the progress of knowledge and manners. They were profoundly religious, and for them God had in the beginning revealed to man the great truths of morality. History, in their eyes, consisted of the increasing degradation of man. Far from being uncultured savages the patriarchs of the Bible and the Greeks of Homer were, for them, the representatives of the golden age of humanity. It was the age of which they were envious. At the beginning of La Bruyère's *Caractères*, the *Discours sur Théophraste* contrasts modern corruption with the primitive state of innocence, modern idols with the great truths ancient man knew by instinct. It talks about the Greek city state with its simple and democratic ways.

This was the level at which lay the real difference between ancients and moderns. It obviously spilled over into literature. The ancient faction remained attached to the qualities of strength and grandeur. Poetry had to accede to the sublime. Not, however, to inflated language and redundant rhetoric, but to that sober greatness born of inspiration, which is present as much in the 'Qu'il mourût' of Corneille as in 'Que la lumière soit, et la lumière fût' of Genesis.

However, this period belonged to the moderns who found their delight in ingenious turns of phrase and in the elegance of the poésie galante that had been fashionable since Voiture.

Part III

Literary Forms

8

Poetry

Poetry before Malherbe

Poetry had its place in French society as it was reconstituting itself after the civil wars, but it was a very strictly defined place. It had, of course, to exalt the newly restored hierarchies and celebrate the king's victories. It had to thunder against his internal and external enemies. It also had to sing the praises of the official religion, and nobly to develop the themes of the gospels and liturgy. The king and his ministers had their own poets. They were rewarded, or more precisely paid, with ecclesiastical livings, pensions and gratuities. Some of the highest members of the nobility liked to have their poets too. They expected them to praise their families and exploits. Sometimes these paid poets were also asked to compose some satire against one of their patron's enemies. More often they were asked to address a few verses to a lady the king or a nobleman had embarked upon conquering, which caused certain nasty people to comment on the strange tasks the Muses were being called upon to undertake.

Some writers had acquired quite a reputation in this kind of poetry at the beginning of the century. They were known as the 'poètes du Louvre'. Chief among them were Cardinal du Perron and Bertaut, who was bishop of Sées. After 1601 they were joined by Vauquelin des Yvetaux and, after 1605, by Malherbe.

The career and work of these poets most strikingly epitomise an entire period of French poetry. They were in the employment of the court. Du Perron and Bertaut were showered with ecclesiastical dignities and livings. Vauquelin des Yvetaux was tutor to the Duc de Vendôme and later to the Dauphin. When Malherbe came to live in Paris the king asked the Duc de Bellegarde to ensure that the poet had his board, a valet, a horse, and a thousand livres as pay.

The 'poètes du Louvre' were thus employees of those in authority and worked to order. Political events dictated the subject-matter of their odes, in which they exalted the authority of the crown. They wrote étrennes, dirges, and epithalamia, on the occasion of the various events – illnesses, deaths, births, and marriages – that occurred in the royal household. Vauquelin des Yvetaux and Malherbe more than once composed poems in which the king addressed one or another of his mistresses.

The characteristics of French poetry at that time derive naturally from the fact that it was a kind of official literature. It was basically oratorical and developed with eloquence the main themes of politics and religion. It had nobility. But it would be difficult to discover in it any of the emotional elements one finds in the great poems of Ronsard and which so often arouse the reader's admiration. The picturesque is missing too, and the poets seem to be unaware of the existence of nature and of the fact that it is beautiful. Nor is there any emotional content in their love poetry, and it is very clear that the poet is speaking on behalf of someone else. It would be unjust to accuse all these poets of hypocrisy. On the other hand the reader fails to find in them the warmth of real conviction. This is hardly surprising. Cardinal du Perron was known to believe neither in God nor in any faith. Malherbe was perhaps as sceptical in matters of religion as he was in politics. One must not be naive enough to believe that he admired all the great noblemen he praised. He called Concini 'l'esprit sacré' when Concini was in power. When he was no longer in power he called him an 'excrément de la terre'. Then he praised the Duc de Luynes to the skies, but after his death he called him 'cet absinthe au nez de barbet'.

After the magnificent achievements of the Pléiade the decline is obvious. It corresponds to the decline in the history of civilisation of the ideals of the European Renaissance. It was an orthodoxy that had been restored and not a faith. The new order conquered men's minds and caused men's actions to conform to its requirements. But it achieved this by compelling docility and submission. Poetry needs different sources of inspiration.

Official poetry, confining itself to a small number of subjects which it developed with rhetorical flourish, was not the only kind of poetry that was written during the reign of Henry IV. What is generally known as satirical literature also had a vogue at this time.[1] The term is ambiguous, however, and covers a number of different kinds of writing.

In the first place it signifies a literature that was defamatory and full of personal insults of rare virulence. It cannot be explained only by the climate of brutishness reminiscent of the military encampments which dominated Paris at the end of the civil wars. Men like Sigogne[2] and Berthelot were particularly good at it.[3] Structurally their satires continued the tradition of the sixteenth century. They were generally octosyllabic and in groups of eight or sixteen. In other words they were not in the Roman tradition.

Sometimes, rather than attack people, such writers might describe objects. For example, they might describe the nose of a courtier. Or they considered the *Anatomie du manteau de cour*. Besides being outrageously impudent, they could be remarkably picturesque. They reflected the influence of Berni and his Italian followers.

This kind of satirical poetry did not, as might be thought, seek to set itself up in opposition to the work of the 'poètes du Louvre'. It represented a different, and complementary, aspect of contemporary society, in which praise and defamation were expressed with equal extravagance, and in which the same men could show feelings of supreme piety and pour out obscenities without incurring ridicule. Malherbe and Mainard wrote verse for the *Parnasse satyrique* without feeling that they were therefore denying their other work.

Mathurin Régnier makes sense in this context.[4] There are historians who made him into the leader of a satirical school, in which Sigogne, Motin and Berthelot were supposed to have been his disciples. They did not see that the alleged leader of the school was very much younger than those who were supposed to have been his students. Mainly, however, a mere look at his satires must convince one that their implacable alexandrines link him with a quite different tradition, namely that of Roman satire.

He was in fact a humanist. In his verse he imitated Bertaut,

Du Perron, and his uncle Desportes. He said that Ronsard was his poetic ancestor. Most of the time his satires were 'discours moraux', in the tradition of the Romans. His subjects are honour, human folly, and the incoherence of reason. His favourite model is Horace.

Yet he belonged to his time. He knew his Italian contemporaries, the satires of Dolce and Alamanni, the picturesque pieces of Berni. He did not think that he was betraying humanist poetry by finding inspiration in them. What he added was a spicy note. For that reason he might be thought to have got rather close to the style of Sigogne in verse like *Mauvais gîte* and *Macette*. But the intention of his poetry was entirely different. He complained in his poems of the contempt into which poetry had fallen through the activities of brutish and uncouth poets. At the same time he expressed regret that other poets had put their services at the disposal of the mighty to help them in their adulterous associations; it was not hard to understand whom he had in mind.

He did not care for Malherbe. But their enmity was not based on the causes attributed to it for a long time. It is not true that Malherbe was the incarnation of order and classical reason, and that Régnier was the symbol of anarchy in literature. On the contrary, Régnier was much more attached to the great traditions of the ancients and the humanists than Malherbe. So much so that, unlike Malherbe, he refused to follow the fashions of society at the end of the civil wars. He refused to take his criteria of good taste from the new élites who, he felt, invoked reason because they did not know the ancients. The only authority he recognised was that of the past, and not that of elegant aristocrats. That was the difference between Régnier and Malherbe.

It is therefore no use looking to Régnier for an illustration of the new trends in French poetry. He was too attached to tradition to reflect the desire for the modern that characterised certain sections of French society at the time of Henry IV. That desire was reflected in the poets we now call 'baroques'.[5]

The name is not unjustified. In this context it certainly does not imply absurdity or bad taste, and it is one of the most valuable achievements of recent historiography that it has conferred upon baroque poetry the rank it deserves. It saw its function essentially in the pursuit of effect. The baroque poet did not confine himself to heaping image upon image and metaphor upon metaphor. He wanted them to be startling and explosive. He wanted them for the shock they provide to the reader, not for the emotions they might be able to arouse. Talk about 'les flammes de l'amour' was far too tame for him. He preferred to make it 'les tisons' and 'les mèches'. He also used antithesis to make his impact.

According to Colletet, two men stood out in the development of the new poetic style. They were Sponde and Laugier de Porchères. Sponde has been neglected for a long time, but thanks to the edition of his works by Professor Alan Boase and the valuable commentaries it contains he is now well known and properly held in high esteem.[6] Laugier de Porchères is chiefly known for his sonnet *Sur les yeux de Madame la Duchesse de Beaufort*. When it appeared it was hailed as the most brilliant expression of the new style. Once the baroque fashion was over, it was despised as extravagant. To us today it seems very quaint, its extreme ingenuity no longer shocks. We are tempted to say that it is enchanting.

Baroque style shocked those who remained attached to tradition. The reaction against it began early. The 'poètes du Louvre' condemned it. Cardinal du Perron merely thought it barbarous. He castigated 'vicieuses' metaphors, which is what he called expressions like 'tisons d'amour' or 'mèches d'amour', because he thought it improper to 'descendre du genre à l'espèce'. The reaction against the baroque poets was led by two men, Jean de Lingendes and Malherbe. It was they, said Colletet, who forced poets like Sponde and Laugier de Porchères to give up their positions of eminence. Colletet thought it a happy victory, because these two new authors 'avaient bien plus de raison et moins de pointes' than the others. What was more, their Muses had polish. Others, like Vauquelin des Yveteaux and Mathurin Régnier, reproached the baroque writers for their odd imagery, their habit of juxtaposing words that were then left without literal meaning. 'Paroles disjointes', Vauquelin said. 'Paroles mal jointes' said an epigram attributed to Mainard. Régnier meant the same thing when he talked of words that were 'mal joints et mal collés'. Colletet provides an important clue about the decline of the baroque fashion in poetry. He said that around 1610–15 Laugier de Porchères' sonnet had lost its appeal.[7]

Malherbe

Against this historical background, the nature and significance of Malherbe's work becomes much clearer.[8] Boileau's famous words 'Enfin Malherbe vint' show the ignorance of this legislator of Parnassus in matters relating to French literary history. Malherbe was neither the only one, nor indeed the first, to react against the poetic style he condemned. What distinguishes him from the others is the dogmatic form of his doctrine, and the unjust scorn he had for Ronsard, as if the latter had been a baroque poet. It was an error that Cardinal du Perron and Bertaut did not commit.

Malherbe's doctrine was particularly rigorous about poetic forms. He restricted himself almost entirely to odes, stanzas (stances) and songs (chansons). He liked to have a large and varied number of strophic forms. It must be said that, in this field, he himself achieved some admirable results. On the other hand, he was very scathing about long sequences of alexandrines and, more generally, about all pieces of isometric verse.

His main preoccupation was language, and it is here that his work connects most clearly with the social evolution of the kingdom. He believed that the most important quality of a language must be its 'purity'. He therefore dismissed everything that did not belong to the usual vocabulary of the social élite, that is the most enlightened and reasonable parts of the court and the upper strata of Paris society. It was for the same reason that he dismissed the poetry of the sixteenth century. He could not bear its archaic expressions, its Greek and Latin borrowings, its verbal innovations. But he also condemned, in this same context, the Provençal and Gascon turns of phrase that had found their way into the court as a result of the recent wars.[9]

Malherbe used this 'purified' language to create a new style, whose principal feature was to be its douceur. This word was constantly used by contemporaries in their references to

Malherbe's works. Its meaning can be readily understood when one remembers the reproaches addressed to the baroque writers at this period: 'Paroles disjointes', 'paroles mal jointes', 'mal joints et mal collés' words. Malherbe's douceur is the opposite of that abrupt style with its combinations of explosive words.

Malherbe's style went well with his essentially oratorical form of poetry. In fact, Malherbe was not greatly concerned about the themes or, if one may put it so, the subject matter of his poems. What he concentrated upon was mainly a kind of stately lyricism. His odes are about the king's victories, and marriages, births, and bereavements in the royal household. His paraphrases of psalms are endowed with the same kind of eloquence as his political odes. Some of his contemporaries recognised this and Chapelain, who agreed with them, wrote: 'Ceux-là ne lui ont guère fait tort qui ont dit que ses vers étaient de fort belle prose rimée'.

He died in 1627, just as French poetry was beginning to enter another epoch. He had acquired such great prestige that he was looked upon as the greatest modern poet. His last years saw him surrounded by admirers. In 1626 a Paris publisher had brought out a *Recueil des plus beaux vers* of contemporary poetry. Malherbe and his disciples took up the entire volume. His most important disciples were Mainard and Racan.

Mainard, in particular, personified the traditions of Malherbe. Towards 1640 he composed some pieces that were very much admired: for example, his *Ode à Alcippe* (1642) and his elegy for a *Belle Vieille* (1644). His *Oeuvres* (1646) showed the school of Malherbe at its best.

Racan had greater genius, and consequently a naturally greater degree of independence. But he did remain faithful to Malherbe. He refused to treat Bertaut and Malherbe as opposites, a proof that he saw better than many others that there was a general evolution during his period towards more 'regular' forms and that Malherbe was not the sole representative of that evolution. But there is ample testimony for his continuing links with his master in the poetry he wrote after 1627, for example, the *Psaumes de la Pénitence* and the ode to Richelieu.

Chapelain and Gombauld should also be considered in this

context. The former periodically published some ode to the glory of Richelieu or the victories of Condé, or later, the policies of Mazarin. Gombauld remained most of the time in the tradition of Bertaut and, like many others, could see no reason for thinking that there were any contradictions between the doctrines of Bertaut and Malherbe.

What might be called the unconditional supporters of Malherbe were but the most demanding group among a much larger body of less severe writers whom one could reasonably describe as supporters of a 'regular' form of literature (les réguliers).

There had been writers of this kind during Malherbe's lifetime, writers who refused to have recourse to baroque effects, avoided the excessive use of metaphor, the bringing together of disparate words, the 'paroles mal jointes' of the modernists. Jean de Lingendes, Motin, and Honoré d'Urfé in his poetry had not been followers of Malherbe but supporters of more 'regular' procedures. They too wanted douceur. But they did not restrict themselves to his forms of stately lyricism. They had preserved a taste for bucolic poetry, and they wrote eulogies of country life and were perpetuating a mythological tradition that they had found in Ovid. They used language that was perfectly clear, elegant, and pleasantly harmonious. The baroque was alien to them. They showed that it was possible to be 'regular' without being strictly like Malherbe.

That was the path followed towards 1625–30 by a number of young poets who called themselves the Illustres Bergers.[10] They belonged to the new generation that was born around 1600. Some of them were to attain at least a solid and enduring reputation, if not glory. In particular there were Guillaume Colletet, Godeau, Malleville and Philippe Habert. They were 'regular' in the strictest sense of the word, though specifically in the most essential realm of language where they were purists. They shunned the excessive use of metaphor associated with the baroque; when they did use a metaphor they made sure that it had lost its ability to shock or puzzle, so that in fact it amounted to no more than an oratorical trope. They confined their audacity to talking about the fire and flames of love, and calling its dire effects a prison. But they did not blindly follow the examples and doctrine of Malherbe. They could not bring themselves to condemn Ronsard, and their attitude towards that great poet was like that of Cardinal du Perron and Bertaut. They used to meet in the presence of a great humanist who, like Du Perron, encouraged them to acquire learning, worthy maxims, and lofty ideals.

The Illustres Bergers split up after a while, as young men usually do after having shared for a time the same tastes in poetry and a few ideas. But a tradition continued to exist which may be termed Malherbian or 'regular'. The most respected poets of the period belonged to it. Thanks to Chapelain they swamped the Académie Française. They were not sectarian. They allowed themselves, and others, great latitude in the selection of poetic themes and forms. During this time, which covers the whole of Richelieu's period of government and goes well beyond it, poets continued to write odes and stanzas, as well as paraphrases of psalms in the manner of Malherbe. Most of them, be they Gombauld, Malleville, Tristan, Scudéry, or Vion d'Alibray wrote a great number of sonnets. Elegies, too, which had been neglected since Malherbe, again came into their own, particularly with Germain Habert and Malleville who thus continued the tradition of the Illustres Bergers. Metamorphoses had also come back again in great numbers. This phenomenon can be accounted for by the fact that, around 1620, Ovid had become fashionable again. The vogue lasted for the next twenty years without a break. Saint-Amant had written his famous *Métamorphose de Lyrian et de Silvie* before 1627. Metamorphoses are to be found in the *Guirlande de Julie* in 1633. The *Métamorphose des yeux de Philis en astres* (1633) by Germain Habert was considered to be one of the masterpieces of modern poetry. Finally, at this period, there was the new form of the madrigal, imitated from the Italians, which enjoyed increasing popularity with its 'galants' themes and irregular versification.

All these poets used a style which conformed to the examples of Bertaut and Malherbe. Their sentences were usually periodic. They preferred parallels to antitheses. They did not refrain from the use of metaphor, but they only employed the simplest. They did not want their thought to be hidden by dazzling language.[11]

It might perhaps be thought that there is something disturbing about making banality into a virtue. But there was a serious reason for it. It might even be held, without trying unduly to accommodate the facts, that it constitutes one of the basic elements of classical aesthetics. For it means that the essence of a work of art is made to reside in its pathetic evocativeness. When our contemporary aesthetic theorists maintain that the pleasures of poetry are purely intellectual, they imagine that they are classical when in fact they are baroque. The critics of Richelieu's time were well aware of this. Chapelain condemned intricate metaphors that were more like riddles ('l'entassement d'expressions figurées') because he said that poetry must not be an amusement for the mind but must, on the contrary, 'toucher les passions'. The reproach he addressed to the moderns was that the pleasure they gave was entirely intellectual; they delighted the mind and made it 'aiguiser ses yeux'. He disapproved of the love of metaphor of the baroque poets because their metaphors were not the source of emotion but in fact prevented feeling from arising at all. What he wanted was that poetry should reach men, not in their intelligence but in 'la tendresse des âmes'.

The poets of the reign of Louis XIII

The prestige of Malherbe, and the tradition of 'regular' poetry that had been established before his death and flourished thereafter, might lead one to believe that from about 1615 the baroque impetus had disappeared, to leave the poetic field entirely in the hands of the followers of Malherbe. The facts are very different. Even before the death of Malherbe, and as early as 1620, there was a revival of baroque poetry. This was the work of writers without talent, but the best poets of the young generation adopted the principles of baroque aesthetics. Mainard, Racan and Gombauld were respected names, but the young generation at the court and the young poets who haunted the bookshops in the rue Saint-Jacques were excited about Théophile, Tristan, Saint-Amant and Scudéry.

This fact is of cardinal importance for the history of French poetry. If one believed the oversimplified picture that critics used to draw of classical literature, one would be left with the idea that Malherbe's doctrine had been taken over by the entire century, that Mainard and Racan were for thirty years the only poets of any importance, and that only a few odd people managed to escape the influence of Malherbian doctrine. Today there can be no doubt that the best poets of the period were precisely those whose inspiration came from baroque examples and not from Malherbe.

The second baroque period was not identical with that of Henry IV. Saint-Amant and Tristan did not write exactly as Sponde and Laugier de Porchères had done. They were not quite so intent in their search for strong effects. They rarely used frenzied hyperbole and other literary extremes. They preferred the ingenious. They took it far, as they also did their search for the vivid. All in all, however, they were sensible.

It was largely by their choice of themes that they were really baroque. The theme of beautiful eyes had provided the subject matter of eleven poems in the *Parnasse* of 1607. Hair, as a theme, had come in at the same time. A feeling for plastic beauty and the vivid inspired a number of brilliant images in Laugier de Porchères. Gold, silver, and precious stones fill his verses. They appear again in the baroque poets of Louis XIII's reign.

Théophile de Viau played an important part in this baroque renaissance. The new generation was entranced by him for many years. He was no follower of Malherbe, nor even really a 'regular' poet. Those who did not like him thought his poetry 'scabreux', his inspiration 'inégale'. These terms had very specific meanings in the literary language of those days. They signified that Théophile did not care about 'régularité', strict 'liaison', and continuity, as the taste of good society demanded. Also, his themes were very much more varied than those of Malherbe had been, and he did not hesitate to evoke funereal visions as the baroque poets had done. His treatment of love and nature was highly original. His descriptions took the form of a series of impressions that were registered in all their disjointedness and vivid immediacy. The youth of 1623 admired his work for the new freshness it brought to French poetry.

But his career was brief, and he lacked time to do the work of which he was capable. Instead, it was his friend Saint-Amant who brought about the reorientation of French poetry.[12]

Influenced by the Italian *moderni*, particularly by Marino, he had published a number of mythological poems prior to 1630 which he presented as 'descriptions'. According to his friend Faret, he gave that name to 'de riches tableaux où la nature est représentée', and he took poetry to be a 'peinture parlante'. His pictures were usually rich and gay, full of gold, silver, pearls, and rubies. But, like the baroques, he liked to evoke macabre scenes as well. His poetry also wrote about ruins, hanging skeletons, poisonous animals, and nocturnal birds in 'la lumière sombre de la lune'.

Saint-Amant, after 1627, added a new note to this kind of poetry. He deliberately turned to subjects that were well-known. He described tavern scenes. He went so far as to describe a cheese, and he wrote a poem about the vine. But these new poems in no way signify a decline into extravagance or vulgarity. Saint-Amant knew all about art, and he certainly knew the Flemish painters. He also rather liked Italian Bernesque poetry. He wanted to compete with the burlesque writer Tassoni. As he saw it, he was amusing his readers with verse that was lively, full-blooded, and ingenious.

All this was a far cry from the poetry that had derived from Malherbe and that his most faithful disciples were continuing to write. But it would be false to suppose that Saint-Amant had set himself up in opposition to the supporters of 'regular' poetry. He agreed with them about what mattered most to them, and he was like them in wanting to use all the resources of the French language. He stated explicitly that the quality of a piece of poetry depended on the quality of its language and that there was no real poet who was not also a 'maître absolu de la langue', who did not know 'toutes les galanteries, toutes les propriétés, toutes les finesses, toutes les moindres vétilles'.[13] In the circumstances, one can understand why Chapelain had only admiration and fellow-feeling for Saint-Amant, and soon had him admitted to the Academy. Himself well-versed in Italian poetry, Chapelain was able properly to appreciate a poet who introduced into French literature the piquant elegance of Berni and Tassoni.

Like Saint-Amant, Tristan knew his Italian moderns. In particular he admired Marino. Urbain Chevreau wrote: 'Notre Tristan, qui admirait toutes les visions du Marin . . .'.[14]

This explains why Tristan in his verse praised the flame-like waves of blonde hair, the pearls and rubies of a beautiful mouth, and why he insisted on celebrating the mysterious beauty of a Moorish slave-girl or the elegance of a young widow in her sumptuous and sombre finery. Later he was to write one of the most beautiful descriptive poems to be found in French literature, *La Mer*, all irridescence and imagery.

Tristan was not afraid to take his descriptions far into the realm of metaphor and subtlety. His verse repeats some of the most daring turns of phrase of Marino. A widow becomes, for him, a beautiful, animated night. It would be wrong to make excuses for him. Rather should it be said that his boldness is infinitely racy and that it could offend only the strait-laced.

The works of Malleville and Scudéry do not bear comparison with those of Saint-Amant and Tristan. They do, however, have the same inspiration. For Scudéry, one of the main objects of poetry is to evoke beautiful shapes and harmonious images. Malleville at times imitated Marino. He used the theme of the beautiful widow. Like Marino, too, he took the theme of the beautiful beggar-woman, and treated it in a long series of stanzas.

Germain Habert must be added to these names. He is neglected today, but his contemporaries thought his work one of the most remarkable expressions of French poetry. Much later, at the time of the quarrel between ancients and moderns, his *Métamorphose des yeux de Philis en astres* was used to prove that French poetry was superior to that of the ancients 'en esprit fin, et doux, et délicat'.[15]

That much-admired *Métamorphose* had been composed in 1638. It was baroque. In fact, it was extremely so. Except for rare moments when the intended effects appeared to be oratorical and pathetic, the poem was caught up in a constant stream of metaphors, riddle following hard upon riddle. The *Elégie sur un bracelet de cheveux*, by the same author, was again entirely baroque, seeing the theme as a spiritual maze, as threads, beautiful treasures, as the bonds of yesterday and the trophies of today. The poetry of Germain Habert provides us with a useful landmark, since it proves that the second wave of the baroque was still alive in 1640 and that people were still attracted to it. Père Le Moyne's *Peintures morales* were written at the same time and in the same pure baroque style.

The second baroque period, which was of great significance for French poetry, occurred at a time when the disorders of the war and the ensuing anarchy were no more than a bad memory, but when individual initiative remained strong and poets to be admired did not have to conform at all costs to rules of 'good taste' and 'good form'. No doubt Saint-Amant was not that pillar of the taverns he has been made out to be, but he did keep gay company in the group that called itself the Goinfres (i.e. the good fellows). Tristan had lived an adventurous life for very many years and he continued to shun the world of high society. Scudéry informed everyone that he was above all a soldier. It was the social position occupied by these poets which explains the curious originality of their work and their happy combination of a great feeling for 'taste' and a yet greater need for personal expression.

As social life began again in France, poets had to think again of pleasing those who mattered in society. Poetry had to adopt new forms. Society poetry (poésie galante) responded to that need. Vincent Voiture provided it with its earliest and best models.[16]

He had been presented to Mme de Rambouillet in 1625. From that moment he devoted his time and talent to amuse the marquise and her friends. But he was much more than an entertainer. He was well versed in ancient literature, the writers of Italy and Spain, and the French novels of the past. It is not quite clear what he thought of French literature of the recent past. One contemporary wrote that 'il ne pouvait lire nos fadaises'.[17] But since he had made it his job to amuse, that was the task to which he applied his considerable talent.

It was Voiture who conceived the idea of galanterie and, above all, it was he who established its tradition and literary forms. He broke with what remained of the heritage of Petrarch. But he refused to be led into the baroque instead. Galanterie, for him, meant a graceful game, in which wit, ingenuity, and a lightness of touch combined with a very slight vibration of the poet's sensibility. It made its effect through delicate compliments and did not wish to be thought unfeeling. But it did not wish to be taken entirely seriously either.

That was galant poetry as Voiture practised it. Some of his pieces are exquisite. The best among them are not those most often quoted and which were inspired by Italian and Spanish poets. They are certainly excellent, but there were other poets at that time who could do just as well. The kind of poetry which is peculiar to him, for example the *Stances du garçon*, are a subtle mixture of wit and sensuality. And there is, for instance, the fantasy on a blue and black shoe, or the stanzas for Anne of Austria, an astonishing combination of familiarity and respect, emotion and lightness, admirable delicacy and appropriateness of tone.

For the frequenters of the Hôtel de Rambouillet Voiture wrote rondeaux, ballads, songs on popular themes, and letters in the language of former days. As they became known they provided entertainment for the whole of Parisian society, and they were taken as models of elegant banter. They were imitated, until the end of the century, by the poets who wrote for galante society.

Voiture's contemporaries recognised the independence he showed in his choice of literary forms. Tallemant wrote that Voiture was the first to introduce 'libertinage', i.e. free thought, into poetry. As an example he cites the fact that before Voiture nobody had written irregular stanzas, 'soit de vers, soit de mesure'. It is indeed true that Voiture was very high-handed in his treatment of the traditional poetic techniques. He showed the same independence in his use of language.

He also changed the kind of treatment poetic themes had been receiving. He transformed them and gave them a new value. The manner in which he dealt with dreams is very instructive on this point. Motin, Théophile de Viau, and the baroque poets had used this theme for mysterious and sensual poetry. The stanzas of Voiture's *Le Songe* were written in a light-hearted and frivolous tone which drew from the same theme entirely new effects.

The period of Mazarin

Changing manners after the death of Richelieu favoured the

progress of poésie galante while the Fronde, and the society to which it gave rise, accelerated it. A new generation of poets was taking the place of those who had been so much admired during the government of the cardinal. After the end of the unrest men like Saint-Amant and Tristan belonged to a past age and even seemed a little ridiculous. Two collections of *Recueils de vers* were published after 1652 which provide the best picture of the new society and the kind of poetry it demanded. In both, the *Recueils* of Champhoudry as well as those of Sercy, poésie galante is omnipresent.

These poets of the new generation were 'regular'. They accepted the authority of Chapelain, Conrart, and Balzac. They were in no way baroque. For instance, when they felt like writing descriptions of nature they avoided the juxtaposed notation which was characteristic of Saint-Amant and Tristan. The baroque use of metaphor was alien to them.

But they introduced a new element into these 'regular' forms of expression which reflected the transformation manners had undergone in the society for which they were writing. They went even further than Voiture. They were not content with substituting galant banter for the expression of passionate feelings. For them love was a game. The lover had to remain free and lucid. No tears or sighs for him. He sought to charm for amusement, but his heart was not involved. Historians of manners must look closely at this kind of libertinage, which is intellectual rather than sensual, and which foreshadows very clearly the manners of the Regency and the novels of Crébillon.

The most gifted of these poets was certainly Sarasin, who was the real successor of Voiture.[18] He did not actually like him, but that was for personal reasons. But he did imitate him extensively. Like Voiture he used a style reminiscent of Marot; and he wrote ballads and songs and playful épîtres as Marot had done. He had an agreeable, delicate, and unaffected wit, and his poetry is as good as Voiture's.

There are certain works of his one must read before one can appreciate the full extent of his culture, and the solid and great poetry he had it in him to write. He knew Virgil well. He admired the 'grand Malherbe', and he expressed his wish to take up 'la lyre qu'en mourant Malherbe nous a laissée'. We must remember him when we meet the system-builders who contrast the classical and Malherbian tradition with those whom they grossly misname the précieux poets.

The same could be said of his friend Pellisson. His poetic talent was not particularly great, and he only wrote verse to amuse his friends. But his ideas were sensible and his taste sound. He infinitely admired Homer. Horace was his bedside reading. He did not need Boileau to tell him that Terence was preferable to Plautus. What he liked in Voiture was his 'très galant et très délicat' spirit, matched by a 'mélancolie douce et ingénieuse'.

In other words the best of the poètes galants did not deserve the scorn showered upon them by certain critics. Still, it cannot be denied that there are obvious dangers when poetry is reduced to being merely a game to amuse the social élite, and these dangers were not always avoided. Poets had to demonstrate their ingenuity. Not the ingenuity of the baroque, with its strong and explosive effects. But the insipid ingenuity that amuses the guests of the salons. And it had to have its share of frivolity, which it had in fact abundantly. For the rhymsters who were fashionable around 1655, poetry was little more than something that accompanied a basket of fruit or deplored the death of a chameleon. The same frivolity prevailed among the poets at the kind of court held by Foucquet. When Mme du Plessis-Bellière's parrot died Foucquet himself took the trouble to write a sonnet on that grave subject, and his friends imitated him.

The language and style of these poets were lax. They showed their inability to work with the economy and brilliance of expression of their predecessors. Their imagery was poor and banal. Their lyrical forms tended to be free to the point of anarchy. Charles Sorel noted, with much truth, that the new poets went in for irregular forms of versification and arranged their rhymes as the spirit moved them.

Some names are notoriously connected with this kind of frivolous poetry which, after Voiture's attractive verse, marked such a sad decline. There were Montplaisir and Mathieu de Montreuil, as well as, unfortunately, the rather discerning and sensitive La Sablière who never succeeded in being more than merely sensitive. Chiefly, however, there was Benserade. After the death of Voiture he was considered to be the wittiest of the poètes galants. In 1649 the ladies of society exalted his sonnet *Job* over Voiture's *Uranie*. That 'querelle', as it was called, was a sign of the fact that the elegant ways of 'galanterie' no longer satisfied a number of poets. They were called the coquets, and they were then fashionable. *L'Almanach des Coquettes* and the *Reveil-matin de la Coquette* appeared at this time. Faithful to sound tradition, Charles Sorel deplored that the Muses were becoming galantes 'à la persuasion des Poètes coquets'. All the best poets shared this indignation. Sarasin and Scudéry mercilessly poked fun at the outrageous frivolity of Foucquet's circle when it spent its time making bouts-rimés about the death of that famous parrot. But, so far as the ladies of fashionable society were concerned, Abbé Cotin and Mathieu de Montreuil, who filled the pages of the *Recueils*, were great men.

It is this kind of poetry, i.e. coquetterie, that too many historians call précieuse. This is not just misuse of language but nonsense. It takes a good deal of undiscriminating thinking to confuse the sophistication of thought and style of the précieuses with the frivolous graces of the coquets.

Although the coquets poets represented the most characteristic attitudes of their society they did not represent all of them. Two other forms of poetry also appeared at that time of which the historian must take note.

Within the space of a few years a number of epic, or more exactly 'heroic', poems were published in French. Between Père Le Moyne's *Saint-Louis* of 1653[19] and Des Marests de Saint-Sorlin's *Clovis* of 1657, five other heroic poems had been published. The rather too famous *Pucelle d'Orléans* by Chapelain – on which he had worked for twenty years, but which did not appear until 1656 – was thus not an isolated case.

It was an odd enterprise, this attempt to resuscitate a poetic form that was all too obviously antiquated, and it met with general indifference. Readers were unanimous that it inspired implacable boredom. Even if the poems had been better, they would still not have been appreciated by a society that was pervaded by the spirit of modern coquetterie. Lucid critics were able to recognise that particular reason for their failure. Costar recalled that the taste for the frivolous even swamped contemporary music, that all the society of his period wanted was 'de petits airs aisés et faciles'. He added that it was the same in poetry. Huet explained the failure of the epics by the fashion for galante poetry. Epic poems, he said, were judged in terms appropriate to sonnets and madrigals. 'Notre nation, notre âge, notre goût sont ennemis des grands ouvrages. Nous sommes dans le siècle des colifichets.'

But perhaps these epics could be interesting precisely as protests against a society of that kind. Tired and sick of the frivolity of the coquets poets, some writers seemed to feel the need to defend French literature against that kind of degradation. They wanted it to rediscover a more substantial form of beauty. Des Marests de Saint-Sorlin and Père Mambrun made no bones about their dislike for the frivolity of the moderns. They even went further and criticised certain forms of 'régularité'. Des Marests spoke of pedantic minds who 'font consister toute l'excellence d'un ouvrage en la seule politesse plutôt qu'en la haute majesté'. Père Mambrun went to war against those who looked at syllables under the magnifying glass to count caesuras and check on hiatuses.[20]

They were thus against the prevailing aesthetic climate. But they still thought of themselves as moderns, and even felt that they were alone in offering French society works that could properly be compared with those of the ancients. Tasso and his *Gerusalemme lìberata* were their inspiration. Their idea of superhuman greatness was not derived from Jupiter or the Gods of Olympus but from the Christian God, from angels and demons. Thus the Christian supernatural replaced mythology. They justified that change by pointing out that they were writing for a modern and Christian society. We shall see that, when the quarrel broke out between the ancients and the moderns, it was the epics of this period which provided the basic topic for debate.

Nor can one ignore the existence, during the same period, of another form of poetry, the burlesque.[21] Italian in derivation (*burla*), the word meant joke. The models were Italian as well. They reflected the taste for derision and parody which is an Italian tradition and which showed itself with particular force during the baroque era. Bracciolini had written his *Scherno degli Dei* in 1618, in which he spoke slightingly of the Olympian Gods. The works of Tassoni and the burlesque epic by G.B.Lalli were well known in France.

French burlesque was not, however, a simple imitation of the Italian models. It reflected contemporary taste for racy sophistication of language. They liked Marot's style at the Hôtel de Rambouillet, and Voiture made the 'épîtres en vieux langage' very fashionable. This was also the kind of language that French poets who were writing burlesque wanted to achieve.

Burlesque style reflected an aspect of contemporary French taste. It had links with the baroque in that it expressed its liking for fun and irreverence as well as its feeling for colour. On the other hand one should not believe systematic historians who try to link it with the political anarchy of the Fronde. To prove them wrong one merely has to look at the date at which burlesque made its first appearance. *Raillerie à part*, which appeared in 1629 in Saint-Amant's *Oeuvres*, was already a piece of burlesque. In 1633 Saint-Amant was to bring out the *Poète crotté* which is full of burlesque. Many of the *Caprices* had been written before 1642, and thus before the death of Richelieu. And the *Requête des Dictionnaires* (*c.* 1636) by Ménage can also be said to be burlesque, while Sarasin's pleasant piece *La Souris*, which was written before 1644, served as a model for burlesque poetry.

But it was Scarron who, in 1643, really brought the burlesque into fashion. That was the year in which he published a *Recueil de quelques vers burlesques* and, in the following year he brought out *Typhon* which was the first French burlesque epic. Encouraged by his success, he presented the public after 1648 with his songs of *Virgile travesti*. During the years that followed a large number of burlesque poems appeared, written by men like Brébeuf and D'Assoucy, and others less known.

Heroes and Gods were the main targets of this baroque literature, but not the rules of good poetry. Writers of the calibre of Tristan, Boisrobert, Sarasin, and Ménage guaranteed the respectability of the burlesque. In 1644 Balzac devoted a study to it. There is no doubt that the burlesque was at that time in the eyes of the intellectual élite an elegant and racy art form.

But it was killed by its own success. The most vulgar and flat-footed rhymsters were attracted to it. During the Fronde pamphleteers used the burlesque to make fun of Mazarin. It became a habit to deal with the most serious subjects in burlesque verse. In 1649 someone published the *Passion de W.S. en vers burlesques*. Good writers who had earlier not disdained using burlesque themselves were not slow to condemn that kind of aberration. In 1649 Scarron talked about it as a disagreeable cloud which was threatening the empire of Apollo. The fashion did not last long and, already in 1652, Pellisson noted that the humanities were beginning to rid themselves of this kind of excess. By 1655 the burlesque fashion was no more than a bad memory.

Poetry under Louis XIV

At the beginning of Louis XIV's personal rule there was consequently no conflict between a classical group and one that stood for indiscipline and extravagance. The conflict which did exist was between a kind of society poetry that was coquette, and a view of poetry that involved it in the search for truth and dignity. However, the latter approach had only given rise to the pedestrian poetry of men like Cotin, Cassagnes, and Boyer, in which they celebrated events such as the peace of the Pyrenees, the convalescence of the king, and the conquest of Franche-Comté or Holland. But poetic effervescence had to be looked for elsewhere; for example in the elegant and witty poetry of the coquets, who sought to please the frequenters of the salons. However, the trouble with these poets was that they lacked not only genius but even talent. The little poems by Abbé Testu and Montreuil were written in colourless and flabby language whose frivolity was bound to nauseate anybody with a feeling for real literature and its needful dignity.

At about this time a new conception of poetry appeared and spread. Mlle de Scudéry was one of the first to state its requirements. The poet, according to her *Clélie*, must seek 'plutôt d'exciter la tendresse et de toucher le coeur que de plaire et de divertir'. From this she concluded that verse must contain 'encore plus de passion que d'esprit'. The lines therefore had to be 'nombreux et naturels'.

This conception of poetry is reflected in some of the works of the period. Segrais' eclogues (1660) were meant to move the reader rather than dazzle him with wit. They tried to hide the effort and skill which went into writing them; it might even be said that they were too successful in this respect. Comtesse de la Suze was animated by the same ideas in her elegies, and it was in that spirit that they were taken and admired in their day. A contemporary said of them that they contain 'tout ce que la passion peut inspirer dans les coeurs et fait dire aux amants les plus tendres, avec des expressions qui étaient inconnues avant qu'elle se mêlât d'écrire en vers'. The comtesse replaced the literature of madrigals and over-ingenious sonnets with passionate poetry of sentiment.

But sincerity can end up by being immodesty. Mme de Villedieu was very audacious indeed in her eclogues and elegies. Her verse speaks of the violence of her desires and jealousies. This was a manner very similar to that of the *Lettres portugaises* which appeared during the same period. Her poetry was neither précieuse nor galante, and made a strong impression on the public between 1665 and 1675.

However, it was in Mme Deshoulières that her contemporaries saw the representative of this new kind of poetry.[22] She in no way admired wit, ingeniousness, or artificial elegance. Her heart belonged to nature, feeling, melancholy reverie. She invented a life of innocence, far from the tumult of towns, free from hurtful passion, entirely actuated by the purest feelings. No doubt this poetry did not reflect the habits of polite society in her day. But it did bring out the reaction of the more serious sections of the nation which were led to break with all the frivolity and artifice, in favour of feelings which were simple and natural, and which countered social conventions with authentic values that placed them squarely before their real destiny, the eternal laws of all things, and the inevitability of death.

This poetry, which reflected a desire for withdrawal from the hectic commerce of social life, assumed growing importance during the second half of the reign of Louis XIV. For Versailles had ceased to dazzle the French. It was nothing more than the enormous administrative centre that kept the kingdom going. Those with a taste for independence turned away from it, and the great families of the princes preferred to live on their own, in the midst of their cours galantes.

Abbé Chaulieu was the poet of this society which was being created outside the official orbit. For him, as for Mme Deshoulières, only the life of feeling had meaning. He had no time for wit and could see only cold antitheses and sham in much of modern writing. Chapelle had been his first teacher. From him he had learnt that everything in human life is vain, be it work, goods, or honours. The only true and precious things are the charms of solitude, the beauty of a landscape, the pleasures of a discerning way of life, and friendship.

As regards poetic expression, he thought that an easy and natural way was all that mattered, that verse should be a kind of music, and that there were no rules to tell one how to introduce measure and harmony into poetry. Only a delicate ear could judge such things.

It is a pity that this kind of poetry of sentiment, leading from Mme Deshoulières to Chaulieu, is too often neglected. Of course it lacks the sure touch of the sublime as well as audacity. But it has purity and elegance, and that vibration of the soul which is perhaps worth more than the fervour of romantic passion.

La Fontaine

There were two poets in the seventeenth century whose work was of such importance that they deserve to be studied in their own right: La Fontaine and Boileau. Their work will be better understood if they are studied against the background of their society and its intellectual climate.[23]

La Fontaine was born in 1621 and, like Molière, belonged to the generation that had grown up under the government of Richelieu. Like Molière, too, he was well-educated, and he was well-versed not only in poetry but also in moral and political ideas, and in speculative philosophy. So far as we know, his first contact with the world of literature was made in 1645, in a small circle that had been formed by the lawyer Patru, Tallemant des Réaux, Pellisson, and Furetière. They were independent-minded. They hated Mazarin and the war policy. Patru disliked the financiers. When the Fronde had been defeated and the men of business had triumphed in Parisian society and were gathering the men of letters around them, Patru and several of his friends remained uncompromising in their hostility.

This was less true of La Fontaine. For, although he knew the facts about life in society, he felt able to make agreeable social gestures without losing his independence of mind. When his friend Pellisson became Foucquet's private secretary, La Fontaine allowed himself to be wooed by the generous chief of the intendants and composed a number of charming poems for him. And when, later, Foucquet was arrested and convicted, La Fontaine was one of those who remained loyal to him.

In the circles he frequented the literature of stories was a favourite, and some of them were pretty broad. But, on the whole, this was merely a game, and the main preoccupation was with the way the story was told. La Fontaine himself wrote some stories. In 1664 he published his first *nouvelle* in verse, adapted from Boccaccio and Ariosto. He went on to write others. These became increasingly daring until, finally, the police had to intervene. In right-thinking society La Fontaine was considered to be a scandalous writer. The less prejudiced, like Chapelain, merely saw in his *Contes* the perfected art of story-telling, and they did not hide their admiration.

At the same time, La Fontaine had friendly relations with people who were under the influence of Port-Royal and, in 1665, he was turning Latin quotations from a translation of St Augustine into French verse. This was not to be his only association with Port-Royal. He collaborated, in 1670, in the compilation of a *Recueil de poésies chrétiennes et diverses* published by Port-Royal.

Towards 1660, his friend Patru had written some fables in prose and had made them a vehicle for social and political satire. Also, Le Maître de Sacy had been publishing a school edition of the fables of Phaedrus, which had brought him great success. La Fontaine decided that he, too, would publish some fables in French verse. It seems that he also had another reason for writing these which had not much to do with literature. The Dauphin was beginning his studies. Aesop's fables were part of what might be called pedagogic literature. La Fontaine could hope that his book would attract the attention of those who were to undertake the task of educating the young prince. The *Fables choisies mises en vers* appeared in 1668.

They were not, and were not intended to be, a picture of French society. It is not true that when he wrote about the lion La Fontaine was thinking about Louis XIV, nor that the fox represents the courtiers. That interpretation, so tempting in appearance, misrepresents the intentions of the author when he published his volume in 1668. At that time, the only kind of morality he wanted to put in his fables was that of Aesop. This means that he was expounding a very simple form of wisdom, one that was founded on the ancient wisdom of man. As in Aesop, this wisdom taught that, in this world, right is on the side of might. La Fontaine shows us crooks, like the fox; hard and unfeeling beings, like the ant. Nice people, of whom there have been many since Rousseau, have had great misgivings about the morality of the *Fables*. Their indignation would have seemed silly to La Fontaine.

His fables were not a picture of French society but of all society. The lion did not represent the king but the powerful man who is strong and rich and who tyrannises little people. He might have been a minister, but he could just as easily have been the governor of a province or simply a local squire. The fox was not specifically a courtier but the crafty man who talks well, whom one can meet in all societies, and of whom simple folk are rightly distrustful. This was the wisdom of all the ages. But it is possible that a man of the seventeenth century might have connected it with Augustinianism. For the latter did maintain that society had been abandoned to its violence by God, and to cunning and cupidity. It also taught that these vices of society were incurable, and that there was no salvation save outside this life. The pessimism of the *Fables* squared with that of Port-Royal, and it is understandable that La Fontaine had good relations with the Messieurs.

He returned to the *Fables* a few years later. Two more volumes appeared in 1678–9, comprising books VII–XI. By this time La Fontaine kept different company. On the one hand he frequented the little circle of Mme de Montespan and her sister Mme de Thianges. There he met La Rochefoucauld, Mme de Lafayette, Bossuet, Racine, and Boileau. These names would be enough to show what kind of reputation he was enjoying at that time. On the other hand, he had obtained the most useful and gracious patronage from that admirable woman, Mme de la Sablière. She was learned without being pedantic, and surrounded herself with philosophers, doctors, and voyagers. La Fontaine lived in this milieu for a number of years.

The *Fables* of the 1678–9 collection show the influence of his new friends. Most of all that of Mme de Montespan, to whom they are dedicated. While the collection of 1668 was not a picture of French society, that of 1678–9 was the picture of the monarch's world. It did not flatter. It showed the king surrounded by a crowd of intriguers busy tearing each other to pieces, deceiving the prince, pushing themselves forward at the expense of others, caring nothing for the public good. It showed the members of the clergy, selfish and anxious only for the privileges of their class. It showed the monks, financiers, the provincial administrators. It contained fables about ministers, about magistrates, and about newly-rich bourgeois obtaining their letters of nobility. Well before Montesquieu, La Fontaine had recognised that what makes the monarchic machine work is vanity. He also noted the new fact which was then changing the character of the monarchy, namely the quest for profit, the desire to get rich, to acquire ever more money, ever more luxury, ever more quickly.

In Mme de Montespan's circle this change did not go unnoticed; indeed it was commented upon without indulgence, but it is unlikely that anyone tried to understand its causes. The scientists and philosophers of Mme de la Sablière's circle were better equipped to look at this question scientifically. They were anti-Cartesian in the sense that they did not think it possible to deduce the nature of reality rationally from general principles directly apprehended by the mind. They were, rather, followers of Gassendi. In other words they believed that science is based on organised experience. La Fontaine was a Gassendist.

Of course, La Fontaine did not intend to reduce the fable to the level of a philosophical appendage. But he did not hesitate to talk in his fables of atoms and infinite voids. He also gave his views on the intelligence of animals, maintaining that Descartes' position was indefensible and contradicted by the facts. His *Discours à Mme de la Sablière*, at the end of the ninth book, is a piece of beautiful philosophical poetry. In it he expounds Descartes' mechanistic doctrine and provides examples to show how arbitrary it is. Instead he proposes Gassendi's thesis, according to which there is a material soul, the quintessential atom, as subtle as light, which his friend, the Gassendist Bernier, said was 'une espèce de milieu et de lien pour unir l'âme raisonnable avec le corps'.[24]

Similarly, the morality that underlies the new collection of fables is no longer the same as that of the previous Aesop-inspired ones. It is that of the sage as understood by Gassendi's doctrine. It enjoins one to distrust public opinion, prejudices, and enthusiasm. It teaches that one should limit oneself to acting with prudence and resignation, and that it is pointless to rebel against the order of things and the abuses which are part of the texture of the social order. Thus, while the morality of the first collection of fables testified to La Fontaine's loyalty to the ancient tradition of wisdom, that of the second showed a much clearer understanding of what it involved.

This basically Gassendist, and thus Epicurean, morality assigned an important rôle to friendship. Understood as the union of minds and hearts, it considered friendship as an authentic social link, contrasting it with such drives as ambition and cupidity. La Fontaine treated this theme most admirably. The fable of the Deux Pigeons contains the idea that was most precious to him.

He was a great artist. He was a very cultured man, certainly the most cultured writer of his time. He was intimately acquainted with the authors of Greece and Rome, as well as with those of the Italian Renaissance and the French story writers of the sixteenth century. They had taught him most exquisitely how to handle his language. Unlike the other writers of his period, he had seen how much the search for purism in language can impoverish it. He greatly enjoyed words and their sounds. His vocabulary is very wide, his syntax supple and varied, giving his fables a unique place in a century that threatened its writers with abstractions and rigidity. He himself recognised this originality, and the most intelligent among his contemporaries understood and admired it. Indeed, they were perhaps less impressed by the lessons pointed in his fables than by his narrative skill that was a revelation to them.

Boileau

The life and works of Boileau illustrate most strikingly the changes in French society between 1660 and 1715.[25] When he began his literary career he never thought of becoming the legislator of Parnassus nor the official poet of the monarchy. On the contrary, he liked the company of independent-minded and cynical men to whom he enjoyed reading the satires he had composed. For he had visions of becoming the Juvenal of his time. He had an older brother, Gilles Boileau, who had made a name for himself some years before by publishing a frightening piece of satire against the poet Ménage, and who had always shown an inclination towards the most caustic kind of satire. Boileau very early accompanied his brother among people who greatly relished poking fun at well-known writers, people with established reputations, and academicians.

If there was one thing these mischievous men particularly disliked, it was the coquette poetry then so fashionable in society circles. They laughed at the authors of madrigals, sonnets, and galant impromptu verse. They expressed their preference for great and serious poetry whose tradition went back to Malherbe, Mainard, and the later Gombauld. They very naturally applauded Molière when, on his return to Paris, he staged his farce about the *Précieuses*. This hostility they also extended to certain aspects of French society as it was then developing. They loathed the financiers and had no respect for the rich bourgeoisie that was then setting the tone. They saw that the middle reaches of the bourgeoisie to which they themselves belonged had been the great losers in the religious wars, and they were unable to reconcile themselves to that fact.

This was the mentality one discovers behind Boileau's first *Satires*. In the earliest version of what became the *Ire Satire* he attacked Foucquet and the other financiers of his time. That nice man Pellisson got the back of his hand for no better reason than that he had become secretary to Foucquet. Then, in 1663, he wrote a satire in praise of Molière and the *Ecole des Femmes*, in which he took the opportunity to maul some of the fashionable poets, like Ménage, Scudéry, and Quinault. None of this showed particularly great courage, because the financiers were at that time mercilessly persecuted by the royal government. But, also in 1663, it came to be known that Colbert had decided to give gratuities to a number of writers, and that he had asked Chapelain to draw up a list.[26] This provided the occasion for much agitation. Those not on the list were up in arms. Gilles Boileau and his brother were among those who had been forgotten. This incited Boileau to write his satire *Muse, changeons de style*. . . . It attacked Chapelain. It named a number of poets who were then much applauded but who were merely poor rhymsters. It was at this time that certain parodies were in circulation which not only attacked Chapelain but also had the temerity to inveigh against Colbert. The public was convinced that 'le cadet Boileau' had something to do with them.

He was a wicked man. He wrote more satires in which he launched out against reason, i.e. dogmatism, and against the prejudices of the nobility. Even in his more innocent pieces, in which he tried to be more like Horace than Juvenal, he found ways of saying something disagreeable about the poets of his time in the middle of descriptions of some ludicrous meal or the disadvantages of life in Paris. He chose his victims more or less at random. But the most concentrated attacks fell on Chapelain, Cotin, and Quinault, men who at other times would have been called official poets.

His contemporaries could not understand what Boileau was about. They suspected that he was rather a thoughtless character who was making himself the imprudent spokesman of 'un certain parti', which probably meant that of Furetière, Chapelle, and Molière. In 1666 polemical pieces appeared which attacked the young satirist and sought to make him the target for the wrath of the royal government. One of these, probably the work of the charitable Abbé Cotin, accused Boileau of endangering civil order, and of undermining the respect citizens owe the authorities, the religious hierarchy, and parlement. Specific mention was made of barbs Boileau aimed at the archbishop of Paris, the counsellors of the parlement, and the lawyers. It was also noted that Boileau had even shown disrespect for the king, for he had inveighed against the poets in receipt of gratuities who had, after all, been thought worthy of that honour by the king. Finally, the author called upon the civil lieutenant of Paris to put an end to such a scandal.

Boileau, without a doubt, took fright. By 1668 it was clear that he had changed his tune. He had obviously decided not to take any more risks. He had given up writing satires. There was one, on women, which he already had in draft form. He ceased working on it.

Fear alone was not responsible for his newly found wisdom. He no longer had the same friends. High society was now his haunt. Mme de Lafayette and La Rochefoucauld in particular had welcomed him, and he could now be found reading his verse at the house of the Duc de Brancas in the presence of the social élite that included Mme de Sévigné, Mme de Lafayette, Segrais, and Guilleragues. It is probable that, from 1668, Mme de Montespan and Mme de Thianges had become his patrons.

He had also, at this time, entered the circle of philosophers and scientists that had been formed by the Premier Président Lamoignon.[27] Here seriously-minded Christian men met as a kind of private academy, which was without doubt more workmanlike than the urbane and frivolous Académie Française. They used to meet, at fixed dates, to discuss historical, literary, moral, or political topics. The very fact that Boileau had been allowed to join shows that he had ceased being a satirist.

He was now becoming interested in the épître as a genre, for which Horace had provided him with excellent models. He used it as a vehicle for moral ideas, and sang the praises of royal enterprises. In his lines on the passage of the Rhine he aspired to the sublime. He addressed one to Antoine Arnauld on the subject of human respect. His epistle to Guilleragues expounded his conception of wisdom. At the same time, as if to demonstrate his peaceful intentions, he wrote the most inoffensive of poems, the heroi-comic *Lutrin*. True, he found a way of inserting a few verses in which he made fun of his old enemies, but by then he was reported to be settling down. In 1674 Louis XIV let it be known that he wanted to meet Boileau. It was the beginning of a long period of favour.

Boileau had thought of writing an *Art poétique* as early as 1669. It was another way of becoming the French Horace, and it was less dangerous than satire. In any case, the members of

Lamoignon's academy liked to discuss the problems of poetry, and to compare what the ancients had thought about it with the views of the moderns. It also gave Boileau the opportunity of using some more unpleasant invective on the writers he did not care for. The *Art poétique* was sufficiently advanced by 1672 for Boileau to be able to give some readings of it in society circles. It finally appeared in 1674. The views he expressed in it were not new. They were the inherited doctrine of all Malherbe's followers. They had been put forward in the first half of the century as a means to achieve discipline and as a body of rules. These rules had been accepted for thirty years and nobody was thinking of questioning them. The Malherbe faction had objected to the artificial and gimmicky character of poetry, and had recalled the need for dignity and solidity. And because galante and worldly poetry also expressed the drive towards modernity, Malherbe's school had pointed to the need for maintaining links with the ancients and keeping them as models.

That was also Boileau's position in the *Art poétique*. One of the most inflammatory pages of his poem is the one on which he derides the cold galanterie of the contemporary rhymsters. When he advises that one should always have one's eyes firmly fixed on 'bon sens' he is thinking of all the poets of the salons whose aim it was, on the contrary, to invent the most ingenious frivolities. And when he speaks against galant fatuity, he expresses his objection to a kind of literature that had fallen to the level of a salon parlour-game.

These were the points on which he had felt most strongly. As for the rest, he showed himself remarkably liberal. At first sight it might have seemed that he only accorded recognition to poetic forms used by the ancients. But he also spoke with evident affection of the simplicity of the rondeau, the old rules for ballads, and of the tender sweetness of the madrigal. Similarly, he conceded that tragedy could depict 'tendres sentiments', and love, and when he talked about the ode he thought it natural that it should sing of 'un baiser cueilli sur les lèvres d'Iris'. Thus, rather than reproach Boileau for excessive dogmatism, one might properly note with regret that he was in some respects inconsistent.

It must be admitted that Boileau was not of great intelligence.

This becomes very clear if one compares his *Art poétique* with the very vigorous pages that Abbé Claude Fleury had devoted to the same questions, or even with the works of Père Rapin on literature. Fleury and Rapin belonged to Lamoignon's Academy, so that Boileau who was often in their company certainly knew their views. But he was unable to assimilate them in their entirety.

Yet, if his *Art poétique* very soon acquired the status of a code for true literature, and if the university for over two centuries sought to illuminate by its means the masterpieces of Molière and Racine, it was because it reflected the faith that a large part of French society had continued to keep with solid and serious traditions, with principles of abiding value and workmanship that were also applied to literature. When the poem appeared it seemed that the time had come for resisting the craze among literary men for urbanity, with its attendant frivolity, false ingeniousness, and galanterie. During the romantic period, the *Art poétique* was still used as a defence against false genius, the facile, and the pretensions of modernity. It is only when one places the poem into the context of the changes that were taking place in society, and consequently in its tastes and ideas, that one is able to understand the authority it acquired and the influence it exerted.

What must, however, be regretted is that the *Art poétique*, having been lauded to the skies, distorted the literary history of the seventeenth century and falsified its perspective. People came to say that classical literature had come into being with what was called 'l'école de 1660', a school whose master was supposed to have been Boileau. From that assumption it was deduced that, without Boileau, Racine and Molière would not have written their masterpieces. The work carried out by Richelieu's generation to lay the foundations of classical literature was completely ignored. Corneille was treated like a ninny. Boileau was praised for having destroyed the burlesque and preciosité, although he had literally nothing whatever to do with the decline of either. The *Art poétique* is an interesting reflection of the tastes and literary ideas of a part of French society between 1670 and 1680, but as a picture of classical literature it can only mislead.

After the *Art poétique* and Longinus' *Traité du sublime*, which was published in the same year with voluminous arguments, Boileau looked like a serious writer. He was able to count on the active protection of Mme de Montespan. In 1677 he became historiographer of the king. In 1683 he was brought into the Académie. It contained a good many of his former victims who had not forgiven him. But the king had made it very clear that he wanted the election of Boileau.[28]

For a long time Boileau wrote nothing. It was not until 1694 that he returned to satire. This was on the occasion of the re-opening of the quarrel between ancients and moderns. The ladies of society had, naturally, taken the side of the moderns. They loved Quinault and Cotin, and they knew these gentlemen better than they did Homer. It was against them that Boileau wrote his satire *Femmes*. A furious diatribe, it united all the moderns against him. But he did not want to start a war, and he proceeded to write two épîtres which testified to his need for tranquillity and his pacific intentions.

He had thus returned to poetry. But his preoccupations had widened and become more serious. The essential element in his life was no longer the writing of verse, but the working out of his position on problems of morality and religion.

Like many other Frenchmen of his class, i.e. the traditionalist bourgeoisie, he had recognised that the nation was in the grip of a grave crisis. The Jesuits, the majority of the episcopate, and the ultramontane faction were seeking to introduce into France forms of life which went against the best traditions of the kingdom, and the government of Louis XIV was under their control. Christianity was being shaped in the image of Rome and Madrid and stripped of its strong moral virtues. Pascal had, earlier, condemned that evil in his *Provinciales*. Now the danger had become evident. The only thing one could now do was to turn round and fight the enemy who thought he had already won. In 1698 Boileau published his epistle *De l'Amour de Dieu* in which he put the case for traditional Christian morality against the ultramontanes. Then, between 1703 and 1706 he wrote the satire *L'Equivoque*. It was an impassioned diatribe in which Boileau talked movingly about the eternal struggle between the forces of light and those of darkness, of the city of God and the city of men. It would have been surprising if the publication of this satire had been allowed. The Jesuits took care of this problem, and the royal government with great docility forbade its publication.

When one realises that Boileau had been a kind of official poet of the régime this disgrace assumes great significance. It reflects how the monarchy had changed during the last part of the reign of Louis XIV, the rôle that was played during that period by the ultramontanes, and the growing division between the public and the royal government. One would completely misunderstand Boileau's last works if one saw them only as the capricious products of an old man who meddled in theology. He was not a Jansenist, and the Five Propositions surely left him cold. But, like the rest of the enlightened part of the nation, he felt that traditional French values were being compromised by the ultramontanes. When he was told that the *Equivoque* could not be published, he knew that the game was lost and that traditional France had been defeated. Two months later, in March 1711, he was dead.

9

The theatre

Of all the literary forms of the seventeenth century, it was the theatre that provided the surest path to glory.[1] The novel was considered to be an inferior genre that barely counted as a part of the humanities. Lyricism appealed only to a very small circle and did not reach the general public at all. On the other hand, a tragedy or a comedy, if successful, was enough to make an author famous.

The theatre and society

During the first twenty-five years of the century, the audience that flocked to the Hôtel de Bourgogne was apparently mainly popular.[2] The scholarly research of Professor John Lough has in recent years been directed to rebutting this traditional view. But contemporary evidence really seems to be too strong to be left unconsidered. Of course, the young gentlemen of the court did frequent the boxes, and they were accompanied by women who might have belonged to respectable society, but the tone was set by the audience down below in the pit, which was largely made up of clerks of the courts, pageboys and lackeys. There were even 'pauvres artisans' among them who, according to an account of the end of the sixteenth century, liked to meet in the pit well before the start of the performance to play cards and throw dice, to amuse themselves through 'devis impudiques', and often to quarrel. Although women ventured into the boxes, and even there only when wearing masks, none would have dared to go into the pit.

The situation changed around 1630, and there is ample evidence for this. We are told that in 1634 'les femmes les plus sages et modestes' had only one desire: to go to the Hôtel de Bourgogne.[3] In 1636, Mairet was happy to see that 'les plus honnêtes femmes fréquentent maintenant l'Hôtel de Bourgogne avec aussi peu de scrupule qu'elles feraient celui de Luxembourg'.[4] We are told that, at that time also, the 'bourgeois' and 'honnêtes gens' were to be seen in large numbers in the pit. In 1657 Abbé d'Aubignac reminded his readers that, fifty years earlier, an honest woman could not have dared set foot in the Hôtel de Bourgogne, with the implication that such scruples had long been lost in good society.[5]

An analysis of theatre audiences between 1630 and 1660 shows that they came from very different sections of the population with very different kinds of background. There was 'le peuple et la cour', 'le courtisan et le bourgeois', and 'les savants et le peuple'. Even the lower sections of the people continued to go to the Hôtel de Bourgogne. Some chroniclers mention shop assistants, pageboys, and very often lackeys. These people mainly went to see farces for a good laugh, or 'vilaines bouffonneries', and were only mildly interested in tragedy. They behaved badly, and talked all the time, if they were not whistling or shouting. Soldiers would on the slightest pretext draw their swords and interrupt the performance. But there is a curious account by Loret which also lists ambassadors, presidents of assemblies, dukes' ladies, bankers, merchants, bourgeois women, and soubrettes.

Merchants in particular seem to have been represented in large numbers. Drapers and haberdashers of the rue Saint-Denis, big dealers on the Paris market, all affected to be enlightened lovers of the theatre. We are told of some forty or fifty of them who around 1660 would not miss the performance of a new play. Fifteen or sixteen of them could even boast to have seen all the plays performed in Paris over the previous thirty years, and their opinions were listened to with respect. These bourgeois might book a box for their wives, but they themselves preferred to be down in the pit.[6]

It was the pit that decided the fate of a new play, its success or failure. Not that section of it, of course, that was composed of the 'petit peuple', 'le menu peuple', the 'racaille', which, as Chapelain put it, 'passe en apparence pour le vrai peuple et qui n'est en effet [i.e. in fact] que sa lie et que son rebut', but the bourgeois and the important traders. They had not read Aristotle and Scaliger. But, as Abbé d'Aubignac would have put it, they lacked neither natural insight nor an inclination towards virtue. They were not conscious of all the implications of art, but they could sense them. Their good sense constituted a tribunal that made no mistakes.

It goes without saying that the well-born folk installed in their boxes despised the pit. Charles Sorel noted well before Molière that if one wanted to damn some witticism all one had to say was that it would raise a laugh in the pit. But Sorel added that such scorn was misplaced, that the pit contained 'de fort honnêtes gens'. He even said that 'la plupart de nos poètes' would not be seen anywhere else. The bourgeois of the rue Saint-Denis had gained a kind of authority over the public. The plays they allowed to succeed from their places in the pit also usually proved successful with the occupants of the boxes, and until 1660 the taste of the court did not challenge that of the town.

That challenge nevertheless had to come the moment Versailles sought to be the centre of the entire intellectual and artistic life of France. Then it often happened that a play was successful at court but unsuccessful in town. Of course, prejudice had much to do with this and Tralage tells us that 'les gens de cour et surtout les dames affectent de mépriser ce que les bourgeois ont estimé'. That, he added, 'a plus l'air de qualité et marque un génie supérieur; à peine le bourgeois a-t-il le sens commun'.[7]

It would therefore be pointless to spend much time trying to discover the reasons for these disagreements when they happened to arise. It is, however, worth considering what the brothers Parfaicts wrote about this. According to these excellent historians of the theatre, the court expected tragedies to provide political interest and nobility of language. The town, on the other hand, demanded 'le vrai et le sentiment'. The court wanted orderly and lofty plots and well-written plays. The town, when it came to comedy, was not averse to plays that had little more than a compelling comic interest.

In Paris the audiences remained very much the same as in the early part of the century. One of Mme de Sévigné's letters of 1672 said that though the pickpockets, pages, and lackeys were no longer to be seen in the pit because they were in the army, at least the shop assistants were still there.[8] In 1700 a note from D'Argenson remarked that, among theatre audiences, one would find 'gens de collège, de palais ou de commerce'. No doubt this explains the dreadful behaviour of the pit till the end of the century. Spectators had long had the habit of yawning during parts that bored them. By 1686 they began to use whistles. Things became so bad that the government had to step in. From 1696 the whistlers had to spend a few days in prison.[9] From a date historians have not managed to determine with precision, lackeys were restricted to the third and last row of the gallery, which was called the 'paradis'. The day was to come when they were refused admission to the theatre altogether.

The organisation of opinion

It can be said that until 1660 public reaction was spontaneous and opinions were freely formed. Of course, there were intrigues in the salons, and conspiracies. Chroniclers write of ladies who acted as an author's patron or, conversely, undertook to destroy the reputation of a play. But these were merely gestures of friendship or personal animosity.

From 1660, however, a spirit of rivalry appeared that had hitherto been unknown. It is said that Quinault was the first to introduce the custom of soliciting approval, and Boyer, his rival, did the same. Rightly or wrongly, Molière's enemies accused him of having tried to gain approval for his plays through private approaches to important persons and of having organised private readings of his plays to ensure their success. They also said that he sold tickets at reduced prices.

Then the literary press was born, and it very soon established the reign of literary friendships, kindness to those one liked, and corruption. In the *Mercure galant* one meets the warm, approving review and the review that is ironical, full of ill-will and poison. In the contract of association between Thomas Corneille and Donneau de Visé for the *Mercure galant*, the two gentlemen set down an agreement concerning their respective share in the sums of money and gifts in kind that they were going to receive from authors. A 1671 text informs us of some thirty professional critics in Paris, self-appointed judges of new writing, who praised or denigrated, and authors had to pay a heavy price to secure a kind word for their work.

The theatre and the royal government

At the beginning of the seventeenth century the theatre was considered to be one of the traditional forms of culture. It was one that princes had to encourage and that it behove the upper classes to frequent.[10] More than once Henry IV and his courtiers attended performances at the Hôtel de Bourgogne. But this testified to no genuine interest or enlightened taste on the part of either king or courtiers. The court at the Louvre, before Richelieu, showed its preference for the royal ballets. There it could satisfy its taste for luxury which it pushed to baroque extremes. In any case the verse plays performed there made them laugh, providing ribaldry and indeed a kind of obscenity that titillates even today.

This situation changed as soon as Richelieu was in a position to mould affairs in his own image. Henceforth the theatre received much attention from the government, and its prestige was to make it into the noblest literary form and intellectual activity. Since the end of the preceding century there had been in existence a privileged group of actors called the Comédiens du Roi. It was little more than a name. After 1630 the Comédiens du Roi were given an assured income of 12,000 livres which was regularly paid. Apart from that group, Richelieu authorised the creation of another company, the Comédiens du Marais. Their leader was Montdory, in whom Richelieu had a personal interest. The royal government intervened in even the day-to-day affairs of the two groups. It also selected their new members. Thus, in 1634, a royal order transferred four actors from the Marais to the Hôtel de Bourgogne.

After Mazarin's death groups of actors continued to receive royal support. But they were not treated equally. The Comédiens du Roi continued to receive their 12,000 livres. Those of the Marais got nothing. When Molière installed himself at the Palais-Royal he was given an annual subsidy of 6,000 livres. It is intriguing to note that, at the same time, Louis XIV gave 16,000 livres to a group of Italian actors for whom he had a particular liking.

The royal government did not, however, at this time intervene regularly and continuously in the affairs of these groups. But it could at any time take measures affecting them that it thought appropriate. Since it had become general policy to centralise authority, it was to be expected that the theatre would sooner or later be reorganised.

In 1673 the Marais was closed by police order. Taking advantage of the death of Molière, the authorities handed the Palais-Royal theatre over to Lully. Molière's companions were ordered to combine with what remained of the Marais group to form a new company.

That was only the first stage. In August 1680 an order of the king brought about the definitive reorganisation of the theatre. A single company was to bring together the Comédiens Français. The Italians were given the old Hôtel de Bourgogne. The Opera, for its part, continued as before.

Also, for the first time, all the actors were made subject to the same rules. The First Gentlemen of the Privy Chamber were given charge of the theatres. It was their task to accept or reject plays the actors wanted to produce, to cast the plays, deal with the actors' accounts, and to ensure that they received each week a report of the activities of the companies and of their projects.

Later these rules were thought to be inadequate. The religious faction demanded, in 1697, that 'commissaires examinateurs' should be appointed to appraise plays before they were performed. In 1701 all new plays had to be submitted to the lieutenant-general of police. Soon afterwards plays were sent for approval to a paid censor. Censorship thus had officially come into being.

Two different kinds of consideration should be distinguished behind the series of measures which first led to restrictions upon the liberty of the theatre and then to the complete abolition of that liberty. The government of the crown and the police were engaged upon a policy of centralisation and reorganisation. They wanted to give the theatre, as they were giving everything else, an overall organisation and make it impossible for it to disturb public order. But, at the same time, the religious faction thought of the theatre as an essentially dangerous institution that was incompatible with the spirit of Christianity. For these people it was not a question of regulating the affairs of the theatre but of introducing such drastic restraints upon its activity as to bring about its eventual suppression.

Since Richelieu the theatre had succeeded in winning the respect of French society. Plays were models of dignity and morality. Most of the actors were perfectly 'honnêtes gens' who conducted themselves with dignity and decorum. That there were exceptions to this does not affect the truth of these observations for the profession as a whole. Nevertheless the religious faction and the Jansenists continued to regret the existence of the theatre and were bent upon its destruction. From 1685 they began to exert pressure on the government. Actors came to be subjected to all kinds of persecution. In 1687–8 the priests of Paris managed over a number of months to prevent the Comédiens Français from finding a site for their new theatre. These same priests also began to make difficulties about giving actors Christian burial. The case of Molière had at that time been an isolated one. It soon became general. In 1696 priests refused absolution to actors. From 1697 they began to refuse actors the sacrament of marriage. In 1694 the religious faction openly declared war. Bossuet and the Sorbonne anathematised the theatre. Preachers pointed out to Parisians that they could not go to the theatre without committing sin.

Needless to say, the majority of the French did not support these views. Neither the archbishop of Paris, François de Harlay, nor Père de la Chaise, the king's confessor, shared this fanaticism. The people of Paris, faced with the polemics of their priests, reacted with good sense: they went to the theatre with increasing frequency. But the religious faction could count on the support of Mme de Maintenon, and was thus certain that the king would be favourably disposed towards its aims. The majority of the Paris clergy supported the religious faction.

Thus its enemies were able to hope that a royal decision would soon put the theatre out of business. In 1694 it was only through an intervention by the archbishop of Paris that the king was stopped from taking precisely that unpopular step.

He managed to convince the king that it would be unwise to refuse the Parisians a distraction to which they were particularly attached. There were even officials in high positions who, far from advocating the closure, advised the king to increase the number of playhouses. But the danger remained. In 1697 Dutch gazettes announced that the court of France was only waiting for the end of the war before it would 'supprimer toutes sortes de spectacles'.

In such circumstances, the theatre could not be expected to retain the vitality it had enjoyed throughout most of the century. In 1696 the Duchesse d'Orléans noted that, since the priests had been preaching with such ferocity against the theatre, there were far fewer good actors than before: 'Ces pauvres diables s'imaginent qu'on va les chasser d'un instant à l'autre, et ils ne s'appliquent plus à leur métier'. Baron, the most famous actor of his day, took fright and retired in 1691. Members of the court no longer dared to be seen at a play. Only the bourgeois were still in evidence.

Tragedy and tragi-comedy before Corneille

The study of the development of dramatic literature within a society involves an analysis of the relationships between the theatre, the authorities, and public opinion. But it must also shed some light on the tragic and comic forms in which the spirit of the period successively expressed itself.

At the beginning of the seventeenth century tragedy reigned supreme. It had a faithful following which showed no signs of wanting to abandon it. During the reign of Henry IV fifty new tragedies were written and performed. They were in the humanist tradition and it is easy to see that the admired and infinitely imitated master at that time was Robert Garnier. His plays followed the fashion of taking their subject-matter from ancient history and the Bible, and sometimes from more recent times. They tried to respect the requirements of the three unities. They also retained some of the characteristics of humanist tragedy, particularly the chorus, the long monologues, the noble and moral tone.

But in a society whose tastes had profoundly changed and which was much less the product of ancient culture than of brutal passion and violence, it was inevitable that tragedy would lose many of the features that had made for its nobility. The usual subject now was no longer the misfortunes of royal personages but atrocious tales of incest, rape, of men assassinated and whose hearts were offered in spectacle to the audience. At the same time the rules of drama underwent a revolution. The unities were gradually abandoned since they were incompatible with the theatre of action. Even the division of plays into five acts was no longer universally maintained. Choruses were disappearing. The old conventions were no longer being observed, so that the stage itself provided pictures of rape, murder, and battles. Monologues became shorter. Subjects were no longer exclusively quarried from the Bible and antiquity but also from romantic literature. It has been calculated that during Henry IV's reign one-third of the new tragedies were of that kind.

Certain writers of that period wrote plays of some merit; for example Claude Billard, Jean de Schélandre, and Monchrestien. But the playwright who won general admiration and who dominated this entire era in the history of the theatre was Alexandre Hardy. He started to write early, around 1595. Thirty years later he was still writing tragedies. He wrote an astonishing number and in 1628 he boasted of having written as many as six hundred and needed only a fortnight to add another title to his enormous list. However, only thirty-four of his plays remain in existence.[11]

Hardy's tragedies provide excellent examples of the nature of the French theatre during the first quarter of the seventeenth century. They show no systematic break with humanist tragedy. Hardy was obviously anxious to respect to the best of his ability the rules he had inherited from the previous century. It is also clear that he wanted to observe the conventions of good taste. Further, he kept the division into five acts, ended most of his acts with a lyrical chorus, and even sometimes succeeded in keeping his plays within the narrow confines of the unities.

But the pressures of the new taste often got the better of him, and then Hardy was not afraid of writing plays in which the action took place over the period of a month or more. Sometimes he even gave up the unity of action, so that one of his plays turns out to have three distinct plots. Some of his tragedies have no chorus. Above all, Hardy at times allowed himself to be attracted to subjects that are atrocious and violent. In *Scédase* two poor girls are raped and, odd though this may seem, they are raped on stage.

Beyond Hardy's frequent disregard of the rules, and beyond the violence that was now being tolerated on the stage, one can see the general direction in which tragedy was developing. For the writers of the previous century the essence of tragedy lay in the misfortunes of a famous personage. It was the gods who initiated the action and man was reduced to being a sighing victim. With Hardy the theatre tended to become the spectacle of a struggle, the place in which human energies are unleashed. Tragedy ceased to bear the mark of the sacred.

These characteristics of the works of Hardy reflect the most significant changes in modern society. His contemporaries did not see this. His somewhat archaic language prevented them from doing so. Having been brought up on humanist literature, Hardy wrote as people no longer spoke in 1620. The new generation could not bear his colourful and verbose language, his mythological allusions and references to ancient history. It found in him neither the douceur nor the 'regularity' it had made its ideals. Between 1626 and 1628 there were pamphlets which brought the rift between the old author and the new style into the open. It is characteristic that it was among the professors of the university that he had his last admirers and the guardians of his reputation.

The first indications of change had thus begun to appear. Contemporaries chiefly pointed to two plays which were immediately seen as manifestations of a new style: *Pyrame et Thisbé* by Théophile de Viau, probably performed in 1622, and the *Bergeries* by Racan, perhaps written in 1620 but certainly published in 1625. But there were very few if any technical innovations. In *Pyrame et Thisbé* there was no real connection between the scenes, the tirades were too long and too numerous, and the poet showed himself unable to make the action seem to progress. The novelty was in the tone, the quality of the style, the modernity of the feelings and ideas it contained. Those were the points that the audience noticed.

Classical tragedy is sometimes presented as having sprung from the ruins of Alexandre Hardy's theatre and the 'irregular' forms of dramatic art as they had been practised during the first twenty-five years of the seventeenth century. But, although it is true that there was indeed a revolution in the French theatre at that time, this was not with the aim of setting up the reign of tragedy. The new genre that was then born was called tragi-comedy.

It was an ancient name. To the Romans it had meant a play in which gods and men were jointly involved in a comic adventure. In sixteenth-century Italy it had acquired two meanings which were kept distinct. It signified a play with a happy ending. But it could also be a play in which tragic and comic scenes existed side by side. Some tragi-comedies had been written in France. They juxtaposed the various conceptions of the genre. The subject was romantic, the ending happy, and the tragic was mixed with the homely.

For a long time these tragi-comedies remained few in number, and historians can only find four in the entire reign of Henry IV, and only one between 1619 and 1624. From 1627, however, they began to multiply. Between 1630 and 1635 there were thirty-five that called themselves tragi-comedies. They also happen to be the plays that were most successful at that time, and there was a team around Pierre du Ryer which won a considerable reputation through having provided the public with tragi-comedies.

The characteristics of these plays were clearcut. First and foremost the subject was romantic. This word does not merely mean that the plays were full of adventurous action and theatrical surprises, and that disguises and unusual happenings crowded in upon each other. It means that the subjects were usually taken from Greek stories, Spanish and Italian literature, the *Amadis* and *Astrée*, and not from Greek, Roman or modern history. A play about Mary Stuart was a tragedy, a play in which a young man was led to kill the father of the girl he loves in a duel a tragi-comedy.

The second characteristic is the complexity of the plots and the prodigious variety of vicissitudes suffered by the persons in the plays. There is no attempt to have the action of the play develop around a central character, or to reduce it to one basic situation which progressively reveals its logical implications. On the contrary, tragi-comedy likes to provide as many sources of emotion as possible. There is a play by André Mareschal which contains five duels and two attempts at murder. Most of the principal characters are injured, five others killed before our eyes. Two women fight a duel. The heroine and her page are attacked by four ruffians. They kill four of them but the heroine is injured and the page killed. The 'diversité' of tragi-comedy was considered to be perfect when it no longer had a live principal hero or, more precisely, when he was replaced by another in every act.

'Diversité' also took the form of mixing tragedy and comedy, the serious and the funny. The young writers liked such a combination which had been introduced by the Italians and which went better with the 'délicatesse' of the moderns than the pity and terror of the ancient tragedies. So far as they were concerned, the variety of moods was not the result of freedom run riot or lack of ability. For them it constituted refinement.

The Greeks, and the Romans after them, had confined the plots of their tragedies to one place and a single day. Humanist tragedy observed the same rule. The authors of modern tragi-comedy paid no regard to this. They wanted to remain free. For their liberty enabled them to produce effects that would otherwise have been impossible. There was a play, in 1631, that took the audience from Lyon to Marcilly; another from Bohemia to Silesia. The plot of a tragi-comedy could last a month or even years.

One of the most striking aspects of this kind of play was the number of scenes of physical violence, duels, and assaults. Authors were not content with just narrating such events. They put them on the stage for the audience to see. They could be sure the latter would never tire of this kind of spectacle, and that it was the most violent scenes that would be the most admired.

It is not the case, as has often been claimed, that this kind of tragi-comedy, as it developed from about 1627, was just a spectacle for the people. It was written by the most reputed authors who were solely writing for 'honnêtes gens'. The people liked adventure and good sword work, but all the young nobility liked that too. Tragi-comedy evoked passionate feelings which were also refined, feelings that a young nobleman could also have experienced. Its language was that of Théophile, Racan, and Mairet. Thus, if it broke with the humanist tradition, this was not because it sought to be popular. It was intended to be modern and portray modern feelings and ideas, with all their fervour and elegance.

After 1628 the public was able to applaud the tragi-comedies of a group of authors who were young and very talented. They were Pierre du Ryer, Auvray, Rayssiguier, André Mareschal, and Pichou. Pierre du Ryer possessed the strongest personality in the group. For a number of years they were not content with providing new plays. They also published prefaces which were like manifestos. Their main tenet was the need for freedom from rules. For a few years tragi-comedy occupied almost the entire French stage. There were other writers who were working along the same lines. One of them was Corneille, and his play *Clitandre* gives the modern reader an excellent idea of what tragi-comedy was like in those days.

At the very time when the triumph of tragi-comedy seemed assured the renaissance of tragedy was in fact beginning.[12] Not humanist tragedy as it had been understood in the second half of the preceding century, that tradition had definitely been abandoned and no one thought of returning to it. What was coming into being was a form of tragedy that was based on the essentials of the ancient models, respected the unities, demanded concentration, nobility, and decency, and which dealt with subjects that had been taken from mythology and history.

The movement seems to have begun around 1625, and its origins are diverse. One aspect of its origins might easily escape notice, but it was important. At that time the pastoral in France was a form of tragi-comedy which, also, was without rules. But two men, who had much influence in the world of letters, Cardinal de la Valette and Comte de Cramail, greatly admired the Italian pastorals, the *Aminta* of Tasso and the *Pastor fido* of Guarini.[13] These pastorals obeyed the rules and conformed to the unities. In 1628 they persuaded the young author Mairet to write a pastoral of this kind. One can also assume that Chapelain used his influence towards the same end.

Another writer, Pichou, also wrote a 'regular' pastoral in which Richelieu took a personal interest. The *Sylvanire* of Mairet was performed in 1630 and had an immense success. Mairet published it in 1631 with a manifesto-like preface.

All this was still in the realm of the pastoral, and what was new was merely that it was tending to conform to the principle of the three unities. But, at this time, literary circles were also casting doubt upon the merits of tragi-comedy. The first evidence for this goes back to 1625. Then, in 1627, a manifesto appeared which defended tragi-comedy. It was in the form of a preface by François Ogier to Jean de Schélandre's *Tyr et Sidon*. Three years later Antoine Godeau wrote a long letter to Chapelain in which he expounded the case of the defenders of tragi-comedy. This letter no longer exists, but Chapelain's reply does, and this enables one to know exactly what the two theses were about. When they are analysed it becomes clear that tragedy is inspired by the Greek conception of a work of art, a conception which relies on the great traditions of Greece and Rome as they had been revived, maintained, and interpreted by men who combined humanism with the spirit of the moderns. Tragi-comedy, on the other hand, is linked with the second baroque period that has already been discussed in connection with lyrical poetry. The essential principle of tragi-comedy is pleasure. The essential principles of classicism are nobility and grandeur; it despises the search for effects and has a demanding sense of decency. It subordinates the work of art to a single idea which is its essence.

These were, then, the basic elements in the conflict between the defenders and the opponents of tragedy. The real meaning of the conflict can now be understood. It was not simply a question of theatrical technique and dramaturgy. French society as it was evolving under Richelieu no longer tolerated the influence of the baroque, at least in its loftier spheres. It was indifferent towards its most attractive qualities for it wanted great ideals, noble aims and attitudes and language to reign in all things. It wanted what it called reason, which meant the domination of universal values over the promptings of feeling and imagination. It is because French society was in the process of becoming classical that tragedy was rapidly taking the place of tragi-comedy.

There was a moment when it looked as if tragedy would disappear altogether. In 1634 the repertory of the Hôtel de Bourgogne consisted of sixty-nine tragi-comedies and only two tragedies. In the same year, however, the young Rotrou put on his *Hercule mourant*, which was a 'regular' tragedy inspired by Seneca. He had read the play to Chapelain and the members of the future Académie Française. These 'divins esprits' encouraged him in his work, and the public was won over. Then, at the end of that year, Mairet staged his *Sophonisbe*, with its subject from Roman history and strictly in conformity with the requirements of the 'doctes'. The success of that play marked the revival of tragedy. In 1635–6, historians tell us, there were as many tragedies performed as there were tragi-comedies. Three of the tragedies of the time ensured the success of the new dramatic form: the *Mort de Mithridate* by La Calprenède, *Lucrèce* by Pierre du Ryer, and, above all, Tristan's admirable *Mariane*.[14]

It was thus with public approval that classical tragedy was progressively conquering the French stage. But it must not be thought that the public had been won over completely. There is proof to the contrary. Contemporary accounts show that the unities, particularly the unity of place, found no great favour with audiences, and that the latter preferred changes of scenery and of décor. In 1632 Rayssiguier wrote 'La plus grande part de ceux qui portent le teston à l'hôtel de Bourgogne veulent que l'on contente leurs yeux par la diversité et le changement de face du théâtre [i.e. of the stage]'. Similarly, Pierre du Ryer wrote that the public wants to have its eyes flattered 'par la diversité et le changement de la scène'. Again, Scudéry wrote after the success of his *Prince déguisé*: 'Le superbe appareil de la scène . . . la face du théâtre qui change cinq ou six fois à la représentation de ce poème . . . tout cela est capable d'éblouir par cet éclat les yeux les plus clairvoyants'. Victory for the rules was not achieved by the public.

It had been achieved by the 'doctes'. It was they who had convinced the authors of the need to apply the rules. In this, the influence of Chapelain and Abbé d'Aubignac had certainly been decisive. But they had taken care to appeal to reason and experience. They stated clearly that 'les règles du théâtre ne sont pas fondées en autorité, mais en raison', and that they are not based on authority but on 'le jugement naturel'. To be sure, this was the language of reason that they had discovered in the great critical writers of humanism, for example in Scaliger, Vossius, and Heinsius.

The authority of the 'doctes' might, however, not have been enough. But they were backed up by the tremendous impetus Richelieu had given to the intellectual life of the period, and, in a sense, it was he who had imposed the rules. No doubt the cardinal had greater preoccupations than the unities, but he did want the dramatic arts to give pleasure to an élite, not to the people. This becomes clear from a note in the margin of the manuscript of the *Sentiments de l'Académie* concerning the *Cid*. He said: 'L'applaudissement et le blame du *Cid* n'est qu'entre les doctes et les ignorants'. The public which applauded Corneille's masterpiece was for him only an ignorant crowd whose admiration proved nothing about the value of the play.

The men of letters around Richelieu shared his views. Abbé d'Aubignac explicitly connected tragedy with the existence of an élite formed of 'personnes de naissance ou nourries parmi les Grands'. He maintained that men in monarchic society 'ne s'entretiennent que de sentiments généreux et ne se portent qu'à de hauts desseins, ou par les mouvements de la vertu, ou par les emportements de l'ambition; de sorte que leur vie a beaucoup de rapport aux représentations du théâtre tragique'. Des Marests de Saint-Sorlin, a close collaborator of the cardinal, also expressed great scorn for the 'indocte et stupide vulgaire', the people whose mind 'si grossier et si extravagant' can only appreciate 'les nouveautés grotesques'. Tragedy had been approved and supported by Richelieu because it corresponded exactly with his ideas about the aristocratic character of dramatic art.

Corneille and contemporary tragedy

It is in the context of the progress of French tragedy at the time of Richelieu that the works of Corneille are best understood. He reached the height of his genius between 1637 and 1642, at the time when tragedy was formulating its laws, and the greatness of the *Cid*, *Horace*, *Cinna*, and *Polyeucte* lies in their having expressed an ideal of heroism with which French society was then preoccupied. Too many historians and critics have given definitions of Corneille's concept of heroism that are too ingenious by half. Some have seen it as a kind of essence of heroism of which Corneille was merely supposed to have deduced the implications. Others have taken the plays of Corneille to be a stage in the development of an abstract concept, of the *a priori* idea of the hero. But if one really wants to enter Corneille's world of heroism one does better to remember the climate of French society in his day rather than to indulge in abstract reasoning.

At the time of Louis XIII and Richelieu, the nobility did not look upon the moral life as a compelling duty, as a body of laws to which one had to submit. The only thing it recognised as meritorious was the taking of risks, living dangerously, having the feeling of exaltation. It did of course talk about duty, but it was about the kind of duty which enjoins a generous heart to go to the extremes of honour and of its demands. It was convinced that the kinds of duties made for the common man were of no concern to it. This was not because it felt it had the right to do as it pleased. On the contrary, it was because its birth had imposed upon it the higher virtues.[15]

These ideas, which were originally those of a class, were in fact then shared by all those Frenchmen who were dreaming of a life that was ardent and generous. There has perhaps never been a time when the French as a whole turned with greater conviction to a heroic conception of life. Richelieu encouraged this with great care, since it fostered the ideal of strength. It was not the bourgeois virtues that were going to win the wars that he had begun. Rather would it be the virtue of courage, a feeling of honour pushed to its limits, and the desire for glory.

Corneille was all the better prepared to express this characteristic of his time for having been the pupil of the Jesuits, who taught him to look on life as a battlefield on which glory was the just reward for the manifestation of strength. According to his masters, and in his own opinion too, true religion reveals itself in this way also. The Catholicism of the Jesuits exalted the Christian hero, the man who conquers heaven in the same way that Alexander and Caesar conquered the world, and he finds his reward the day the Roman Church proclaims him a saint and erects above the altar his triumphant picture showing him being carried to heaven by the angels and crowned by the hand of Christ.

Even the philosophy of the period used the theme of heroism. It advocated generosity. It taught a morality of liberty, disdain for imposed duties, and supremacy of the will. The generous man is one who refuses to accept slogans, who agrees to live dangerously in a world full of the commonplace, who accepts the notion of duty only if it accords with an inner imperative and not merely with a social rule.

Corneille expressed the heroic aspect of his century with exceptional grandeur. Rodrigue, Horace, Auguste, and Polyeucte are fired by heroism, whether their prime concern be with honour, their country, or religion. It was a sublime sentiment, that was pushed beyond the limits of reason and went well beyond the requirements of duty. There is no law that tells Polyeucte to bring down the statues of the gods. In fact, far from there being one, the Christian Church forbade that imprudent gesture. But Polyeucte does not obey a duty laid upon him from outside. He gives effect to an inner demand which is entirely his own, and which places him among the heroes.

It is only if we isolate Corneille's works from their period that we are tempted to misunderstand his tragedies and see in his heroes, as some critics have done, no more than 'fanatiques réfléchis' that are possessed by but one idea, beings devoid of passion who mechanically obey their 'reason'. Corneille did not find his heroes in books. He was aware of, and wanted to depict in his tragedies, the great heroic inspiration of the French of his time. It was certainly a strangely passionate period, in which a sense of honour all too often demanded the sacrifice of a cherished life, and the desire for glory inspired plots and plans for assassination, as well as the purest acts of heroism.

Corneille succeeded in expressing the spirit of his period with genius in so far as he succeeded in creating characters that were alive and full of deep humanity. He did the opposite of what a number of critics have alleged. He did not make his heroes all of a piece, obsessed by the idea of a duty to be done. On the contrary, they are torn by conflicting passions, and even the love of country assumes in them the violence of a passion. In the hearts of Rodrigue and Chimène love is in conflict with the sentiment of honour, but that sentiment in these generous characters is itself a passion which is more demanding than any other. Curiace is torn between his patriotism and friendship, and he expresses his plight in words that must move us and that do move us if we know how to read Corneille without thinking about dramaturgy and dialcctics, if wc only contemplate the examples of humanity he puts before us. And one cannot fail to be moved by the terrible struggle that tears Pauline apart as she has to decide between her love for Sévère and her ties with her father and husband.

La Bruyère made a great mistake when he said that Corneille had painted men as they ought to be. But the mistake helps one to measure the distance that separates French society of Richelieu's time from that of the end of the seventeenth century. It takes someone totally ignorant of the lives of the French between 1630 and 1640 to miss the point that there were many who were prepared to push their sense of honour to the same extreme limits as Rodrigue. The inhuman hardness of the young Horace is not at all a virtue of man as he ought to be. But at the time of Richelieu a French nobleman was not entitled to assess the demands of the state as against the calls of family ties, friendship, or love. Later on the character of the French was to lose its toughness. Their hearts softened and they became nicer people. In La Bruyère's day they could no longer understand Corneille.

Perhaps 'regular' tragedy, whose rules were at that time beginning to be accepted, was not the best medium for the expression of moral grandeur and heroism. Corneille only adopted the form because he had to. He had at first tried other ways, and his *Clitandre* was very free in the dramatic structures it used. But it should not be thought that Corneille was hamfisted in the way he applied the rules. *Le Cid* shows that he could apply them to perfection. It has been possible for a long time to cast doubt on this fact, because it was not known that the unities that applied even to tragi-comedy differed from those of tragedy. And the *Cid* is a tragi-comedy. But the quarrel about the *Cid* showed Corneille that he would have to pay too dearly for any further refusal to obey the rules insisted upon by the 'doctes', and that the world in which he lived did not confer success on those who merely pleased the 'peuple'. In *Horace, Cinna,* and *Polyeucte* he showed that he could work within the rules of classical orthodoxy as well as anybody.

Corneille was too much immersed in the climate of his time for him not to want to reflect its romantic inspiration. After *Polyeucte*, and for a period of about ten years (1642–51), from *La mort de Pompée* to *Pertharite*, the tragedies he wrote have the common characteristic of reflecting a romantic conception of life and art. It is true that many of them remain tied to historical subjects, like the tragedies of Richelieu's time, *Nicomède* in particular. Often, however, they merely used historical names in plots devised by their author, which is the case with *Rodogune*, where Corneille dared on his own admission 'feindre [i.e. make up] un sujet entier sous des noms véritables'. For all that, these tragedies were modern and romantic.

They were so even in their most debatable characteristics. The modern romantic hero was in love. He was galant. So, in *La mort de Pompée*, we see Caesar resting from his battles by writing madrigals, and Nicomède found it quite natural to leave the battlefield for the love of Laodice. The situations in which these heroes were involved remind one constantly of contemporary novels, for example those of La Calprenède. Thus, a passing reference in the historian Baronius gave Corneille the idea of *Héraclius*, i.e. children substituted for each other and the dangers of incest. Events in *Rodogune* – the poisoned cup, the stabbed young man who whispers the name of his assassin without being able to make himself understood – take one far away from *Horace* and *Cinna* and are very much in the romantic tradition.

There is no difficulty in recognising the weakness of this conception. It does not lie so much in the alleged improbability of the plot. Rather is it to be found in the arbitrariness of the work of art as a whole, where the poet is no longer working within the confines of either history, or real psychology, or indeed the real world, but in which he freely invents exceptional characters with which he could be sure of earning the applause of his contemporaries because they would find in them the refinements of heroism and galanterie of their dreams.

The moment tragedy came to depend on admiration and no

longer put on the stage victims of destiny, as in Greek tragedy, but tough, healthy human beings, it was clear that it had to have well-knit plots. Dogmatic critics have condemned Corneille, particularly for the works of this period, because of his alleged clumsiness, uncertainty, and obscurity. But one should, on the contrary, admire him for the extraordinary mastery with which he succeeded in dominating his complex plots and enabled his audiences to grasp them. Above all, it is absurd to speak of clumsiness, as if the very essence of romantic tragedy did not require a vast array of obstacles in the way of the hero.

He has also been reproached for having incredible plots. It is obvious that Corneille could not accept the idea of having credible plots, in the sense in which the theoreticians of classicism understood that concept. This he explained in a note at the beginning of his *Héraclius*. The only kind of credibility he was prepared to admit was the coherence of his heroes, and their actions had to conform in a credible way with their character as it appeared from the start of the play. On the other hand it was the author's job to invent his characters as he thought fit. He might, if he chose, confer upon his hero strength beyond the ordinary and which, in consequence, is not credible. This may seem to be a paradoxical maxim, but it was an obvious one in the context, since it signified that the truth of the tragic hero could be neither ordinary nor common, and that the obstacles he had to surmount could have nothing in common with the little mishaps which make up the life-story of the majority of men.

Although tragedy coincided with the mentality of French society before the Fronde, it had to change with the changes that took place subsequently in the country. So much so, that Corneille stopped writing for the theatre after 1651. Historians have tried to find reasons for this silence in Corneille's private life. In fact, however, it was tragedy as such that was at that time in a state of crisis, and other authors had stopped writing too. In the three years 1649–52 the two Paris playhouses put on only six new tragedies. Corneille had stopped for the same reason as his colleagues.

It was seven years before he returned to the theatre.[16] By then the situation had radically changed. The incredible success of *Timocrate* by his brother Thomas, at the end of 1656, had shown that the crisis of tragedy was over. Foucquet was pressing Corneille to break his silence. In January 1659 he presented *Oedipe*, and thereby inaugurated the last period of his career as a dramatist. After fifteen years, in 1674, he came to the conclusion that he had better bid the theatre a final goodbye.

During this last period he wanted to create a kind of tragedy which was not exactly like either the masterpieces of the great classical era or his own earlier romantic tragedies. They were political tragedies. They were about the great interests of state, their characters were heads of state, illustrious warriors, and ministers and princes of the blood. They were about the passions of ambition and vengeance, and love only appeared if it was intimately linked with a political enterprise, to thwart it or bring it to its final fruition.

The political concerns he put on to the stage were not just a series of commonplace and vague, rhetorical maxims. They were thinly veiled topical political issues of the French monarchy, treating of the state of the kingdom after the end of unrest and at the beginning of peace. In *Oedipe* Corneille attacked the notion that it was up to the people to determine justice. In *Attila* there is a magnificent speech about the great destiny of the French monarchy and the inevitable decadence of the empire. In *Tite et Bérénice* one finds a flattering account of royal policies, and the picture he gives of Attila was very obviously intended to make one think of Louis XIV, at once peace-loving and redoubtable, who was able to make Europe tremble without having recourse to arms.

Corneille's tragedies therefore showed complete support for the policies of the new reign. They exalted authoritarian monarchy and applauded the pursuit of prestige. They provided the French with a magnificent picture of a state in which peace had been re-established and had made possible gestures of reconciliation and clemency. *Sertorius*, that admirable play, cannot be properly understood unless one is aware of the secret intention behind it. Corneille wanted to remind the French that at the time of the civil wars it was sometimes difficult to know where one's duty lay, that errors were committed in that respect which were not criminal, and that it is good to forgive.

It cannot fail to become obvious to anyone who re-reads these tragedies of Corneille's old age, that this great man wanted to make these masterpieces the supreme expression of the conscience of the nation in the early years of the personal reign of Louis XIV. Their failure proved him wrong. *Oedipe* had an honourable reception, but *Sophonisbe* was given a cold welcome, while it appears that *Othon* and *Agésilas* had only moderate success. *Attila* was a cruel flop. It was in fact so cruel that Corneille stopped writing for three years. He came back with *Tite et Bérénice*. *Pulchérie* was unsuccessful, and *Suréna* brought only modest success. It was then that Corneille decided that the time for definite retirement had come.

It would be an oversimplification to explain the final failure of Corneille as a result of his having exhausted his genius. The tragedies of his old age are full of magnificent scenes and of innumerable passages containing those 'sublimes beautés' that Mme de Sévigné enthused about. They presented the French with scenes whose topicality was obvious. But a literary work, though it may seek topicality, cannot be limited to allusions or to the exposition of ideas. It is more important for it to comply with the expectations of the generation for whom it is written. The generation of 1660 did not want anyone to speak to them of themselves, their recent trials, and their hopes for the future. They did not want to hear any more political talk. They wanted the theatre to arouse their emotions and make them weep at the sight of moving passions. Saint-Evremond, with great acuteness, saw that the spectators of those days only liked grief and tears. Only the pathetic could arouse them. It was for this reason that, rather than old Corneille with his political tragedies, they preferred the emotional works of Racine.

The works of Corneille therefore covered several periods in the history of French tragedy. But they did not smother all dramatic life around them, and it is to the rest of tragedy that we must now return to see how it developed after 1640. 'Regular' tragedy had succeeded in conquering all before it, its principles were fixed, it no longer had to grope its way. This must be borne in mind so that one avoids the mistake of thinking that tragedy had not reached its high point until after 1660. But since it was closely linked with the development of French society which was then undergoing great changes, tragedy too changed.

In the years following *Horace* and *Cinna*, the splendid examples they provided inspired other writers. The best authors of the period – Gombauld, Rotrou, Du Ryer, and Tristan – wrote tragedies at that time which tried more or less closely to follow those of Corneille. Roman history alone supplied more than half their plots. Several plays staged episodes of Greek history. The fashion of Cornelian tragedy lasted until the Fronde. But then it stopped abruptly. It was not just Corneille who kept away from the theatre. Tristan put on one comedy and one pastoral, but no tragedy. Pierre Du Ryer did likewise and returned to tragi-comedy. Writers who were highly esteemed, like Boyer, Desfontaines, Gilbert, and Mareschal felt discouraged and wrote nothing.

It would be too easy to explain the decline of tragedy through the anarchy of the Fronde. The public had recognised some of the obvious faults of the genre before the unrest had begun. Wits were having fun with all those appeals to the gods, those monologues, and all the stage-whispers and futile rhetoric. When the tragic hero announced that he was going to kill himself and then proceeded to do nothing about it, they did not feel pangs of emotion.[17] They laughed. The Fronde was not responsible for this state of mind, for it had existed before it. But the Fronde did accentuate it. Parisians saw too clearly the pitiful reality that had been hidden behind the prestigious façade of the aristocracy. It was henceforth impossible to make them believe in all those alleged heroes. They had seen with their own eyes that they were unreliable, weak, selfish, and greedy.

Tragedy revived as abruptly as it had declined. But it was a new kind of tragedy. If one likes one can call it galante tragedy, so long as one realises that it was essentially romantic, that it found its inspiration in the tragi-comedy of 1630, that it differed from it only in its acceptance of the rules, and that its defining characteristic was that it mixed traditional romanticism with the new galanterie.

The first of these plays performed in December 1656, and the one that started the fashion, was *Timocrate* by Thomas

Corneille. The subject had been taken from La Calprenède's *Cléopatre*. It was extravagantly absurd. The audience had to be infinitely credulous. Yet the play was a success, indeed one must regretfully take note of the fact that it was one of the successes of the century.

There was thus a new tragic genre, and authors had merely to exploit its possibilities. Thomas Corneille, however, had no illusions about the merits of his *Timocrate*. He had the frankness to admit that the success of his play was perhaps due to 'l'injuste caprice' of the public, which was incapable of distinguishing 'les faux brillants' from real beauty.[18] This did not, however, stop him from putting on *Bérénice*, based on the *Grand Cyrus*, and which was no less absurd than *Timocrate*. That was followed by *Darius* in which one could see the king of the Persians hiding under the name of Codoman. Romantic improbability was here pushed to lunatic extremes.

At the same time Philippe Quinault was giving up writing Spanish comedy in which he had, all the same, achieved honourable successes. He began to write galantes tragedies. His first was *Amalasonte*, in 1657, and soon after he presented his *Feint Alcibiade*. Even Scarron could not quite resist the fashion, and Boisrobert also succumbed to the temptation.

That was the position of tragedy when Louis XIV began his personal rule. It exactly reflected the taste of the period and the state of mind of the French when they had restored their social life after the Fronde. Their world, ruled by the financiers, was no longer the world of Richelieu. It cared little about the great interests of state. The virtues of strength, austere greatness, and dignity touched by tenderness made no appeal to it. It wanted elegance, galanterie, and refinement, however pointless. It had peculiar ideas about heroism, probably because it did not quite believe in it; it saw it as an attractive idea. Now that the Fronde was vanquished, the Paris bourgeoisie went to the theatre for romanticism of a kind that did not even try to take itself seriously. Abbé d'Aubignac left a useful hint about the successes of romantic tragedy. He wrote that the plays of Thomas Corneille, 'n'ont été que des escroqueries pour nos bourgeois'.

Tragedy was supreme. Writers who wanted to make a quick

reputation presented the public with plays that combined memories of Corneille with the most threadbare effects of romanticism. Quinault continued as before, and the great Corneille returned to the theatre. Some of their plays called themselves tragi-comedies for the simple reason that the ending was a happy one, but they did not really differ from tragedy. Twenty-two new tragedies and twelve tragi-comedies have been counted between 1659 and 1666.

Apart from the giants – Corneille who was ending his career, and Racine who was beginning his – two names characterise the tragedy of that period: Thomas Corneille and Quinault.

Over a period of eighteen years, from 1660 to 1677, the first of these playwrights produced twelve tragedies and tragi-comedies.[19] They showed some skill and talent for inventing scenes of pathos and striking phrases, but it would be impossible to discern in them any coherent conception of tragedy. Thomas Corneille did not opt for either political or sentimental tragedy. A few powerful scenes remind one that he was the brother of the great Corneille; others make one think of the worst improbabilities of romantic tragedy. In any case, as a writer he plagiarised everybody. There are all too precise reminders of his brother, of Quinault, of Boyer, and even of Racine.

Quinault, during this period, went on writing romantic tragedies whose essential elements were the substitution of children, disguises, and people finally recognising each other.[20] He could, however, write something rather better than that, and nearer the Corneille formula. In 1671 he gave up writing tragedy, and began composing libretti for operas for which Lully wrote the music. He achieved new triumphs in that sphere.

Other names could be added. Abbé Boyer, Michel Le Clerc, Jacques Pradon, all provided the French theatre with works whose mediocrity was not always apparent.

The time of Racine

Racine emerged from the midst of a crowd of mediocrities. He too was of his time, but he dominated and surpassed it.[21]

He began working for the tragic theatre with his *Thébaide* in 1664. The play did not merely fail to contribute anything new, but it had not even caught up with developments in the realm of tragedy. It was reminiscent of the plays of Pierre du Ryer and Rotrou that the public had applauded around 1640. It included a large number of tirades about politics. Polynice inveighed against government by the people. Creon justified absolute government in the name of reasons of state. Etiocle expounded the doctrines of Machiavelli. With a little imagination the audience might even have taken Creon for Mazarin. There were moments in the play that recalled Condé's exile in the Netherlands. It was an odd mistake for a beginner to make. Since the Fronde the Paris public had lost interest in politics.

The *Thébaide* was therefore a failure. But Racine had learnt his lesson. Since Paris wanted mainly romantic and galante tragedy he provided it with *Alexandre*. He used the themes and methods that were at that time bringing Quinault his triumphs. The characters had no occupation other than love, and tender talk concerning it. Alexander was inspired by a 'beau feu' in his projected conquests, and the conquerer of Asia was entirely preoccupied with the problems of passing messages of love into the camp of the enemy. Romanticism was apparent in the smallest gestures of the characters. If they talked about love it was in terms of sweet tenderness punctuated by a wealth of ardour and sighs, like the characters of La Calprenède. And if they were aiming at achieving glory it was not because they were giving a moment's thought to the positive results of their exploits, but for its own sake, and for the satisfaction of presenting it to the woman they loved.

Alexandre corresponded so well with the taste of the period that it could not fail to win acclaim. It was first performed in December 1665 and had a big success. But it was two years before it returned to the stage. In November 1667 Racine presented his first masterpiece, *Andromaque*.

In fact, the difference between *Alexandre* and the new play was immense. There were a number of reasons for this. The most obvious was certainly that Racine had discovered the real character of the society for which he was writing. Until this time he had been an obscure young man who was friendly with some bright people whose audacity consisted of poking fun at silly innocents. He really only knew about life through books. But, in 1667, he was received by Henriette d'Angleterre, had conversations with her, was introduced to Mme de Montespan, and thus entered a world where he became acquainted with at lcast some of the less public aspects of le grand siècle. At the same time he had an affair with the most famous actress of the day, Thérèse du Parc. She had connections with a number of rather worrying people whose habits were to be revealed to the public in the *Affaire des poisons* ten years later. As Racine was beginning to understand society he was also beginning to understand himself. His relationship with Thérèse du Parc taught him what passion was about and gave him a taste of the nature of jealousy. He saw that man was not really like the characters of a tragedy. That discovery led to *Andromaque*.

The reaction to *Andromaque* shows how much his contemporaries had been repelled by the characters of the play; the characters are unlike those usually encountered in the tragic theatre at that time. Pyrrhus looked to them so little like a king as he went about indecisively losing his temper, brutal and timid in turn. Nor could they understand how Orestes could fulfil so badly his mission as ambassador, and that he could sacrifice it for the sake of his passion. Andromaque shocked them too They thought her 'étourdie'; they reproached her for not being more rational and prudent in her conduct. They regretted that Hermione cared too little about the requirements of honour, and that she did not even for an instant rejoice at having been avenged.

One is not always aware of the degree to which Racine revealed the hidden depths of his society, because one is too often deceived by the appearance of majesty of the monarchy, its respect for étiquette, and its apparent conformism. That was Stendhal's mistake in his study of Racine. He saw the court of Louis XIV through the eyes of the Restoration. But we now know the reverse side of le grand siècle, and the frenzied passions the appearance of majesty tried to hide. In his masterpieces Corneille had given a true picture of a society that was anxious to perform the most estimable actions, and was inspired by a heroic conception of life. But what had been true in 1640 was no longer so at the time of Racine, and most writers have not had the lucidity to see it. It is thus not surprising that Andromaque struck them as scandalous.

They were given even greater cause for indignation in December 1669, when Racine presented *Britannicus*. It could have been a completely political tragedy. The subject dealt with the Emperor Nero and that formidable woman Agrippina. The fate of the empire and the world was going to be decided during those brief hours, and the will of one of history's great monsters was to come into collision with the domineering habits of his mother. Instead, Racine brought out the human realities that lay hidden behind the political drama. He showed a vicious young prince, impetuous, given to sudden frenzied passion, trembling before his mother, feeling stifled by her, and only finding the strength to rebel against her because he had been aroused by a young girl he had seen by torch-light. And Racine showed an old woman who saw that her power was crumbling and who was unable to do anything about it, who loved her son as if he were her property, who behaved even more imprudently as she saw him slipping away from her, and who tried in vain to keep him.

Racine took the audience into a world no writer had previously dared enter. But when one reads the correspondence of the period, the pieces of polemic that were being printed in the Netherlands about the court of France, the *Histoire amoureuse* by Bussy-Rabutin, and the memoirs – for instance those of Primi Visconti – one sees that this is no imaginary world, and that Racine put on the stage a collection of human beings whom he must have created in the image of some of those encountered in monarchic society.

Moreover, society at this time was beginning to take stock of itself. This was of course less visible in mediocre authors than in those who were more observant and lucid. And it was no accident that most of the latter were in some way connected with Racine. La Rochefoucauld was the most significant name among them. There is little difference between La Rochefoucauld's conception of the passions and that of Racine as it appeared in his first masterpiece. Agrippina's love for Nero is compounded of the will to dominate and to possess, which is the definition that the author of the *Maximes* also gave of love. Similarly, passion appeared in *Andromaque* and *Britannicus* as an irresistible force, an irrational attraction, and the heroes and heroines of Racine loved with a kind of fury that was accompanied by a clear awareness of the madness of what they were doing. This was also the 'amour d'inclination' discussed by the philosopher friends of Mme de Sablé, and whose terrible consequences they had noted. At that time, too, Bussy-Rabutin was speaking of the indignities certain forms of love involved, and Guilleragues was writing his *Lettres portugaises*. It was not long before Mme de Lafayette, in her *Princesse de Clèves*, was to tell of a woman consumed by a love she refused These intelligent observers had discovered something which Corneille's generation had not suspected. Towards 1670, French society had ceased to believe in free will.

When, in answer to an invitation from Henriette d'Angleterre, Racine wrote *Bérénice*, he owed both his real subject and his understanding of the interplay of the passions to contemporary society. For, beneath the names of Titus and Bérénice, one discovers the passion Louis XIV and Mazarin's niece[22] – afterwards to be the Connétable Colonna – had for each other. They had loved passionately, but the superior demands of the state had militated against their love. Corneille, on the same subject, gave us noble speeches of two heroic souls. Racine had a better knowledge of the great of this world, and his characters reveal themselves as two irresolute people who are incapable of following through decisions previously made, and who are completely in the grip of passion.

But Racine remained under the spell of his great rival. It is clear that he wrote his tragedies with one eye firmly on Corneille or, more precisely, to do better than he while following the same lines. This was obvious in *Bajazet* and almost excessively so in *Mithridate*. In *Iphigénie*, however, new preoccupations appeared which were to show themselves with still greater force and clarity in *Phèdre*. He was no longer content with merely substituting for Corneille's strong-willed and forceful heroes passive characters who were dominated by their passions. He turned to Greek tragedy and made the real subject of his last tragedies the intervention into our lives of the mysterious powers that dispose of the fate of the world. Iphigénie and, in particular, Phèdre are victims of the gods. At the time Racine was thinking also of writing an *Alceste* based on Euripides, which shows how much tragedy was becoming sacred drama for him. Racine seemed to be defying the moderns in taking this road. The moderns wanted tragedy to exalt the freedom of heroes and their greatness. They thus wanted it to be entirely human and devoid of the sacred. In French society at that time, though it was apparently pervaded by Catholicism, it was the religious aspect of Greek tragedy which repelled audiences. According to Saint-Evremond, the presence of the gods filled the ancient theatre with a spirit of superstition and terror, a spirit that teaches men to recoil with fear before every danger. To moderns like Saint-Evremond, the Greek myths were repugnant, barbarous, dangerous, and opposed to the feelings a human being worthy of the name ought to have.

It is therefore tempting to conclude that Racine, in returning to these myths, was taking up a position contrary to that of the moderns. The truth is less simple. The taste for the profusely complex and for pomp, which had been in evidence for a number of years in the most diverse media of artistic creation, had brought with it a limited revival of mythological plays. This was particularly so in opera.[23] In 1671, the performance of *Pomone* showed that opera had fallen for the Greece of mythology. In 1672 Lully and Quinault put on the *Fêtes de l'Amour et de Bacchus*, in 1673 *Cadmus et Hermione*, and *Alceste* in 1674. *Les amours de Diane et d'Endymion* and *Le mariage de Bacchus et d'Ariane* were other contributions to the same movement. So, Racine was catering for a general taste when he evoked ancient Greece and her legends.

But the way in which Racine treated the examples of ancient Greece was rather different from that of most people and, in a sense, even its negation. What opera audiences were applauding was the triumphal affirmation of love and life in the midst of infinite luxury, the realisation of dreams of power, and the joy of the beauty of woman. Racine, on the other hand, saw in Greek tragedy the image of man dominated by inhuman and evilly-inspired fates, punished for defects for which he had no responsibility.

This was a vision of the world which Racine had no doubt drawn from within himself. But it was also in tune with the pessimism of the Augustinians; the Greek concept of destiny corresponded to the predestination of the Jansenists. It also corresponded to the new conception of man which arose in the middle of the century, and which found expression in La Rochefoucauld's *Maximes*. It was a strangely pessimistic conception that accounted for all human action in terms of the promptings of the passions, refusing to believe in disinterested gestures and all forms of aspiration towards higher ends.

Thus in *Iphigénie*, and even more in *Phèdre*, Racine expressed the pessimism which pervaded some of his contemporaries underneath that façade of optimism erected by the majority of them. However it must be said that Racine went further in his tragic view of life than any other contemporary Phèdre is not just a soul who had been refused grace She was damned in advance and the gods wanted it so; they wanted positively both her crime and her fall. Racine had gone back to the God of the bible for his notion of tragedy, to the God who said that it was He who saved and who damned. No other writer would have dared offer his contemporaries that terrible image of God. One is here in the presence of that rare kind of genius who accepts the intellectual climate of his time while at the same time extending it to its outer limits and imparting to it an impulsion of power which could come only from him.

Racine's silence after *Phèdre* is perhaps only a mystery if one forgets the atmosphere of the period, the declared hostility of the court to the profane pleasures of the theatre. Racine stopped writing tragedies because he had become devout and wanted to align himself with Mme de Maintenon. The two plays he wrote after his retirement from the theatre, *Esther* (1689) and *Athalie* (1691) show the way society had changed since the royal government had allowed itself to become the docile instrument of the religious faction.

There is certainly no lack of grandeur about the vision he presented of the Christian faith in these two plays: a small group of predestined people in the midst of a crowd of sinners, and the pure constantly threatened with persecution. His characters were people leaving the joys of the world to seek refuge in obscurity and silence, the better to be able to meditate upon the divine verities. That was the picture Racine no doubt had of religion, and many ardent souls shared it.

Paradoxically, it was precisely at this period that the purest souls were being persecuted by the royal government. Racine was aware of this, and with great courage he alluded in his tragedies to Port-Royal. Jansenist writers had, before Racine, condemned Aman, the criminal, and compared Mardochée with Antoine Arnauld. The story of Athalie recalled the tribulations of Port-Royal, the monastery half abandoned, its friends discouraged, the momentary triumph of the Jesuits. The sad grandeur of Racine's two holy tragedies is perhaps the truest and most striking expression of the monarchy of France at the end of this reign and epoch.[24]

Racine's withdrawal from the theatre after 1677, and his two final religious tragedies for the convent of St-Cyr twelve and fourteen years later, are in their way symbols of the decadence of French tragedy from about 1680. This decadence gradually manifested itself and could not finally escape the notice of contemporaries. The failure of his *Artaxerxe*, in 1682, persuaded Boyer to retire. Pradon was being ridiculed by the critics and, when he died in 1698, he had already ceased to count for a decade. The great noblemen who patronised the theatre were doing what they could to find new talent. Abeille, La Chapelle, and Du Boulay showed in turn their utter incapacity. Another writer, Campistron, appeared around 1683–5 to have some talent, but he soon gave up writing. La Grange-Chancel, a newcomer, passed for a great man for a while, but in 1706 the public saw in him no more than 'le singe de Pradon'. Between 1705 and 1715 Crébillon conferred a semblance of life on tragedy by providing a large number of scenes of violence and by exhibiting frenzied passions.

It must be clear that this kind of continuous, profound, and irremediable decadence must have had causes of a general nature, and that it cannot be explained merely in terms of a lack of genius. The most visible cause was the public's indifference. It had stopped being interested in tragedy. This lack of interest can be translated into figures. In the fifteen years 1660-75 the number of tragedies actually performed was sixty-three. During the fifteen years that followed it fell to thirty-three. It was not only the authors who were discouraged. Actors were led to present as few tragedies as possible. In 1712 the government intervened. It obliged them to alternate comedies and tragedies. The receipts of the Comédie Française for that period are known to us. They show that, apart from a few exceptions of short duration, tragedies were played to houses that were half empty.

It is not difficult to explain the public's lack of enthusiasm. For a start, authors kept on repeating indefinitely the dramatic formulae they had inherited from previous generations. They were no more than manufacturers working to patterns. There was an Italian comedy that made fun of them, the *Arlequin misanthrope*. According to it, 'Tel qui n'a pas appris à lire fait des poèmes dramatiques en vers et en cinq actes.'[25] A revolution was called for but the writers were incapable of providing it. In any case the intervention of the authorities would have prevented them from doing anything of the sort. The least departure from orthodoxy was prohibited, only the most conventional works were allowed. Campistron at one time wanted to depict Don Carlos' murder by Philip II. He was stopped from doing so because royal sentiment could not tolerate such a subject. So Campistron went to Roman history and found an analogous subject in *Andronic*. It satisfied the police. But one can understand why the Paris public succumbed more and more to the temptation of the whistle.

This situation throws some incidental light on the relations that can develop between a form of literature and a society in which it goes on subsisting. Here was a society that had been profoundly transformed. Yet its political structures had not changed, and the authorities insisted on maintaining literary forms that had had their significance a long time ago when they in fact did express the spirit of their age. But now they no longer provided a response to any call, so that their existence had become entirely artificial. In such circumstances no writer could give them back the life they had lost. That is what happened to tragedy at the end of the seventeenth century. Voltaire's success in the following century was illusory. In fact tragedy did not die during the romantic era. It had breathed its last well before the end of the seventeenth century.

As tragedy lost its prestige, so another dramatic form, opera, began to gain ground.[26]

First attempts at opera were made around 1640. In that year the Comédiens du roi performed *La descente d'Orphée aux enfers* by Chapoton. It was a production that required a few flights by gods that were carried out with the most rudimentary of techniques. After the death of Richelieu his successor took a particular interest in spectacular plays with music. Mazarin knew what admirable things Italian engineers had done for stage settings. He loved the operas of his own country. He sent for one of the best-known Italian producers, the engineer Torelli, and for the most famous musician, Luigi Rossi. The *Finta pazza* was performed in Paris in 1645. It was not an opera but a play with musical interludes. Its settings were magnificent, and the French were dazzled. In 1647 Torelli produced Luigi Rossi's *Orfeo*, and Mazarin commissioned Corneille to write the words for *Andromède*.

After the Fronde Mazarin had other spectacular plays performed in which music played an increasingly large part. The 'tragédie à machine' was becoming a form of musical art. But the French were not entirely won over. They were not enamoured of music and were much keener on seeing exciting stage settings. They, in fact, preferred the traditional court ballet to Italian opera. They would even rather have plays with songs, which was another art form. Between 1655 and 1660 there were some attempts to set up a purely French musical theatre.

Molière recognised the direction in which the tastes of his countrymen were developing. He interspersed many of his comedies with music and dancing. Critics have often looked with disdain on his comedy-ballets. They thought that when he composed them he merely obeyed the injunctions of the king. The opposite was without doubt the case. He was hoping for the harmonious blending of text, music, and dance, and he worked hard to achieve it. The musical element increased as he progressed from the *Fâcheux* to the *Princesse d'Elide*, the *Amants magnifiques* to the *Malade Imaginaire*. *Monsieur de Pourceaugnac* is a kind of *opera buffa*.

In 1669, a certain Pierre Perrin was given the privilege of opening an 'Académie d'Opéra'. He took on two associates and obtained the collaboration of Cambert, who was one of the best French musicians. In the rue Mazarine he established a very beautiful playhouse, which was inaugurated on 3 March 1671. But the venture had its enemies. In 1672 J.B. Lully acquired the privilege from Perrin and obtained a real monopoly of dramatic music in France. On 27 April 1673 *Cadmus et Hermione*, by Quinault and Lully, was given with grandiose settings by Vigarani in the presence of the king. The following day Louis XIV gave Lully the theatre at the Palais-Royal. From that moment the public accepted French opera as the most attractive art form, and as the medium that best expressed the splendour of the monarchy and of the aristocratic society that was being created around it.

Comedy before Molière

Like tragedy, comedy in the seventeenth century reflects the changes in taste and trends of thought of French society. But while by the end of the century tragedy had lost its prestige with the public and only survived as a result of royal pressure, comedy went from strength to strength.

At the beginning of the seventeenth century comedy was a genre that had been almost abandoned and, for thirty years, the number of new comedies remained infinitesimal. This may seem surprising. It is not, however, too difficult to explain. Performances at the Hôtel de Bourgogne regularly consisted of a five-act play – either a tragedy or tragi-comedy – and finished with a one-act farce. It was the latter which provided the laughter in the programme for the performance. Such farces were hardly literary works. This was so obvious that the actors did not bother to keep the scripts. Today none are left. One can only assume that these farces were partly inspired by traditional French farce, and partly by Italian farces which were then in fashion. Three actors at the Hôtel de Bourgogne had acquired enormous popularity: Gros-Guillaume, Gaultier-Garguille and Turlupin. Gros-Guillaume played the parts of valets and drunks, Gaultier-Garguille played old men in farces, and Turlupin the parts of valets, tricksters, and crooks.

Comic elements were also to be found in pastorals and tragi-comedies. And there were many plays which contained scenes that were on the homely side, or even straightforwardly funny. But they had nothing in common with any of the traditional literary forms of comedy, neither Latin nor modern Italian. There were no pedants, comic soldiers, wet-nurses, or go-betweens. They were, if anything, comments upon manners. Often they were witty and racy. This was for instance the case with Racan's *Bergeries*, around 1620, and Mairet's *Sylvie* (1626).[27] They were charming works which can even today be read with pleasure. The reader sees through the pastoral and tragi-comical elements and recognises the authors' intentions without difficulty. They were not trying to conjure up some illusory Arcadia, but scenes of life in France. And they did this with great delicacy, with an excellent feeling for what is funny without being vulgar. What one admires is the appositeness of the observation of everyday things, the discreet subtlety with which feelings are expressed. These works were not comedies, but they were to give birth to a form of modern comedy.

It was to works such as the above that Corneille turned for his beginnings in the theatre. In 1629 he wrote *Mélite*, and five more comedies followed during the next five years. It is clear to anyone who has read the *Bergeries* and *Sylvie* that Corneille had not created an entirely new kind of comedy, though this has been claimed by some. The homely and sensitive realism which is characteristic of Corneille had charming antecedents in Racan as well as in Mairet. What was new in Corneille's work was mainly that it eliminated from this realism the tragi-comical and pastoral elements it had possessed in the earlier writers.

The result was that realism became much more frank. Corneille amused himself with showing the life of gilded youth in Rouen. Or he might portray at some length certain social types. There was even, in *La Veuve*, the portrait of the young man who had just finished his studies and who did not know what to do with himself at his first ball. His plays also contain colourful Parisian scenes, for example the books hopsaround the Galerie du Palais, their shelves of recent books, the chatter of the pretty salesgirls, and the gossip of the customers.

Some of Corneille's contemporaries followed the same recipe. It was probably in 1633 that Pierre du Ryer put on *Les Vendanges de Suresnes*. Claveret located his *Esprit fort* in the forest near Versailles. Raissiguier staged his *La Bourgeoise ou la Promenade de Saint-Cloud*. Du Ryer's play is certainly the best of these. It is a delightful portrait of the manners of the petty bourgeoisie of Paris on holiday, as they take a walk on the outskirts of the city.

It is odd to note that, despite its very great merits, the comedy of manners thus conceived had only an ephemeral existence. Corneille gave up writing in that idiom after 1634 and went on to other things. It is known that the public was too preoccupied with the heroic and romantic to get much pleasure from looking at scenes from everyday life. But the comedy of intrigue attracted it a little more. This was noticed by Rotrou and Mairet.

They looked for their models in the literatures from Rome, Italy, and Spain. They preferred to derive their comic effects from romantic situations, which they took from their models, rather than from the portrayal of manners and characters. The basic situation from which they worked often involved pirates, kidnapped girls, the substitution of infants, and disguises. But instead of turning them into tragedies, they tried to draw comic consequences from them by pushing them to the point of absurdity, by exhibiting the confusion to which they could give rise, and by the use of cases of mistaken identity and other misunderstandings. Most of these comedies cared so little about realism that they kept the old characters of Latin comedy, the parasite, the pedant, the swaggering soldier, and the old servant woman.

Though this was the state of the comedy of intrigue between 1630 and 1640, it should not be condemned out of hand. Many of these comedies have much verve, interesting material, and well-chosen language. The *Galanteries du Duc d'Ossone*, presented by Mairet in 1636, is very much the best example of the genre. It had a deliberately mad plot and was full of excellent analyses of character and manners, but all France knew that the real Duc d'Ossone had been a little crazy. The other comedies of the period are less good, but several plays by Rotrou and Scudéry are every bit as romantic as the public wanted them to be, and they are in no way to be despised.

Despite certain novel aspects, comedy remained on the whole the prisoner of tradition. Around 1640, imitations of Spanish comedies helped to renovate some of its types, subjects, and language. Except in a few plays by Rotrou, the really sustained effort at providing something new came from Boisrobert's brother, D'Ouville. He knew both the Spanish language and literature very well and, in quick succession, he brought out five comedies between 1639 and 1645, in which he had borrowed from Calderón, Lope de Vega and Montalvan. They were tremendously successful, and they set a new fashion. Of the twenty comedies produced between 1640 and 1648, ten were translations or imitations from the Spanish. What is more, the fashion lasted. Between 1645 and 1656, Scarron staged seven comedies which he had taken from Spanish writers. Boisrobert put on nine comedies between 1650 and 1656 which he had imitated from Tirso de Molina, Lope de Vega and Calderón. At the same time, Thomas Corneille wrote seven comedies whose subjects he had derived from Calderón, Rojas, Moreto, and Antonio de Solis y Ribadeneyra. It was in this climate that Pierre Corneille brought out *Le Menteur* in 1643, i.e. after D'Ouville's early plays but before Scarron and Boisrobert, and which he took from a comedy he believed to be by Lope de Vega; in 1645 he presented *La Suite du Menteur*.

These plays were hardly comedies at all but much more like the romantic plays of a rather later period. They were in fact *comedias de capa y de espada*, cloak and dagger dramas. They were all about young men in despair, girls seduced or in danger, and very often about duels and assaults at night. There were heavily veiled women, perilous encounters, and acts of audacious temerity. It was a romantic world of love that did not really intend to raise a laugh.

But it was a tradition of Spanish comedy that comic scenes and burlesque dialogue should come together in the same play to arouse the emotions of the spectator. The element of laughter was very often provided by the valet, whose characteristics were derived from Sancho Panza and were now fixed. They were a mixture of laughable cowardice and gluttony, with a taste for sententious moral slogans full of artless egoism. Sganarelle in Molière's *Don Juan* is of the same type. Molière was not to know that there would one day be critics who would see in Sganarelle the incarnation of good sense and right reason. But the critics' gift for infinite nonsense is traditional.

Most of the comedies of Spanish inspiration did not attempt to hide their origins. On the contrary, audiences liked being transported to some Spanish town, an environment totally different from that of France, where young girls waited on balconies for the men they loved to pass by, and women with mantilla-covered faces carried messages of love. Corneille, however, did not write quite in that idiom in the *Menteur*, which makes his play a notable exception.[28] The action takes place in Paris, first in the Tuileries and later in the Place Royale. He substituted French ways of life for the much-admired Spanish ways that other authors had been careful to preserve. The public might have been surprised, but it certainly applauded.

There was a sudden break with the Spanish tradition around 1656. By way of explanation there is only one piece of evidence. Thomas Corneille had been presenting his *Le Charme de la Voix*, an adaptation from Moreto, and it had been a failure. The reason for this, according to him, was that French taste could no longer take 'ces entretiens de valets et de bouffons avec des princes et des souverains'[29]. French society after the Fronde did not care for dissonance in tone, it disliked mixing the comic with the tragic.

Molière and the end of the century

In November 1658 Molière put on his first performance before the king. Thereafter his plays were in the van of developments in the field of Paris comedy until his death.

When he first appeared on the scene 'grande comédie' or 'la grande et belle comédie' was highly prized by the French. The most fashionable authors were happy to contribute to its success. Among them were Scarron, Thomas Corneille, Quinault, and Boisrobert. 'Grande comédie' was defined by the journalist Charles Robinet as consisting of portraits of passions that had been aroused in the nicest way, of good sentiments, of judiciously scattered moral precepts, of a winning wit, in sum a kind of play from which one could learn something and which at the same time was a source of pleasant amusement.[30]

Since that was what comedy was then about, one can see how far out some historians were when saying that before Molière comedy in France was absurd and vulgar. On the contrary, the enemies of Molière reproached him for having ruined, through his clowning, the traditional values of comedy: dignity and elegance.

During his tours of the southern provinces he had acquired the habit of finishing his performances with a 'petit divertissement'. This had been an old custom of the Paris stage at the beginning of the century and was lost only towards 1642 with the changing taste of society. These 'petits divertissements' were really the old farces. Only the titles are left of these short one-acters, except for two whose text has survived. The latter give us an opportunity to see precisely what kind of genre this was. The scenarios seem to have been extremely simple, and their structure quite uncomplicated but geared to technical efficacy. They gave rise to funny situations, and jests that could draw laughter from audiences of students and clerks from the courts of justice. Molière made full use of this national comic art form.

Nor did he despise Italian comedy. He had written two plays in the provinces which were imitations of Italian models, *L'Etourdi* and *Le Dépit amoureux*. They were very successful when he played them in Paris. They were comedies in five acts, i.e. 'grandes comédies'. They also contained the kind of romantic elements that one found in Quinault and Gabriel Gilbert. Molière had no compunction about writing plays full of romantic and conventional situations for a public that clearly wanted that kind of thing.

At that time he was only an author of modest success. His real excellence was not recognised until, in December 1659, he presented *Les Précieuses ridicules*. Its form was that of a farce. There was only one act, and the plot was simply a joke played on two silly women. The actors wore masks and kept the names that were traditionally given to them in the theatre: Gorgibus, Mascarille, and Jodelet. Some of the jokes did not respect what might be called the proprieties. But the significance with which Molière invested his little play was unusual. He had taken as his subject certain aspects of social life. Neither farce nor 'grande comédie' had done that before. Both genres had confined themselves to quite arbitrarily conceived plots. They aimed at making people laugh without introducing any kind of realism. Molière was the first to bring out the comic element inherent in certain ways of talking and thinking. He showed how absurd some of the romantic notions were that filled the books of the period, and he poked fun at the literary pretensions of the ladies who were holding their salons and the wits who paraded before them. He also made his characters speak a language which was a caricature of that spoken in fashionable circles.

One does not explain the satirical significance of the *Précieuses* merely by pointing to the native good sense of its author. It should be recalled that very much earlier, before the period of his long journeys through the provinces, Molière knew a number of young men in Paris who had been pupils of Gassendi. These men had been very severe in their disapproval of all forms of romanticism. They could not even accept the grand sentiments of tragedy, or the weighty majesty of its language. On his return to Paris Molière went back to his old friends, and he made new ones among people who had already for some years derided the pretty social ways of their contemporaries, the coquets, and the précieuses. Men like Patru, Sauval, Furetière, and the two Boileau brothers were very much in tune with the spirit of the *Précieuses*, and it can be said that in this satire Molière had provided the kind of criticism of fashionable society that these writers had also made.

While *Les Précieuses ridicules* constituted a satire of a particular aspect of contemporary life, the *Ecole des Maris* (1661), and even more the *Ecole des Femmes* of the following year showed the author's ambition to give comedy greater significance and wider scope. He was steeped in the Latin tradition, and Terence provided for him the supreme comic achievement in literature of all time. His upbringing and his friends had made him a humanist and, in his view, a literary work could not be devoid of moral import. Recent critics who can see in Molière only a man who wanted to make people laugh show not only that they are incapable of understanding how complex works of art are, but also a great ignorance of basic ordinary history. Molière, as a humanist, could not conceive of a literature that did not have moral significance.

For that reason he painted, in the *Ecole des Maris*, the adorable portrait of Isabelle, a young woman after his own heart, all subtle mind, delicacy, and modesty. It was chiefly for this reason too that, in the *Ecole des Femmes*, he changed the old theme of the 'précaution inutile' to a condemnation of moral priggishness, a rather splendid affirmation that some human beings have a spontaneous awareness of what is right and proper and healthy.

The *Ecole des Femmes* was therefore not simply a satire on some ephemeral fashion, but an invitation to the audience to learn a timeless moral lesson. Yet it was intimately related to the condition of contemporary society, in which there was a basic cleavage between two rival attitudes. On the one hand there was the traditional attitude, according to which a young girl grew up under the close surveillance of her parents, read only the prayer-book, left the home only to go to church in the company of a responsible person, and knew nothing about the world until marriage placed her for ever under the authority of her husband. On the other hand there was the modern attitude born of the Renaissance – and which had been rapidly gaining ground for about twenty years when Molière was writing – which gave a girl access to intellectual pursuits, let her read society poetry and novels, allowed her to go out freely and have friends. It left to her the responsibility of making something of her life. The main thing was that she was no longer subject to soul-destroying constraints. That was the situation Molière had in mind when he wrote the *Ecole des Femmes*. He presented the issues clearly and was not afraid of offending prejudices and sectarian interests. The result was that the play elicited indescribable fury. One can say that the most admirable part of his later work can be explained by the scandal to which the *Ecole des Femmes* gave rise.

The religious faction was not prepared to allow Molière to get away with his criticism of the traditional ways of life in France, which were closely linked with the religious traditions. Molière defended himself against these attacks by vigorously attacking his opponents: he wrote *Tartuffe*. The polemics caused by the *Ecole des Femmes* took up most of 1663. In May 1664 Molière presented the three acts of *Tartuffe* before the king. The religious faction succeeded in having the play proscribed. Molière did not give up. In 1667 he put the play on again without warning. It was at once prohibited. He waited a little longer, until, in February 1669, it was finally allowed to be performed. Its success rewarded Molière's patience.[31]

Historians have tried to discover who the main adversaries were that Molière was attacking in the play. They considered that Molière was chiefly thinking of the Compagnie du Saint-Sacrement, whose partial responsibility for the condemnation of *Tartuffe* is now established. In the seventeenth century Père Rapin was convinced that Molière had been thinking of the Jansenists, and it is certain that these devout men themselves believed it too. If one remembers the religious situation in France at the time at which the play was written, it can be assumed that Molière was thinking of the Catholic movement as a whole and not of particular sections of it. He knew that the religious faction was determined to subject the private life of all Frenchmen to the rules of the Church and the decisions of the hierarchy. He knew this long before the final years of the reign made it tragically obvious. That is the meaning of *Tartuffe*, and not some kind of criticism of religious ideas or a satire of hypocrisy.

It was also an aspect of social life and not an abstract idea that was behind Molière's *Don Juan.* He wanted to depict the type of free-thinking nobleman as he could daily be seen at the court, where people like the Guiches, the Vardes, and the Manicamps were the source of much scandal. Moreover, Molière introduced the additional refinement of allowing his Don Juan to become devout and thus combine the vices of the debauchee with those of the hypocrite.

Molière's contemporaries realised what he was trying to do in his plays. They said that his comedies were 'd'agréables peintures du temps', that they provided 'des tableaux des choses que l'on voit le plus fréquemment arriver dans le monde'.[32] They also said that his portraits had a moral significance, that Molière wanted to contribute to the improvement of morality. They believed that he wanted to combat 'les défauts de la vie civile' and that 'sa fine morale instruit en faisant rire'. These comments are in clear conflict with the opinion of modern critics. But the latter do not seem to realise that in a century dominated by humanist traditions the interpretations given by Molière's contemporaries came quite naturally.

Le Misanthrope should be looked at in the same light. Taking a misanthropist for his central character gave Molière the opportunity of parading before us the most characteristic types of his society: the agreeable and sceptical man of the world, the nobleman who wants to shine in his little poems, the prude, the coquette, the little marquis. He even went into detail, showing for example the contemporary custom which led those who had a case to plead to call on their self-appointed judges.

Molière thus painted his society, and he did so with passion. For there is no doubt that he took sides. He was no cold-blooded observer. He was without mercy when he depicted the world of fraud, of universal hypocrisy, and of silly vanity. One may be assured that he shared Alceste's disgust. This fact may escape one, because his genius is such that even as he seems to agree with the misanthropist he looks at himself, and he judges himself with the same severity as everyone else. And disgust and anger appear to him as pointless as everything else. Why all that indignation when evil is part of human nature? Why bother to condemn corruption and injustice when the whole of society is predestined to corruption and injustice? Molière would certainly agree with the Augustinians that God left the world to the wickedness of man. The misanthropist is not wrong about human vices and stupidities. He is wrong only in allowing himself to become indignant.

Molière's most valuable works were thus his portraits of contemporary society. But he did not look at his work as the author of the *Comédie Humaine* was to look at his. In this connection it is particularly useful to compare Molière's *Avare* with Balzac's *Eugénie Grandet*. Balzac studied a man typical of his society, a product of his society, who is part of his time in that he inserts himself clearly into the specific social and economic pattern of his particular period. Balzac's miser is a wine merchant of the Loire region at the time of the Revolution and the years that followed it. The moment of history and the geographical location are not just the framework within which the action takes place. They constitute its determining causes without which the character of Grandet would be inconceivable.

When Molière wrote his comedies that type of study was not yet known. The observation of manners in his day meant noting particular characteristics associated with a particular form of society and showing their moral significance. Nobody even suspected that there might be links between these facts and geographical and politico-economic conditions. Whatever may have been said about Harpagon's avarice, they have nothing to do with his society. They reflect the eternal characteristics of avarice as they were able to show themselves in a Parisian bourgeois of the seventeenth century.

Molière continued, until the end of his career, to use his comedies to satirise some of the follies of his contemporaries. And he kept his pugnacity. In *L'Amour médecin* he caricatured the doctors at the court. In the *Bourgeois Gentilhomme* it was the turn of the newly rich commoners. The *Femmes Savantes* attacked the wits and housewives who insisted on parading their knowledge. The faculty of medicine was the subject of *Le Malade Imaginaire*, and he had even thought of taking it out on the faculty of theology. His satire was often pushed home with great audacity. In *L'Amour médecin* the actors had been given masks which were recognisably modelled. In the *Femmes Savantes* the least bright among the spectators could not miss that Trissotin was Abbé Cotin. In the play he had projected about the Sorbonne, one of the actors would have been afflicted with the dreadful jaw that belonged to the venerable Dean of the faculty, the theologian Morel.

But, though Molière is to us principally the chronicler of the manners of his time, he did not confine himself to depicting fashions and silly habits. He was interested in all art forms, and in this respect, too, he reflected certain important tendencies of his period. He was in fact a very learned man. He knew his Spanish literature as well as the works of Italian story-tellers and comic writers. He knew the old French farces and was in no way disdainful of them. The *Commedia dell'arte* provided him with much material.

Also, as has been stated in another context, he was intrigued by a new art-form which corresponded better than any other to the climate of the French monarchy at that time, a period that had glory and prosperity and luxury, and which above all wanted art that dazzled. Molière's comedy-ballets have been traditionally looked upon as inferior art, as if he had written them only to please the king without himself having any real interest in them. His contemporaries were unanimous in denying this. Molière was particularly active in this field, he was groping his way to a form of art in which the spoken word, dancing, and music would come together. One must read *Le Sicilien ou l'Amour Peintre* to realise this aspect of Molière's genius, the extent of his poetic imagination and quest for beauty. This was not the only example, for in his later career such comedies with music and dancing assumed increasing importance in his work and became, indeed, a characteristic of it.

After 1660 the works of Molière dominated the comic stage and its evolution, and on reading the comedies written during that time by other authors it becomes clear that they had his masterpieces at the back of their minds. But they did not all simply follow in his traces, and several forms of comedy continued to exist.

The most important of these other forms, and the one which retained the greatest prestige, was the comedy of intrigue. It continued the tradition of romantic comedy of the previous period, the *commedia sostenuta* of the Italians, as well as Spanish comedy. It was the kind of comedy in which one might see a young girl dressed as a man the better to be able to get near the man she loved. But it should not be thought that these plays were in any way vulgar, though they were romantic and a bit dotty. They deserved the name 'grandes comédies' they were given by their contemporaries. Scarron at the end of his life, Quinault, and above all Montfleury and Thomas Corneille were the chief suppliers of these entertainments. Critics who speak of them with scorn, as if they were extravagant and absurd, merely show that they have not read them.

When Molière came back to Paris, social pressures had already for nearly twenty years made farce impossible. Audiences, composed now of right-thinking citizens, refused to put up with the vulgarities of traditional farce. But the triumph of the *Précieuses ridicules*, which was really a farce though not vulgar, brought about the revival of that ancient comic form. Between 1663 and 1667 twenty-four out of thirty-seven comedies we know about were one-acters, and therefore farces. Very estimable writers like Montfleury, Chappuzeau, Boursault, and above all Poisson, provided the Hôtel de Bourgogne with what had become known then as 'petites comédies'. The only elements these writers had kept of Molière's farces were the schematic structure and the types he used as characters. They had no wish to fill their 'petites comédies' with satirical pictures of a prevalent social folly. They remained very close to the French tradition of farce. Their plays were often little more than an animated fabliau.

Real changes came from another direction. Some comedies had begun to bring on to the stage certain aspects of Parisian life. The capital, in 1662, had introduced the first public transport system. A few weeks later there was a play *Intrigue des carrosses à cinq sous*. At about the same time there was much talk in Paris about a small circle of gourmets. They called themselves the Coteaux, as a reminder of the slopes of Champagne. Donneau de Visé was led to stage a comedy with the title *Les Coteaux* in 1664. This was all a matter of producing something very topical, and there was no attempt at profundity. But it marked an important stage in the development of the theatre. It showed that French society liked to see itself portrayed on the stage. The facts of social life were no longer outside the scope of literature. This was the beginning of what was to be a far-reaching revolution.

It was not long, in any case, before writers began to look more deeply into the society they were depicting. Comedy began to portray new types, financiers for example, or it might describe what it was like in a bourgeois family when the daughter was being married. Champmeslé, in 1671, staged *Les Grisettes*, in which he depicted two young bourgeoises who were not being caricatured but shown as they might very well have been, and amusingly at that. Poisson, in the same year, put on his *Les Femmes coquettes*. This reminds one of *La Parisienne* by Becque, for Poisson's fashionable Parisienne is heartless and unscrupulous, self-seeking and selfishly prudent. She avoids the risks of adventures for reasons that have nothing to do with virtue.

No doubt Molière's rôle in the development of this kind of comedy was important. After all, he had made his début with the *Précieuses*. And this had then been followed by *Tartuffe*, the *Misanthrope*, and *Les Femmes Savantes*. Also, *Le Bourgeois Gentilhomme* and *Monsieur de Pourceaugnac* had been a kind of comedy of manners. But the success of these plays and those of Donneau de Visé and Poisson prove that they coincided with a public demand. They had nothing in common with the earlier romantic and rather absurd comedies. The public no longer wanted to be transported into the realms of adventure. It preferred to be shown amusing sketches of contemporary manners.

Those were the origins of what was afterwards called the comedy of manners, and which went on to thrive after the death of Molière. The other comic genres continued to exist only in the background. A few romantic comedies survived. Sometimes actors put on comedies that were little more than animated tales. The vast majority of comedies after 1672, however, were concerned with showing the manners of contemporary society.

Many of them took up an aspect of recent events. The *affaire des poisons* provided Thomas Corneille and Donneau de Visé with their *Devineresse* (1679). In the following year, after a comet had been giving Paris a fright, Donneau de Visé and Fontenelle staged the *Comète*. Or authors took their subjects from some new facet of social life, as when Hauteroche presented his play *Les Nouvellistes* in 1678.

The public liked it. And, after 1680, what had earlier merely been a new style became a veritable craze. The company of Italian actors was responsible for this sudden change. From that date onwards, they acted plays which, quite shamelessly, held up to ridicule the men and events of the moment. The first of these comedies, *Arlequin Mercure Galant* (1681) revealed the shady dealings of Thomas Corneille and Donneau de Visé in the running of their newspaper. Their success caused the company of the Comédie Française to imitate them, and the comedy of manners had come to stay. It was Parisian life that the authors particularly liked to put on exhibition, and in those days gaming had assumed the proportions of a social menace in the capital. Often it was women of high society who ran the gambling houses. Hauteroche's *La Bassette* (1680), the *Joueurs* by Champmeslé (1683), and *La Désolation des Joueurs* by Dancourt (1687) are commentaries on that phenomenon.

Following the earlier examples of Poisson and Champmeslé, other authors preferred to depict particular types that were new to society. In 1685, *Les Façons du temps* showed a selfish and brutal financier and a young officer whose one wish was to be kept by a rich woman. The following year Baron brought out his *L'Homme à bonnes fortunes*, and in 1687 Dancourt and

Saint-Yon produced their *Chevalier à la mode*. Then, in 1692, Dancourt presented *Les Bourgeoises à la mode*, a cruel account of an adventurer, a number of women who were the bane of their husbands, and young girls anxious to lose their virtue.

This kind of comedy, as has been noted, marked a revolution in the history of French literature, but it corresponded to a profound social revolution. There is no need to repeat that Molière had already filled his plays with a wealth of social detail. They were neither the same manners, nor were his ways of exhibiting them the same, as those of his successors. His old servant-women were continuing an old-established theatrical custom and reflected what remained of a society that was still attached to the old traditions. On the other hand, Champmeslé, Poisson, and Dancourt and others like them give us soubrettes. They are young, witty, charming, and totally lacking in moral sense. Molière's young women were in love and sweet. Those of the new comedy are coquettes, without heart or scruple. Molière did not have any really wicked women. Champmeslé's *Grisettes* shows Crispin making ready for a rich marriage, but completely determined to keep Martine as his mistress as before. What completes the picture is that, in many of these plays, there is not a single honest or even sympathetic character. They are all crooked, greedy, and corrupt.

They are like that because the society in which they live thinks only of money and pleasure. The new comedy is not concerned with character. It looks at men only in the social context in which they live. It no longer makes a spectacle of the man who is avaricious as there have been avaricious men through the ages. It shows financiers, merchants, and young officers. It paints the new social type, the adventurer. It does indeed show old women, but not as 'characters' true of all history, but women of their own time, ready to buy love as they might buy any other merchandise.

To set its characters firmly into their background, the new comedy was prepared to deal with aspects of reality that had hitherto been kept out of literature. The *Rue Saint-Denis* by Champmeslé (1687) is the story of a fraudulent bankruptcy involving a fictitious partnership contract and secret annulling documents. It reminds one very forcibly of the *Maison Nuncingen* by Balzac. *La Rapinière ou l'Intéressé* describes the machinations of a financier who deceives the tax collector and milks the taxpayers. In 1685, the author of *L'Usurier* claimed that he had put into his comedy 'tous les secrets de la banque', and to have described the rise of the 'riche roture'. It would not be enough to say that the 'money problem' was then making its appearance on the French scene. It was more than that. A revolution was taking place which was thrusting into literature the facts about finance and economics, and the reason for this was that French society was then being conquered by these new realities. That revolution was not the work of the nineteenth century and Balzac. It had occurred around 1670–80 and had gathered momentum as the reign of Louis XIV drew to a close.

Historians of literature have mainly concentrated on *Turcaret* by Lesage, which came out in 1709. It is a play that combines the usual characteristics of the comedy of manners, the dishonesty of all the characters, a taste for caustic comment and cutting irony. The types are all old familiar ones, the financier, the adventurer, the crazy old woman, and the young beau. In fact, however, many other plays had gone much more searchingly into contemporary life. The best of the authors of that kind of comedy was without doubt Dancourt. Traditional criticism has scorned him because he seemed to care nothing for good construction. One only has to read him without prejudice to realise how sure his touch was and how full of zest his dialogue. Dancourt's *Agioteurs* (1710) is a far more thorough piece of analysis than *Turcaret*.

It is a law of nature that when the whole of society develops its ideas and tastes in a certain direction, there will be some who refuse to follow the crowd. They are the people who prepare the next phase. This law is confirmed particularly well by what happened in the last fifteen years of Louis XIV's reign.

At that time a number of Frenchmen were unhappy because their society was drawing ever further away from the old traditional values, because it seemed to believe only in money and pleasure, and because it no longer found room for spontaneity and generosity. From about 1700 there was a kind of comedy that it would be proper to describe as sentimental or moralising. After indulging in a prank or two, the characters of such plays would make a great show of repentance. At the sight of virtue they would shed sweet tears. Destouches put on *Le Médisant* in 1715 to teach men to abhor satire. His virtuous wish was certainly shared by many of his contemporaries. The play was well-received and right-thinking people rejoiced in the resurrection of real and healthy comedy. What is known as comédie larmoyante in the middle of the eighteenth century is simply the continuation of this form of virtuous and sentimental comedy that first appeared in 1700.

10

The novel

Forms of the novel at the beginning of the seventeenth century

The novel clearly did not have the place in seventeenth-century society that it was to have in later days.[1] It did not quite belong to what was known as 'la belle littérature'. But that does not mean that only a few people read novels. It was the favourite reading of women, even in the upper strata of society, and we are told that at the beginning of the century women used to take the novels of Nervèze and Des Escuteaux to church with them instead of the prayer book. And there were many novels to choose from, which also shows that they were in demand. To quote a telling figure by way of example, there were sixty new novels in the course of the first decade of the century.

In fact, the novel was a very diverse literary form. There were the novels of chivalry that followed the tradition of *Amadis*. They were crowded with marvellous adventures and heroic exploits. One reads about single combats and kidnappings, and the hero would find himself rewarded for his exploits in the arms of a 'gorgiase infante' with green eyes. Then there were novels that derived from Boccaccio's *Fiammetta*. They were more like short stories, based on a simple plot which was nearly always the same. An ardent love would be born between two young people. The parents would object. The virtuous lovers would submit, but only after having wept plentifully and sighed plentifully. Nervèze and Des Escuteaux were taken very seriously during the reign of Henry IV by a public for whom their stories were not monotonous and conventional.[2]

In the midst of all this abundance and mediocrity there was a masterpiece, the *Astrée* by Honoré d'Urfé. It was published in three parts, in 1607, 1610, and 1619. It was a pastoral novel, its characters shepherds and shepherdesses of the Forez. But they gave no thought to carrying out the tasks appropriate to their condition. They were intended to be poetic characters, belonging to a realm quite different from that of the material world of everyday life.

In that Forez, which was a new Arcady, all their time was spent in love, thinking about love, and studying its characteristics. They pursued these activities with infinite delicacy, and marvellous lucidity. Hylas might defend the cause of inconstant and sensual love, there was always Silvandre to expound sentiments that were of real nobility about the spiritual nature of love, and the high priest Adamas put forward the theories of the Christian mystics.

The success of the *Astrée* was great. It did not just reach the world of letters but French society. In 1626 Mlle de Gournay wrote that the novel by Honoré d'Urfé had become a 'bréviaire aux dames et aux galants de la Cour'. The salons and the whole of high society had been won over. When, forty years later, Mme de Lafayette in her house in the rue Férou received her friends La Rochefoucauld, Mme de Sévigné, and the future Mme de Maintenon, it was often a page of the *Astrée* that they examined for its meaning and beauty.

The novel did not, however, influence only society. It also left is mark on the theatre. During the first part of the century playwrights liked to take their plots from *Astrée*. Nor did they seek to conceal this fact, for the public loved the novel and the playwrights could be sure to please it by transporting its pleasures to the stage.

It must also be said that the novel had important consequences for the development of French writing during the century, and upon its moral outlook. Seventeenth-century man is not the geometer and theoretician some historians have assumed. He is a romantic. He adores adventures and delicate sentiments. He believes in what he calls 'galanterie', which is very much like the sensitivity and refined forms of behaviour and the respect for woman that are such pronounced features of the *Astrée*.

Novels of adventure and the epic novel

The period marked by the government of Richelieu was to see

a new form of novel which historians have named the adventure novel. The name is a good one so long as one remembers that this form of the period 1620–40 is very different from the old adventure novels of the *Amadis* kind.

What explains the disappearance of the sentimental and pastoral novels is the changes that were taking place in French society at this time. In the new, energetic France Richelieu wanted to create, there was no place for lengthy analyses of feelings, nor for the interminable discussions of the shepherds of the *Astrée*. Heroic exploits were wanted, and big battles, and it was these that were to fill the pages of the adventure novels. On the other hand the Frenchman of this period does not conceive of the spirit of war without the refinements of galanterie. The adventure novels catered for this requirement.

But from 1634 onward, the adventure novel underwent a transformation. Or rather, beside the novels in which the author told of the adventures of an imaginary character, there was an increasing number of novels in which the hero was a famous general, or one of the famous kings in history, and their adventures were the military campaigns they had waged and the battles they had won. It was the time when there was a profusion of novels about Darius, Alexander, Mithridates, Vercingetorix, Titus, and Suliman.

These changes in romantic literature corresponded exactly to the changes then taking place in the social life of the French. The aristocratic spirit and the warlike spirit were coalescing. Adventure was now less identified with kidnappings, duels, and swordplay with bandits along some dark road It meant war as it was understood and practised in those days, made up of brief but violent encounters, sudden assaults, skirmishes, war in which the leaders of the army charged at the head of their cavalry, war bloody and joyous all at once, that was interrupted every year at the end of the summer to allow the heroes to return to Paris so that they might be worshipped by the ladies.

That is the novel some historians call epic. Others have preferred to name it heroic and galant. Both names are appropriate, because these interminable narratives were, and were intended to be, prose epics, and all of them have in common the attempt to combine heroic exploits with behaviour that is consonant with galanterie. What they also have in common is that they are unreadable. But it is important to see why they have become so. It is not just that they are too long. It is certainly not because they might be absurd. On the contrary, they tried to be realistic, that is they wanted to tell of exploits that could really have been carried out and they describe feelings a great prince could really have had. The reason for boredom derives from the fact that they correspond too closely to the ways of feeling of a particular social class, of the state of society at a particular moment in history. One can imagine without difficulty that officers in Condé's army found pleasure in these heroic and galant novels that were being published in Paris while they were making war at the frontier. But the fate of this kind of literature was too closely linked with the society for which it had been written. It was inevitable that it should disappear with it.

Some of the novelists of that period became famous. In the field of the real adventure novel, the most famous name was that of Gomberville.[3] His *Polexandre*, with titles that varied with different editions, is a model of the genre, full of battle stories, tempests, and wanderings across continents. La Calprenède and Scudéry made their name in the epic novel. The former produced the ten volumes and five thousand pages of his *Cassandre* between 1642 and 1645. Then, from 1647, he published the twelve volumes of his *Cléopatre*. Hard on his heels, Georges de Scudéry published the ten volumes of his *Grand Cyrus* between 1649 and 1653, and after 1654 his endless *Clélie*. It will not be irrelevant to note that both lived in the entourage of the Prince de Condé, who was the most perfect model of the 'héros chevaleresque et galant'.

The historical novel[4]

Around 1660 there was an almost abrupt change in romantic literature. The new generation felt that it was absurd to use plots that were set in the remote past, whose ways of thought and feeling and expression could not really be known. Boileau was by no means the first to deride the 'héros de romans'. There was no lack of evidence between 1655 and 1660 that a reaction was setting in. But it was not only the historical falseness that shocked the new generation in the works of Scudéry and La Calprenède. It was also the prose epic element in these novels, that is the conventionality of their sentiment, the sham nobility of the characters who were without weakness and without tarnish. Not least, it was also their length. After 1660, the ten-volume volume made way for the short narrative of less than two hundred pages.

But the new novel that set out to provide more truth did not wish to be realistic. The earliest example of the genre, the *Nouvelles françaises* by Segrais (1656), is a collection of historical stories.[5] It does not even wholly avoid the traditional romantic approach. There are still strange coincidences, disguises, and pirates. But there are far fewer than there had been in the earlier heroic novels. The author also placed his plots in periods of history that were closer and therefore more readily understood. They were about England at the time of William the Conqueror and Burgundy at the time of Jean sans Peur. The anachronisms of the *Grand Cyrus* and *Clélie* were thus easily avoided.

It was a woman who first followed Segrais' example. Mme de Villedieu first published *Lisandre*, a collection of galants episodes, then, in 1667, *Anaxandre*, which tells of adventures 'plus galantes qu'héroiques'.[6] This really marked the start of a new style, and Bayle formally recognised her as having originated it. 'Le nouveau goût qu'elle créa subsiste encore', he wrote.

At the same time a lady of the highest social rank and who did not belong to the literary world was writing for her own amusement a short novel, *La Princesse de Montpensier*. She published it in 1662, though without her name, and it obtained considerable acclaim. The story took place in the sixteenth century, at the time of the Valois, and was solely concerned with describing a psychological crisis. There was no trace of romanticism.

From that moment the laws of the novel were fixed for the rest of the seventeenth century. It was to be short. Its action took place in the circles of a princely court. Real history therefore had an important part to play, and the reader was being introduced to intrigues, cabals, and secret negotiations. For this part of their work, novelists of the new kind would study not only works of history, but also chronicles and memoirs of the period they were proposing to write about.

But, upon the foundations of historical fact, they proceeded to construct sentimental plots that were entirely of their own invention. As Boursault wrote at the opening of his *Prince de Condé* in 1675: 'On peut regarder comme autant de vérités les endroits qui ne concernent que la guerre, mais on ne garantit pas ceux où l'amour a quelque part'. Towards the end of the century there was a proliferation of 'histoires secrètes' that explained the great events in history in terms of secret loves of, say, the king of Castile or the connétable de Bourbon. Thus, the novel that had begun from a need for greater truth had relapsed into artifice and unreality. In 1697 Abbé du Bos wrote: 'Notre siècle est devenu bien enfant'.

The works of Mme de Lafayette stand out from among the other novels of this kind, which were on the whole mediocre. After her *La Princesse de Montpensier* she wrote a Moorish novel, *Zaïde* (1669–71), after which came *La Princesse de Clèves* (1667). This masterpiece confined itself to the form of the novel as it had been fixed for fifteen years. The story takes place at the time of Henry II. It describes the intrigues that were being woven at the court of France. The love plot was one of her own invention, but the names of her characters she had taken from memoirs. Her originality lay in the way she depicted love, as a passion, a kind of witchery, a form of enslavement, and it is really in the history of moral thought in the seventeenth century that this splendid work ought to be given a place.

The novel of satirical comment[7]

Not everybody accepted as a true picture of life what most novels presented as such. Those who did not preferred books that told them about everyday reality, even – or chiefly – if it was vulgar or obscene. Historians with a liking for systems have been attempting to connect that kind of interest with the bourgeois mentality. They have said that the romantic tradition corresponded to the existence of an aristocratic class and the realist tradition to the existence of the bourgeoisie. Such oversimplifications can only harm our understanding of history, and it has been shown that the most extravagant forms of romantic tragedy had received their support from the shopkeepers of the rue Saint-Denis. What is true is that the Paris bourgeois naturally looked with suspicion on a literature that exalted the warlike virtues and the splendid manners of high society, and that it was for that reason that he could not be happy with the contemporary novel.

This bourgeois distrust of fantasy was paralleled by other considerations which were rather more literary. Baroque culture had brought about in Italy a literature of parody which ridiculed the values most people admired in the new society. This was a literature that did not mind at all describing things that were vulgar, but it did this only from a desire for authentic realism. It loved the grotesquely outrageous and the crudest effects.

Finally, there was the Spanish picaresque novel, read and translated in France, and having its origins in the new taste for the trivial. It taught the French to appreciate colourful descriptions, and gave them at the same time the idea to describe the lowest orders of society, the world of pickpockets and go-betweens.

A number of novels at the beginning of the century gave an indication of that kind of interest. However, in 1623 there appeared a masterpiece of a quite different order. This was Charles Sorel's *Histoire comique de Francion.*[8] The book contained neither heroic exploits nor elegant galanterie. The hero was in fact a nobleman and not one of those tramps of the picaresque novel. But he was involved in strange adventures and became mixed up with rather frightening people. He despised the great nobles and detested the honest bourgeois. He dared admit that he did not believe in God and that the world's morality was a sham. Seen as a whole, the *Francion* was not a realist novel in the nineteenth-century sense. It had not been Sorel's aim to reproduce with minute precision the condition of people with humdrum lives. But there are some parts of the book which do constitute a realistic portrait in the best sense of that word. When the author described life inside the colleges, or reproduced conversations between men of letters in the bookshops of the rue Saint-Jacques, or when he showed the reader into a literary salon of a bourgeoise, he eschewed exaggeration and mockery. In such situations he was a superb observer.

The success obtained by this novel throughout the whole century and the large number of reprints prove the extent to which the *Francion* reflected the tastes of a section of French society. While there were many among the nobility and the bourgeoisie who were passionately involved with the exploits of the Grand Cyrus, innumerable readers loved the *Francion* whose lack of orthodoxy and frequent irreverence helped them to ward off the illusory pleasures of their contemporaries.

It was not, however, the realistic aspect that drew them to the *Francion*. At about the same time André Mareschal published his *Chrysolite* in which he portrayed with much realism, penetration, and sensitivity the life of a Parisian family. It was an excellent work but had no success at all. Similarly, Charles Sorel published, in 1648, the first part of his *Polyandre*, which provided a curious picture of the Parisian bourgeoisie. Its failure was so unambiguous that Sorel gave up the idea of writing the rest of the novel. The failure might just be blamed on Sorel's faults, the slowness of the story, the heavy emphases in his descriptions. But it is more likely that the public at that time had no taste for simple and unvarnished reality.

Scarron's *Roman comique* (1651–57) has been interpreted as a realistic work. But he nowhere claimed to be giving a true picture of the lives of actors. In this novel, Scarron remained as true to the burlesque tradition as he had been in his *Virgile travesti*. It was intended as a parody of the heroic novel. That is why there are so many blows being exchanged in it, why there is such a wealth of mishaps, those 'orages de coups' which certainly should not be taken seriously but which, on the contrary, openly make fun of the usual exploits of the epic heroes. Similarly, Scarron takes every opportunity to laugh at the impeccable heroes of Scudéry's novels, and at the sighs and daydreams of the lovers in that author's interminable volumes.

The *Roman bourgeois* published by Furetière in 1666 also contained a fair amount of parody. Right from the beginning the author banteringly imitates the style of the epic poets. And it is the desire to parody which accounts for the heavy humour and the rather too numerous exchanges of blows and insults. Unlike Scarron, however, Furetière really did want to describe the concrete facts of daily life. He described the life of the 'gens de chicane', and he endlessly portrayed the negotiations which preceded bourgeois marriages at that time. His description of a religious concert at the Capuchin monks of the Place Maubert is a piece of excellent realism.

But we have said that the time for the realistic novel had not yet come. The *Roman bourgeois* was a complete failure. The public took it to be an aberration on the part of the author.

The portrayal of society in the novel after 1670

There were signs, at about the time when the *Roman bourgeois* was being published, that something new was happening that might one day affect the novel. The French had made the discovery that contemporary life was worth looking at and that it provided all kinds of features that could interest a novelist. Boursault was describing camp-life during the expedition to Crete in his *Le Marquis de Chavigny*. Another of his novels was set in the Mazarin period and took in the Flanders campaign of 1667. In another sphere *L'Amant de bonne foi* (1672) told a bourgeois love story, and *L'Illustre Parisienne* (1679) gave a very vivid description of Paris manners. Caught up in this movement, Mme de Villedieu left the historical novel to others and wrote around 1675 her *Portefeuille* which was full of stories about Paris as it then was. From 1671 a new custom appeared in the novel which became permanent: characters were no longer called Ariston, Athénaiste, or Agenor. They were acquiring French names. In his *La Fausse Clélie*, Subligny initiated this feature. It may seem a superficial novelty, but it reflected a profound change.

Despite appearances, the novels in memoirs-form which were then being published showed the same desire for truth. The most famous author of this kind of novel was Gatien de Courtilz, who was practically an adventurer.[9] He published many such novels between 1688 and 1701. He used much imagination in what purported to be historical tales, but there was no real resemblance between his world and that of the old epic novels. Moreover, Gatien de Courtilz often found his sources in authentic memoirs, and his great knowledge of recent history provided him with a wealth of material.

There were other novels that had appeared after 1660 in which the desire for realism was much more obviously reflected. Their main object was to describe life in the lower orders of society. The pioneer in this field was Préfontaine. In his *Orphelin infortuné* (1660), he showed the scribes of the courts with their threadbare coats, their battered hats, and their down-at-heel shoes. In 1670 he brought out *Les Maîtres d'Hôtel aux Halles* with its pictures of the lives of domestic servants. His *Poète extravagant* was a kind of investigation into the world of prostitutes and pickpockets. It was a significant innovation, but what was particularly revolutionary was that his descriptions were not meant to be satires or parodies. Reality had become worth describing and analysing in its own right.

From then on novelists can be seen studying the material conditions of life. Le Noble introduced the reader to apothecaries, washerwomen, and lawyers. A novel by Passerat of 1695 told of the success among the ladies of society of the dancers of the Opera. Others show the reader the 'petites maisons' of the outskirts of Paris in which rich men were then beginning to receive prostitutes. Le Noble's *Histoire du Vinaigrier* tells us how a vinegar-maker can amass a large fortune and enable his son to make a good marriage.

At the same time as the facts about society, physical facts also began to make their appearance in the novel. Until then, novelists never thought of giving the reader a portrait of their characters. All women were beautiful. If they were virtuous they were fair, if they were not convention made them dark. Now the reader was told that a certain heroine had beautiful eyes but that her mouth was too big and that she had a bad complexion. Of another it was said that she was big and dark, had good eyes, an upturned nose, and fat arms. A novelist writing about a boudoir now described the sofa and the mirrors. If he took the reader to a café he makes sure to inform him that a well-sugared cup of coffee cost four sols and that those who frequented it drank more wine and liqueur than coffee.

It is obvious that a profound change had taken place in the novel. It was to be carried to great extremes. It led to Restif de la Bretonne and Balzac. It created relationships between society and literature that had never been thought possible. The change clearly did not take place in the nineteenth century, nor even in the second half of the eighteenth century. It had begun very clearly in the novels that were published at the time of Louis XIV.

11

Moralists and memorialists

The beginning of the century

One of the traditional preoccupations of French writers is the study of man, the attempt to understand his nature and the motivation behind it. At the beginning of the seventeenth century it was Montaigne who dominated this kind of enquiry. Scholars and scientists openly professed their allegiance to his thought. Among the Dupuy circle there was general agreement that *a priori* conceptions had to be disregarded in the search for knowledge, and that progress in the study of man could only come from the analysis of the beliefs and customs of the ancients and the peoples with whom explorers had come into contact. All of them were agreed that man is not controlled by rational forces, and that his beliefs and customs are the result of education, received opinions, and habit.

That view was not, however, the only one that was current at that time. The Dutch Neo-stoic school was highly thought of in French intellectual circles.[1] It taught that man is above all a reasonable being, that his reason partakes of divine reason, and that it is therefore able to apprehend the eternal truths directly without the mediation of experience. A particularly striking aspect of the doctrine was the concept of Natural Law which, though for the followers of Montaigne it had no absolute validity, they held to be a value that was independent of time and place and was consequently true for all men.

There was another capital point on which the doctrine of the Neo-stoics was at variance with the tradition of the *Essais*. For the learned men who followed Montaigne, the moral life rested on a single principle that was within man himself, and that might be called his desire to live (the concept of *amour-propre* of those days). According to the Neo-stoics, however, God or

Nature had given man, in addition to that desire to live, the desire to further the interests of the species and, more generally, the harmony of the universe as a whole. They took it to be natural for a man to sacrifice himself for his family, his country, or humanity. Or rather, they did not take that to be a sacrifice, since they thought man was fulfilling himself in a superior manner when he subordinated his actions to goals that transcended him.

These two opposing doctrines were of little concern to men outside the world of philosophy and science. In aristocratic society moral preoccupations were of a different order. Writers addressing that kind of society were busy explaining ways in which the reader might please those at court, might increase his prestige so as to obtain the favour of the great. Among these authors were Faret, Grenaille, and Bardin. Their books had titles like *L'Honnête Homme* and *L'Honnête Femme*, and they taught their readers to live 'suivant les maximes de la politique et de la . . . morale'.[2]

It may surprise us that this literature was vastly successful. But it met, of course, the exact needs of its society. In that world in which success depended upon the favour of the great, in which it was the result of slow and prudent manœuvring that would gain one access to them and then win their confidence, it was natural that morality should often be understood as a technique giving access to worldly careers. And since in that society it was neither faith nor enthusiasm that mattered but docility towards the privileged, morality came to be identified with the science of success.

La Rochefoucauld

La Rochefoucauld's *Maximes*, one of the most important and typical works of the century, must be seen against all the beliefs that have just been outlined.[3] The work represents the personal philosophy of a great man. Still, it came to be written in a society which foreshadowed it and promoted its creation.

La Rochefoucauld frequented the circle of Mme de Sablé.[4] It was a world of philosophers and scientists in which one of the favourite topics for discussion was the nature of man and his behaviour. The marquise herself boasted that she was better than anyone else at analysing and uncovering the most secret of motives. Her main interest lay in discovering the finest nuances, clearly to define them, to distinguish between them with precision, and to find for each the most exact description. Her friends were philosophers and scientists mainly occupied with problems of physics, medicine, and politics, as well as with those of education and ethics.

It was in this circle and for his friends that La Rochefoucauld in 1660 began his collection of maxims. He had no thought of publication. But, in 1664, a copy of the manuscript came into the hands of a Dutch publisher, so that all La Rochefoucauld could then do was to provide an authentic copy of his own. It came out dated 1665. Until 1678 several editions appeared, corrected and augmented.

The idea of writing maxims is easily explained by the customs in society circles at that time. People just enjoyed them, exactly as they enjoyed proverbs, portraits, and 'questions d'amour'. It provided occasions for those who frequented salons to 'raffiner sur les delicatesses du coeur et du sentiment'. They took all this very seriously, for although they liked to sharpen their subtle ideas they certainly did not want to court paradox. It was truth they were after. In Mme de Sablé's salon Abbé Jacques Esprit and the marquise herself exchanged maxims, and La Rochefoucauld emulated them.

He had thought out a philosophy of man. It was bitter and sad. He allowed no room for disinterested feeling. Even love was for him no more than a passion to dominate and possess. Friendship he took to be selfish, like love. Bravery, goodness, even humility were in his eyes merely refinements of egoism. Self-interest sufficed to explain them all

The misinterpretation the reader must avoid is to see in the *Maximes* only a personal doctrine that belonged merely to the author, invented by him as a result of the combined influence of frustrated ambitions, private experiences, and moods. This would be a double error. First, there was no need for La Rochefoucauld to invent a moral philosophy that accounted for all human action in terms of self-interest, or *amour-propre*. Philosophers had ceased to believe for some time in the existence within man of a spiritual 'appetition' that might have led him to a search for universal values, a natural inclination towards the good and disinterested action. Hobbes had strongly attacked that doctrine and the intellectual circles of Paris were well-acquainted with his views.

There were other reasons why a philosophy of man that was basing itself on *amour-propre* should find a hearing at that time. Descartes' *Traité des passions* (1649) and the *Caractères des passions* by Cureau de la Chambre, both many times reprinted, had drawn attention to the part played by the 'humours' in the life of man. It meant that the part of free-will and reason had to be thought of as less important than before. The moral life was reduced to no more than a mechanical interplay of passions and consequently of *amour-propre*. La Rochefoucauld was well aware of what an English writer had called the new anthropology. He wrote: 'La liberté est peut-être une illusion', and 'Les humeurs ont un cours ordinaire et réglé qui meut et tourne doucement et imperceptiblement notre volonté'.

Among Mme de Sablé's friends there was lively and courteous discussion of these new ideas. They were particularly concerned with love. There were those who remained convinced of what one might call the Cornelian conception of love, in which the Platonic and Neo-stoic doctrines seemed to meet. They believed in what they termed 'l'amour de connaissance', a love that originates in the recognition of the perfection of the person loved and which, since it is the result of a spiritual conviction, is at the same time an act of pure freedom. Others, however, refused to recognise anything other than 'l'amour d'inclination', that is blind and irresistible instinct which thrusts a human being in the direction of another, a love entirely devoid of spiritual value, and the most violent form of *amour-propre*.

The *Maximes* thus summed up with tremendous power a conception of man that was then emerging from among the philosophers and which was soon to dominate the period. But they also mirrored the state of mind of French society as it came out of the years of unrest into the reign of Louis XIV. The contemporaries of La Rochefoucauld saw in the civil disorders, the failure of liberal hopes, and the triumph of absolutism the proof that man was decidedly the product of his passions and that constraint alone could ensure order. Those who, like La Rochefoucauld, had seen the intrigues of political leaders at close quarters, with their lies, their calculating self-interest wrapped up in noble talk, could no longer have any illusions about the avowed or concealed egoism of the mass of humanity. They decided to draw their lesson from it all. They took society as a form or organisation in which nearly everyone cheated, in which intrigue, ingratitude, and lies triumphed, a world without honour and without generosity. La Rochefoucauld's *Maximes* caused a scandal when they were published, but it was their tone which shocked. Their inherent pessimism was shared by French society as a whole in the years that saw the restoration of privilege.

The Mémoires of de Retz

The *Mémoires* of Cardinal de Retz have the same background. He wrote them well after the Fronde, in 1673–8, in a society in which he encountered Mme de Sévigné and Mme de Lafayette, as well as his former adversary La Rochefoucauld. But the old enmities had become meaningless, and both men were more aware of the beliefs they shared, their common experience of life, and their common melancholy.

The similarity with the author of the *Maximes* extends in de Retz even to a taste for lapidary moral precepts, the habit of expressing moral observations in axiomatic forms that encompass deep truths about the innermost secrets of the human soul. De Retz' intentions were similar to those of La Rochefoucauld too. He went to pains to explain that, though he could sleep well during periods of stress, this was not a sign of courage but rather of total defeat. He had every right to preface the *Mémoires* with the note that he wanted to 'rendre compte de tous les replis de son ame et de ceux de son coeur'.

Like that of La Rochefoucauld, de Retz' method was that which the philosophers of the eighteenth century called analysis. He left no room for the noble but nebulous ideas which reassure the mediocre. For him the human soul was like a piece of machinery whose works could be taken to pieces, and the *Mémoires* constitute a splendid portrait gallery that is characterised by the lucidity of its author who penetrated beyond the appearances of his subjects into the recesses of their hearts.

De Retz also applied this method to politics. The state was a large machine or, as he put it, a clock whose works and weights the politician must get to know. It was the task of parlement to 'modérer le mouvement' but not to impart movement. De Retz thought that the chaos of the Fronde was to be explained by the attempt of parlement to play a rôle for which it was not fitted.

The philosophers of the romantic period were critical of de Retz' mechanical political model. They took him to task for ignoring the profound and unconscious forces that escape analysis but which determine the history of nations. This criticism may be justified in the case of some polemicists of the school of Machiavelli, but certainly not in that of de Retz. He was well aware of the influence of public opinion. He realised that one goes wrong about political parties if one ascribes programmes to them, and, to their leaders, deep thoughts. He knew that in most cases politics is simply a matter of mediating between conflicting interests, blind passions, and collective stupidity. His explanation of the Fronde went well beyond mere mechanics. De Retz often returned to the point that the disturbances broke out without anyone having actually wanted them or foreseen them, that there had not been, as he put it, 'un grain de manège d'Etat' in that revolution. From its outset it had been beyond the control of those involved in it.

It was not merely because he was a highly intelligent observer that de Retz held these views. His post as coadjutor of Paris brought him into closer contact with the people of Paris than any other man. There were others who wrote first-hand accounts of the Fronde, for example Montrésor, Fontrailles, and Lenet. But they never went beyond talking about the intentions of individuals and the conspiracies of cliques. De Retz was alone in having understood that it was the people of Paris who were the real force behind the revolution, and that, while the Fronde might very well seem silly and pointless to anyone seeking precise reasons, it is explained and almost justified by the general conditions of the state and the relations between the social classes within it. It is not really surprising that the petty bourgeoisie of Paris rebelled against the state that had handed it over to the mercy of the financiers, and had made it the victim of a political system that had deprived it of its most prized traditions. It needed no 'manège'. The rebellion was spontaneous.

Since de Retz' *Mémoires* were not finally published until 1717, they could not exercise their profound influence until the eighteenth century. It would, however, be impossible to understand the political thought of the period of the Enlightenment without them.

Other moralists

Lesser moralists, too, managed to impress their contemporaries. In particular there were the Chevalier de Méré, Abbé de Saint-Réal, and Nicole.

The Chevalier de Méré, between 1668 and 1682, published not only *Conversations* and *Lettres*, but also treatises: *De la Justesse, Des Agréments, De L'Esprit, De la Conversation.*[5] The titles themselves give an adequate account of how he conceived the rôle of the moralist. It is entirely socially-orientated. It is a continuation, and the end product, of the literature of the 'honnete homme' mentioned earlier, and of which Faret had for a long time been the most conspicuous product. This shows the limits of the man as well as the points of difference with La Rochefoucauld. Nevertheless, Méré's writings offer an excellent insight into the mentality of his society, or at least in that part of society that remained attached to the old ways. For Méré had been born in 1607 and therefore belonged to a generation that was already advanced in years when his books appeared. They tell us about the picture these people continued to have of the honnête homme: ceremonious, a little stilted, anxious to conform in every way to a very precisely defined code of behaviour.

Abbé de Saint-Réal was mainly a political writer.[6] In 1672 he published a *Don Carlos*, and in 1674 a history of *La Conjuration des Espagnols contre la République de Venise*, both of which are less works of history than essays in political theory. He knew the writings of the Italian *trattatisti* and, like them, he tried to distil general maxims as well as to analyse how states worked. Saint-Réal's thought was very like that of La Rochefoucauld. His work is pervaded by the same pessimism. Man, as he saw him, is only guided by self-interest. But like

La Rochefoucauld, and even more like de Retz, Saint-Réal took his idea further than the school of Machiavelli had done. Self-interest, for him, was not merely what reason says it is, it is even more what the passions and prejudices make it out to be. Hence the all-important conclusion that political science amounts to the science of man and his make-up. Thus, what has to be studied is the human heart, the ways to the human soul, its foundations and periphery. Once we have done that we shall see that the most striking actions are often the result of oddities and follies, and that pure evil, the pleasure of hurting for its own sake are often the motives for our conduct.

One might have thought that there could be little in common between the doctrine of Saint-Réal and that of the good Nicole of Port-Royal. But the same climate had brought these two very different men to the same conclusions. Nicole contented himself with explaining in terms of original sin what La Rochefoucauld and Saint-Réal had explained in terms of the normal interplay of the forces of human mechanics. Like La Rochefoucauld, he saw in amour-propre the source of our alleged virtues, of courage, love of truth, and desire for justice. He also believed that the passions are the real source of our actions.

Nicole transferred his pessimism also into the realm of social analysis, just as La Rochefoucauld, de Retz, and Saint-Réal had done. He was certain that the world was in the grip of injustice and sin. His works allow one to see the degree to which the Augustinianism of Port-Royal was in tune with the moral philosophies that dominated French society after the Fronde and during a great part of the personal rule of Louis XIV.

La Bruyère

The first edition of La Bruyère's *Caractères* in 1688 clearly showed its links with the preceding moralist literature.[7] There were few 'portraits' and what was most obvious about the book was its large number of general maxims in the tradition of La Rochefoucauld. It constantly reminded one of Montaigne, Pascal, and Nicole, while other parts were reminiscent of the treatises about life in society and the best way of getting into the court. La Bruyère's image of man was like that of

La Rochefoucauld. He emphasised the contradictions within us, our weakness, and the part played by the passions.

After the fourth edition, however, in 1689, the emphasis of the book changed. There were more portraits, and these increased with every edition until they finally provided a panorama of French society and, in the words of a contemporary, 'une description des moeurs de ce siècle'.[8] This did not at all mean that the interest henceforth lay in the 'key' to the portraits; that is often of no importance and, more than once, La Bruyère gave one name to a collection of features taken from different sources. His readers liked to look for keys, but in this they were wrong, because the interest of the *Caractères* lies elsewhere.

They portray French society, the world of the court (truly a nation within the nation), the state of the Church, its worldly prelates and elegant preachers, the corruption of the magistrates, the young parlementaires who had become smart. In all this, La Bruyère was simply following the fashion that, since about 1680, had prompted the French to take an interest in the analysis of manners. He was following in the footsteps of playwrights, some of the novelists, and even of some preachers, for the latter were sure to please the faithful if they introduced into their sermons some ingenious and striking description of contemporary forms of behaviour.

What is particularly notable is the firmness with which La Bruyère appraised and condemned his society in these descriptions. He was not afraid of denouncing the selling of offices and pointing out the disastrous consequences of that practice. He condemned the totally irrational differences of prosperity between the various sections of the nation, and the general misery that was in his view the inevitable consequence of the luxury enjoyed by the financiers. He knew and said that war was responsible for the deep malaise in French society, and his readers found no difficulty in seeing that the policy of prestige had obliged the government to hand over the country to the rapacity of the financiers.

The unprejudiced admired the candour of the *Caractères*. Already in March 1688 a journalist was praising the 'noble intrépidité, la liberté vigoureuse' of La Bruyère, as well as 'des maximes d'une grande force et qui sont tirées du bon sens et de la droite raison'. In the *Discours sur Théophraste*, at the head of the *Caractères*, he saw a parallel between the French monarchy and Athenian democracy which 'ressentait la liberté d'un républicain'. That interpretation of La Bruyère is not mistaken, and we are today particularly sensitive to his passionate protests against injustice and the abusive use of power. One is grateful to La Bruyère for having seen so clearly the suffering of the mass of the people, for having refused to acquiesce in it, and for having expressed his indignation at it with some violence. The famous page he devoted to the misery of the peasants still stirs us.

But one must recognise the real meaning of his criticism and the real import of his thought. He was not a precursor of the *philosophes*, he was not in advance of his time. On the contrary, he was in the tradition of the Christian moralists. He was an ardent disciple of Bossuet, and he was a severe judge of monarchic society because he compared it with the happier days of primitive society at the time of the patriarchs. He exalted the old forms of society when nature showed itself to men 'dans toute sa pureté et sa dignité.' He judged the institutions and manners of his century in terms of the ancient humanity of the patriarchs and Homeric Greece. He was thinking of the first books of the Bible and some episodes of the Odyssey when he inveighed against the selling of offices and the luxury of the financiers. He did not admire the institutions of Athens because he was a republican, but because the constitution of Athens and its simple, popular ways and equal citizens seemed to him to be more in tune with pure nature than the régime of the modern monarchies.

Such were the limits of his thinking. But it has a great deal of historical significance. It shows that even within the religious faction there were Christian philosophers who did not subscribe to royal policies, nor to the social order the monarchy had brought about, nor to the moral order which was their consequence. This refusal to submit was only underwritten by a few members of the religious faction at the end of the reign. But their numbers increased and they came to be represented among the clergy and in the university. They were, above all, going to be more radical. Eighteenth-century Jansenism was to find its recruits in their ranks.

Mme de Sévigné

There is nothing arbitrary about linking Mme de Sévigné with the writers who were interested in moral problems. She had of course no desire to propound a moral doctrine. But she was a keen observer of men and society and showed much lucidity in her judgments. She was an eye-witness of French society who liked to record, interpret, and judge character and manners.

She belonged to the generation that had reached its majority at the time of Mazarin, and this shows in her writing. The time of 'la belle Régence' left her with a great freedom of mind, gaiety, and the impossibility of succumbing to the pedantic ways the official world was assuming as the century neared its end.

From about 1665, she was in touch with the greatest men and women of her time, with La Rochefoucauld and Mme de Lafayette, with Mme de Montespan and Cardinal de Retz when he was back in Paris. She also met the writers Boileau, Segrais, Ménage, and she would have seen more of Racine if he had not left her with some doubts about his character. She also knew the Messieurs of Port-Royal, and loved and admired them.

From these contemporaries she learnt all about life at court and in Parisian society. She talked about it to her daughter, who had become Mme de Grignan and, since 1670, lived most of the time in Provence. The letters she wrote to her constitute for the reader a kind of chronicle of France over a period of more than twenty years. They have remained famous in literary history because of their wit, elegance, and gaiety. They no doubt deserve it. But they also have other less obvious merits. Mme de Sévigné was not merely a charming woman who agreeably told anecdotes. She was also an observer who was at once intelligent and sensitive. There is nothing better than her letters to give one a picture of what France under Louis XIV was really like. At first people accepted with some reticence the harsh authoritarianism of the reign. Then the French were simply dazzled, and Mme de Sévigné allows herself to get carried away. Like everyone around her she admired the young king, was impressed by his majestic grace, and applauded his quick and easy conquests. But as the years went by her tone changed. She saw the misery of the peasants, the shocking brutality of the royal administration. She saw the despair of the provincial nobility that was decimated by the wars and was as hard hit as the rest of the people by the general misery. Even for the king she could then muster no more than formal respect, and even that she at times forgot.

She could judge the France of Louis XIV with such lucidity because she did not share its enthusiasm. She was a sincere believer but not devout, and she laughed at the pretensions of religion in France when those in the government assumed airs of the most exalted piety. She had great respect for the Jansenists, but this was not the result of religious fervour. It was rather because she disliked the Jesuits. But it was also because Augustinianism meant for her what it had meant for Pascal, namely a very high and a very pure conception of Christianity, a demand for a higher morality that was not to be met elsewhere. It may also have been because she shared with the best minds of her time the deep conviction that the human condition was a kind of bondage and, like them, she may not have had much faith in human freedom.

Notes

Part One

1 SOCIAL STRUCTURE

1 The Counsellors of State (Conseillers d'Etat) were recruited from Presidents of the Courts, Prosecutors, Advocates General, and Intendants. From these Counsellors were recruited members of the Grand Conseil, the Conseil d'Etat, and the Requêtes de l'Hôtel. In other words, they ran the administration of the monarchy.

2 The main work written at that time on this subject is by the jurist Loyseau, and has the characteristic title *Traité des Ordres et simples dignités* (1613).

3 For the attitude of François de Sales, Bérulle and the religious faction as a whole, see A. Adam, *Les Jansénistes au XVIIe siècle*, 1968, pp. 39–41.

4 The account is by Mariéjol who reproduced extracts of this address to the king (*Histoire de France* by Lavisse, VI, 2, p. 390). The address was presented by the Duc de la Force, having been drawn up by the Comte de Cramail. The latter did not merely play an important part in aristocratic society, but he was also the leading light in a group of men of letters. Régnier dedicated a satire to him as the Comte de Carmaing, which was the alternative way of spelling his name.

5 Lavisse, *Histoire de France*, VI, pp. 3–4.

6 There were some particularly obvious cases: the Condés were practically masters of Burgundy, the Vendômes looked upon Brittany as their own, and the Longuevilles adopted the same attitude towards Normandy.

7 Louis XIV kept the Great Families (les Grands) out of the Conseil d'En-Haut and all the other councils; the only exceptions were the Duc de Villeroi and the Duc de Beauvilliers.

8 Loyseau, in the already cited *Traité des Ordres et simples dignités*, analysed the composition of the third estate. He mentioned in particular the professors of the four faculties, the holders of offices relating to the finances of the monarchy, judges, lawyers and all those having a profession relating to the law (notaries, clerks of the court, prosecutors), and merchants.

9 This relates to a decree of the Council of 13 May 1631 which was read to members of the parlement who had been called to the Louvre. The

decree annulled a parlement decree which had refused to register a royal edict (Lavisse, *Histoire de France,* VI, p. 393).

10 This was precisely the attitude of the high magistracy during the decisive months in 1715; the magistrates refused to discuss theology, and confined themselves to the law. Their point was that Noailles could not be condemned for an act of disobedience which had not come before the courts; to the Jesuit Tellier (the king's confessor), who had maintained that Noailles' disobedience was public knowledge, d'Aguesseau replied that such reasoning was alien to a jurist since 'public knowledge' was not a concept in French law. He also explained that a national council could only be called by the pope or by the established procedures of the French episcopacy; the government, even when backed by some of the bishops in league with the Court, could not do so. We are here in the presence of the conflict between the traditions of the parlement and modern arbitrary power. On this major clash, see A. Adam, *Les Jansénistes au XVIIe siècle,* 1968, pp. 328–30.

11 Lavisse, *Histoire de France,* VI, pp. 159–60 and 162. The nobility had 132 deputies.

12 Two figures allow us to gauge the size of the illicit profits made, quite openly, by the tax-farmers (traitants). When the king created a new office the arrangements for it were made by a tax-farmer; the latter paid the king the sum demanded and proceeded to look around for a buyer, being allowed to make a profit of one-sixth of the original sum paid; in fact everyone knew that tax-farmers actually took a commission of twenty-six per cent.

13 Sauval, the historian of Paris, gives a remarkable account of the situation. He makes a comparison between the decline of the Soissons and Chevreuse mansions (the old and upper aristocracy) and the splendours of those of Amelot de Bisseuil, La Bazinière, Beauvais, Ruart, Guénégaud, and Monnerot, which belonged to the financiers of the period 1655–60. On this analysis, and the facts confirming it, see A. Adam, *Premières Satires de Boileau,* p. 136. The Duc de Saint-Aignan provided a good example of a great nobleman who thought it worth his while to marry his son to the daughter of a financier. In 1662, at a time when Colbert was very vigorously proceeding against the tax-farmers, the Duc's son was engaged to the daughter of Monnerot, who was one of the most dishonoured financiers of the period.

14 During the reign of Louis XIV big firms already existed in forms that were to be further developed later (private firms, limited partnerships, joint stock companies, etc.). Their capital came from members of the magistracy, merchants, and other shareholders, and they gave rise to new hierarchies: foremen, overseers, and directors. But the most widespread form of work was still that done in small workshops and at home.

15 The compagnonnages (work-guilds) were forms of clandestine trade unions, originating in the sixteenth century and expanding in the succeeding century. They had names like *Enfants de Salomon, Enfants*

de Maitre Jacques, Les Gavots, Les Dévorants. Just one example: in Chartres, one-third of all workers were compagnons (Régine Pernoud, *Histoire de la bourgeoisie en France*, II, p. 230).

16 Strikes had become sufficiently frequent and significant in the seventeenth century for the authorities to prohibit them: Paris in 1660, Lyon in 1665, and Dijon in 1667 had strikes dealt with in that way, and the 'masters' (maîtres) of the corporations denounced the strikers.

17 Lavisse, *Histoire de France*, VIII, p. 230.

18 Mariéjol, in *Histoire de France* by Lavisse, VII, p. 339. This was a statement presented to the king by the Paris merchants in 1685.

19 R. Pernoud, *Histoire de la bourgeoisie en France*, II, p. 109, quotes President Bouhier's most detailed account and penetrating analysis of these events: 'The population of the villages, which had previously been content to look after its inherited lands, thought that the towns offered an easier life, and moved into them. The bourgeoisie of these same towns profited from the mistake of the village folk and bought their lands. Since the bourgeois were unable to cultivate the lands themselves they put them into the hands of poor métayers whom they ruined as time went by. Thus nearly all those who live on the land are today poverty-stricken, and the villages much less populated than when they were in mortmain.'

20 This comes from a report of 1660 by the ambassador in Venice.

21 Quoted by Lavisse, *Histoire de France*, VIII, p. 271.

22 *ibid.*, p. 272.

23 In 1675, Marshal Albret wrote in the middle of the insurrection in Guyenne: 'Most bourgeois are no better disposed' than the insurgents in the countryside, 'though they did not dare show their ill-will for fear of imperilling their life and property'.

24 Among the preachers of the period, Father Soanen of the Oratoire was one of the most outspoken about the poverty of the peasantry. He described it in terms which remind one of the famous passage of La Bruyère (A.Adam, *Histoire*, V, p. 193).

25 Although millenarianism was no longer a danger, the civil and religious authorities had not forgotten it; at that time it was known as illuminism and caused some alarm. The real reason behind Saint-Cyran's persecution was not his friend Jansen's *Augustinus*, for the latter had not yet appeared; it was because he was accused of illuminism in false stories that were told about him (A. Adam, *Du mysticisme à la révolte, les Jansénistes au XVIIe siècle*, p. 140).

26 A considerable number of these booklets have been published in the ten volumes of *Variétés historiques et littéraires* by Edouard Fournier, 1855, and they have been well selected to give a properly balanced picture of this kind of popular literature. This aspect of seventeenth-century literature is examined in Charles Nisard, *Histoire des livres populaires ou de la littérature de colportage*. One must unfortunately have a number of reservations about recommending R. Mandrou, *De la culture populaire aux XVIIe et XVIIIe siècles. La Bibliothèque bleue de Troyes*, 1964; its

author, who is apparently unfamiliar with seventeenth-century literature, places Scarron and Cyrano into the first third of the century and attributes *Arlequin empereur de la lune* to Cyrano who had been dead a long time when the Italians first presented it. Also, in talking about the existence of a popular audience for the theatres of Paris, he seems to be unaware of Professor John Lough's basic text *Paris Theatre Audiences in the Seventeenth and Eighteenth centuries*, Oxford University Press, 1957.

27 On the links between popular fairy tales and the literary genre which derived from them, see M.E.Storer, *La mode des contes de fées*, 1928. This book also has a very good bibliography. See also Lucie Félix-Faure Goyau, *La vie et la mort des fées*, 1910.

28 For example, Nisard mentions the *Alphabet de l'imperfection et malice des femmes* by J. Olivier, 1617 (*Histoire des livres populaires*, I, p. 421). A list of complaintes can be found in P.G.Brunet, *Manuel du libraire et de l'amateur de livres*, 1878–80.

29 For an excellent study of the mazarinades see C.Moreau, 'Bibliographie des Mazarinades' and 'Choix de Mazarinades' which appeared in *Publications de la Société d'Histoire de France*, 1846–54, 3 vols.

30 There must of course be no confusion between the somewhat spicy stories of popular literature and rather broader writings like *Muses folâtres*, *Parnasse satyrique*, etc; Charles Nisard seems to make just that confusion, prompted by an old booklet (*Histoire des livres populaires* I, p. 432). So-called satyrique poetry is obscene and not popular, its authors belonging to the Court and writing for it.

31 Balzac's testimony is most important on this topic because he specified the social strata where Ronsard was most admired around 1615–20: he said that it was 'the parlement of Paris, and the parlements in general, the university, and the Jesuits' (A.Adam, *Histoire*, I, p. 24).

32 Queen Marguerite's circle was the one which was most attached to the culture of the Renaissance. Among the great noblemen there were Marshal de Bassompierre and the Comte de Cramail.

33 In his *Histoire comique de Francion*, Charles Sorel amusingly described the taste of college students for novels depicting heroic battles, and for the 'horrible chaplis de géants déchiquetés comme chair à pâté'. On this fashion, which is a legacy of the Middle Ages, see the facts and figures given in A.Adam, *Histoire*, I, p. 102; the topic is studied as a whole in N.Edelmann, *The Attitude of Seventeenth-Century France towards the Middle Ages*, New York, 1946.

34 The galant magistrate appears towards the end of the century. He no longer wears even his black cloak, but a grey coat with a fussy cravat; and he carries a cane. The comedies of the period ridiculed his vanity, his flabbiness, and his libertinism.

35 For facts and figures about the amount of money made by the authors of the period, see H.J.Martin, *Livres, pouvoirs et société à Paris au XVIIe siècle*, 1969, p. 424 *et seq.* Given the erudition of the chapter, it is surprising to find in it a rather odd remark about Corneille. M.Martin accuses the author of the *Cid* of having 'trafiqué allègrement' and 'pas toujours

très honnêtement' in privileges he had obtained through the publication of his works. But the truth is simpler. It was common practice that the author of a play did not publish it until the players had stopped performing it. Thus, when Corneille found that his play was too successful, and that therefore only the players benefited from it for too long a time, he asked the latter for an additional payment of a hundred livres. Since the players unhappily refused, Corneille had the *Cid* published. He was entirely within his rights to do so, even if custom was against him, but people accused him of avarice. More detail in A.Adam, *Histoire*, I, p. 514.

36 Towards 1620 a poem was doing the rounds called *La Pauvreté des poètes*, the work of a little-known rhymster by the name of Boissières; Boissières listed just about all the known poets of the period among those who were poverty-stricken, including Malherbe.

37 The first to have the glorious title 'poète crotté' was Marc de Maillet. For details about him, see Frédéric Lachèvre, *Bibliographie des recueils collectifs*, II, p. 350. Théophile had composed verses about him, and Saint-Amant called him 'the queen's fool' (the queen was Marguerite).

38 For the social condition of the first Academicians, see A.Adam, *Histoire*, I, pp. 221–2.

39 Notes on the poets of the period, including information about their social origins and living conditions, are to be found in the already-mentioned work by Fr.Lachèvre, *Bibliographie des recueils collectifs*.

40 Foucquet's place in the development of literature is discussed in the very important work by V.Chatelain, *Nicolas Foucquet, protecteur des lettres et des arts*, 1905.

41 The list of recipients (gratifiés) of 1663 is contained in *Pièces intéressantes*, by La Place. The big edition of Colbert's *Correspondance* starts only with the June 1664 list.

42 These sentences are extracted from a letter by Huet to Ménage of 17 August 1663 which is preserved in the Bibliothèque nationale, n.acq. fr.1341. f° 157.

2 THE SOCIAL IMPLICATIONS OF POLITICAL HISTORY

1 The following pages naturally do not pretend to provide an account of the political history of the seventeenth century, nor even a synopsis of it. Their sole aim is to help the reader see the different stages of development of the period, and to enable him to place the works of literature into their appropriate setting. To take two examples: the paragraphs devoted to the period of anarchy, which runs from the death of Henry IV to the beginning of Richelieu's ministry, help to give an understanding of the poetry of Malherbe after 1610 and of that of Théophile de Viau; and the account of the 1636–42 conspiracies brings out the significance of Corneille's *Cinna*.

2 This question was recently raised again in the thesis by Etienne Thuau, *Raison d'Etat et pensée politique à l'époque de Richelieu*, Athens, 1966.

3 The *Recueil de Lettres* published by Nicolas Faret in 1627 was for a long time ignored by historians. In fact, most of it constitutes a veritable manifesto from the writers of Richelieu's circle. It contains letters by Malherbe, Balzac, Boisrobert, and Silhon (the Conseiller d'Etat).
4 *Statolatrie* is the word used by Father Claude Clément, a writer of the religious faction, in 1637 (Thuau, *Raison d'Etat*, pp. 95–6).
5 Grotius, who felt himself threatened in his own country and was, in fact, already imprisoned, sought refuge in Paris in 1621 and stayed until 1632, before going on to Hamburg. But, having entered the service of the king of Sweden, he became the latter's ambassador in Paris in 1634, where he stayed until 1645.
6 The basic work on this remains Chéruel, *Histoire de France sous le ministère de Mazarin*, 1883, 3 vols.
7 Amusing examples of Broussel's revolutionary rhetoric may be found in Aubertin, *L'Eloquence politique et parlementaire*, pp. 203–20. He referred to the Queen Mother as irate Juno (*Junonem iratam*), and pretended to have 'the feelings of a real Roman'.
8 The poets became deeply involved; the most famous plays were the *Triolets* by Marigny and his imitators.
9 All these events are narrated, on the basis of evidence from archives and original documents, in vol. VI of *Histoire des Princes de Condé* by the Duc d'Aumale.
10 According to the anonymous author of a *Lettre d'Avis* (1649), this scandalous theory was some thirty years old.
11 Pomponne de Bellièvre was Premier Président at the Paris Parlement. When de Retz was arrested and then escaped from prison, Pomponne de Bellièvre gathered around him the writers who remained hostile to the government; the most important among these writers were Gilles Boileau, Furetière, Godeau, and Sauval. He died in 1657.
12 In 1659 Colbert wrote: 'The king no longer has credit; no one is now doing business with him since it is believed that he must go bankrupt.' He thought the king's difficulties had begun some ten years earlier (Lavisse, *Histoire*, VII. 1, p. 78).
13 This statement by the historian Sauval, comes from his big *Histoire de la ville de Paris*, cited above.
14 The best account of the wars of 1668–78 is still in Lavisse, *Histoire*, VII. 2, pp. 309–45.
15 The various sections of the central administration, their respective responsibilities and the way they worked are analysed in Lavisse, *Histoire*, VII. 1, pp. 149–54.
16 On the constant rivalry between the provincial governors and the intendants see Lavisse, *Histoire*, VII. 1, pp. 165–7.
17 These words were spoken in the house of Lamoignon during a meeting of the group of Christian philosophers who gathered there each week (A. Adam, *Histoire*, III, p. 4).
18 On Colbert's industrial and commercial policies see Lavisse, *Histoire*, VII. 1, pp. 206–66.

19 These criticisms of Louis XIV are most amusingly yet pungently summed up in the thirty-seventh letter of the *Lettres persanes*. See the reference to contemporary writings which shed light on Montesquieu's accusations in *Lettres persanes*, Droz, Geneva, pp. 98–9.

20 Even after the end of the war the debt continued to increase. Military expenditure remained much too high and the financial controller contemplated bankruptcy, and even recommended it to the king. It was to have been a partial bankruptcy of a half or third, involving the suspension of payment of orders and the taking of measures.

21 These accounts are to be found in A. Adam, *Histoire*, V, p. 8.

22 The sentence comes from the novelist Nervèze (1606) and is quoted by M. Magendie, *La politesse mondaine*, 1905, p. 71.

23 M. Magendie, *ibid.*, p. 110.

24 Mademoiselle de Gournay accounts for this 'madness' (folie) in two ways: (1) noblemen were always carrying their swords, and (2) they thought it clever to beat up a peasant or a bourgeois (*Avis*, 1641 edition, p. 241).

25 *Francion*, Roy edition, II, p. 133.

26 *ibid.*

27 Sorel said this of Philémon, and Tallemant said it of Henry I of Montmorency (Pléiade edition of *Historiettes*, I, p. 65) though with some exaggeration (same edition, note, p. 749).

28 Before 1604 officers could sell their offices for a payment of twenty-five per cent of their value, so long as they lived for forty days after the sale had been concluded. The latter proviso created disastrous difficulties for their heirs, and in 1604 Henry IV freed them from it, provided the officers had annually paid one-sixtieth in the form of a tax. If that had been done, the heirs could nominate the new holder of the office. The financier Charles Paulet won the right to levy the tax of one-sixtieth, and the tax became known as the paulette. For practical purposes, this procedure made the royal officers proprietors of their offices.

29 One mazarinade denounced, one by one, the presidents, counsellors, and maîtres des requêtes who had been implicated in the machinations of financiers (Adam, *Histoire*, II, p. 10).

30 See above for details about popular literature and the booklets of the Pont-Neuf.

31 Georges de Scudéry called the people 'cet animal à tant de tetes'; La Ménardière talks about it as a stupid animal that knew no more than the mechanical arts; Desmarests de Saint-Sorlin is entirely scornful about 'l'indicte et stupide vulgaire'. All these writers were members of the group of writers whose task was to spread the ideas of Richelieu.

32 The question is analysed in Adam, *Histoire*, II, p. 2.

33 The new avenues to prosperity were the results of the monetary crisis. Gold and silver coins had become rare, because the variations in the value of money had led to the exporting of gold and silver. Holland, Genoa, and Geneva had become the European markets for precious metals. Paper money, of which there was far too much, had fallen

disastrously in value. Only gambling in shares could bring one a fortune.

3 LITERATURE AND POLITICS

1 At the beginning of this century, although there were 'poètes crottés', opulent rewards were received by those who worked for the Court. Desportes was given the living of a well-endowed abbey, and also lived in a luxurious property at Vanves. Bertaut was principal almoner to the queen, and was made bishop of Séez in 1606. Du Perron became bishop of Evreux, and later archbishop of Sens and a cardinal.
2 These Malherbe verses can be found in the Lavaud edition, I, pp. 205 and 128.
3 *Oeuvres complètes*, by Théophile, Alleaume edition, I, pp. 144–5.
4 *Perroniana et Thuana*, Cologne, 1694, p. 191.
5 On the group Cinq auteurs and the problems it raised, see Adam, *Histoire*, I, pp. 504–7.
6 See texts quoted in Thuau, *Raison d'Etat*, p. 169.
7 On this aspect of Richelieu's work, see Adam, *Histoire*, I, pp. 214–20.
8 On the Siti issue, see the *Mercure* of 1618, p. 268, and the *Mémoires* of Richelieu, II, p. 295. In fact, the two men had merely supported the cause of Marie de Médicis. Luynes had them burnt.
9 For the rules, see E. Coyecque, *Inventaire de la collection Amisson*, vol. I.
10 The so-called *satyriques anthologies* are exhaustively examined in Fr. Lachèvre, *Les recueils collectifs de poésies libres et satiriques* (1600–26), Paris, 1914.
11 The following plays by Du Ryer are full of political tirades: *Arétaphile* (1628), *Argenis et Poliarque* (1630).
12 Letter published by Tamizey de Larroque, *Mélanges historiques*, p. 469.
13 On the very active part played by Cardinal de Retz among men of letters, see Adam, *Histoire*, II, pp. 11–15.
14 Chatelain's very important work *Nicolas Foucquet, protecteur des lettres* has already been cited as giving a complete picture of literary life around Foucquet as well as his entourage.
15 These are the words of Daniel Huet (1674) and Abbé Paul Tallement (at about the same time). For the quotations see Adam, *Histoire*, III, p. 5.
16 La Fontaine, *Epitre à M. de Niert*.
17 On Colbert's policy concerning writers, see the detailed account in Adam, *Histoire*, III, pp. 9–12.
18 *La Muse historique* was republished in the nineteenth century by J. Ravenel and E.V. de la Palouze, 5 vols., 1857–91.
19 See the excellent little book by Pierre Mélèse, *Donneau de Visé*, 1936.
20 See B.T.Morgan, *Histoire du Journal des Savants*, 1928.
21 In Paris this decision led to the separation of the police from the judiciary. The newly-created post was called 'Lieutenant général du prévot de Paris pour la police'.

22 Quoted by Adam, *Histoire*, v, p. 6.
23 Louis Honoré, *Une boutique de librairie à Toulon sous Louis XIV*, Cannes, 1937.
24 On this question, see Pierre Mélèse, *Le Théâtre et le public à Paris sous Louis XIV*, 1934.
25 On Chavigny de la Bretonnière, see the *Variétés* by Fournier, vol. VI, p. 209. These *Variétés* reproduced the text of his pamphlet *Le cochon mitré*, which was a cruel attack on the bishops of the period.
26 On this new and important phenomenon of social life, see Fr. Funck-Brentano, *Les Nouvellistes*, 1905.
27 E. Hatin, *Les Gazettes de Hollande et la presse clandestine*, 1865.

4 SOCIAL AND LITERARY LIFE

1 *Journal* by L'Estoile, dated 5 February 1595.
2 See particularly the Lavaud edition of Malherbe, *Poésies*, vol. I, pp. 64, 78, 190.
3 On Queen Marguerite's group see Simone Ratel, *Revue du XVIe siècle*, années 1924 and 1925.
4 Quoted by Magendie, *La politesse mondaine*, p. 121.
5 The Hôtel de Rambouillet has been studied by Emile Magne, whose two volumes *Voiture et l'Hôtel de Rambouillet* (1929–30) are exceptionally well researched.
6 Quoted by Magendie, *La politesse mondaine*, p. 125.
7 'Déconfiture des rondeaux' is found in a letter by Chapelain of 12 February 1638 (*Lettres*, I, p. 198). A *Recueil de divers rondeaux* was published in 1639. On the metamorphoses, see Magne, *Voiture et l'Hôtel de Rambouillet*, II, pp. 183–4. See also the *Discours* on the metamorphoses in Abbé Cotin, *Oeuvres galantes*, II, p. 312 *et seq.*
8 This important question was the subject of the thesis by M. Magendie, *La politesse mondaine*. In 1630, Faret published *L'Honnête homme ou l'Art de plaire à la Cour*, which was his main work; Magendie republished it in 1925.
9 See P. Mesnard, *Histoire de l'Académie Française*, 1857, but also the *Histoire de l'Académie Française* published in 1652 and republished with excellent notes by Ch. Livet in 1858.
10 Camus, *Issue aux Censeurs*, following *Alcime*, quoted by F. Brunot, *Histoire de la langue française*, II, p. 32.
11 On the ballets and Italian operas of Mazarin's period, see the two works of Prunières, *L'Opéra italien en France avant Lully*, and *Le Ballet de Cour en France*, 1913.
12 The aims of the Académie are described in Pellisson I, p. 101.
13 Quoted by Magendie, *op. cit.*, p. 484, referring to the *Mémoires*, I, p. 395.
14 A. Adam, *Histoire*, III, p. 24.
15 The Messieurs du Marais included members of the great noble families like Candale, Brissac, Fontrailles, Aubijoux, as well as young members of the parlements like Bauchaumont, Coulon, Camus, and Broussin.

16 See the *Mémoires* of Goulas, II, p. 457. The reference there is to M. d'Aubijoux. The other libertin Mme de Motteville calls an 'honnête homme' is Fontrailles.
17 See Lenet, *Mémoires*, and the accounts contained in the Duc d'Aumale's *Histoire des princes de Condé*.
18 The *Grande Description de l'état incarnadin* is in the fourth *Recueil des pièces en prose* by Sercy, 1661, p. 221. The book is the work of Foucquet's entourage.
19 On the 'Samedis de Sapho', see principally the excellent book by G. Mongrédien, *Mademoiselle de Scudéry et son salon*, 1947.
20 This concerns the poet Isarn (sometimes spelt Ysarn or Isar) and M. de Doneville, son of a president and man of letters.
21 In particular, there is in vol. 10 of the *Grand Cyrus* a very lively response from Mlle de Scudéry to an attack by an unnamed enemy (the latter appearing only under the romantic pseudonym Damophile).
22 R.La Thuillère, *La Préciosité, étude historique et linguistique*, I, 1966. However, the book which allows us the best insight into préciosité is *Roman de la Précieuse* (Abbé de Pure, 1656–8 and republished by Emile Magne in the series *Textes Français Modernes*).
23 *Dialogue de la Mode et de la Nature*, 1662.
24 Quoted by Sauval in his account of the Précieuses; among other quotations: débiaiser ses sentiments, décontenancement, servir importamment.
25 On the salon of Mme du Plessis-Guénégaud, see Adam, *Histoire*, II, pp. 46–7.
26 On the salon of the Duchesse de Richelieu, see *ibid*, III, pp. 34–5.
27 This comes from Brienne, *Mémoires*.
28 The princely courts during the second half of the reign of Louis XIV have been described by Desnoiresterres in *Les Cours Galantes*, 4 vols., 1860–4.
29 See Ch.M.Jourdain, *Histoire de l'Université de Paris au XVIIe et au XVIIIe siècles*, 2 vols, 1888.
30 It would be a mistake to take it for granted that all seventeenth-century writers had a knowledge of Greek. They often used bilingual editions in Greek and Latin. La Bruyère, for instance, is known not to have used the Greek text of Theophrastus but Casaubon's Latin translation. Racine alone was an excellent Hellenist.
31 Quoted by J.Lough, p. 87.

Part Two

5 RELIGION, SOCIETY, AND LITERATURE

1 If, apart from their public expression, one wants to gain an insight into the real feelings of the French bourgeoisie about these problems, one should start by reading the *Journal* by L'Estoile, the *Lettres* by Guy Patin,

as well as those by Chapelain. These three bourgeois are eminently representative of the ideas of their class.

See Dagens, *Bérulle et les origines de la Réformation catholique* (1575–1611), 1952.

3 On François de Sales and the religious literature which propagated his ideas, see H.Bremond, *Histoire littéraire du sentiment religieux*, 12 vols., 1916–36.

4 This extraordinarily strong and characteristic letter is reproduced in Adam, *Les Libertins au XVIIe siècle*, pp. 156–7. The letter was found by R.Pintard and published by him in his thesis *La Mothe-le-Vayer, Gassendi et Guy Patin*, 1943, pp. 64–5.

5 On Port-Royal, apart from Sainte-Beuve, *Port Royal*, one must not forget A.Gazier, *Port-Royal*, 2 vols, 1922.

6 On the ultramontanes and their campaign against the Augustinians in 1649, see Adam, *Les Jansénistes au XVIIe siècle*, pp. 193–6.

7 It might be thought that the traditional interpretation of the bull was shown to have been mistaken when M.Henry published his *Vie de François Bousquet* in 1889, and which he based on evidence from archives. He showed that the pope had clearly stated that the bull was issued at the same time as the *Augustinus* and not against either it or its author, and that Bousquet quickly informed the French authorities of this fact. Nevertheless, the French authorities were so dominated by the religious faction that they paid no attention to this, and the pope himself finally acquiesced and solemnly asserted the reverse of what he had told Bousquet.

8 On the close links between the moral thinking of the bourgeoisie and the *Provinciales*, see Adam, *Les Jansénistes au XVIIe siècle*, pp. 221–7.

9 This was finally demonstrated in the 'Grands Ecrivains de France' edition of the *Provinciales*. There is, on each page below Pascal's text, a complete replica of the casuists' propositions, so that no mistakes are possible.

10 The most striking example is the Drouet de Villeneuve affair. The latteo was a theological student who had supported the ultramontane cause. The parlement intervened and pronounced its verdict which the Sorbonne accepted, except for the theologians from Saint-Sulpice.

11 This unfortunate young man was denounced by a priest from Saint-Sulpice, condemned to death on 26 August 1662, and burnt to death on 1 September; powerful pleading on his behalf had proved useless.

12 Mme de Maintenon wrote in 1690: 'Le roi se porte à merveille. Sa santé et sa sainteté se fortifient tous les jours'. And in 1714: 'Son zèle pour la religion augmente' (quoted by Lavisse, *Histoire*, VIII, 1, p. 280).

13 It is difficult not to realise that the war against England was prompted by Catholic rather than by political considerations. Three lines in the prologue of Racine's *Esther* prove that this was his conviction, too: the king of France was said to have armed himself to fight God's war and for God's rights.

14 These accounts can be found in Adam, *Histoire*, v, p. 90.
15 This is the way Loret put it in his *Gazette rimée* of 1657.
16 Father Caffaro, of the Congrégation des Théatins, had published a letter in the spring of 1694 called *Lettre d'un théologien* in favour of the theatre; it has been alleged that its real author was Boursault. Bossuet was so incensed about it that he had the unfortunate monk banned, and himself published *Maximes et Réflexions sur la Comédie*.
17 On this question, which bien-pensants historians prefer to ignore, see O.Douen, *L'Intolérance de Fénelon*, 1874, which is based on authentic documentation.
18 See the important work by Raymond Schmittlein, *L'aspect politique du différent Bossuet-Fénelon*.
19 On Bourdaloue, the significant book to consult is E.Griselle, *Histoire critique de la prédication de Bourdaloue*, 1901.
20 On Mascaron, see the useful thesis by L.L.Lehanneur, *Mascaron d'après des documents inédits*, 1878.
21 The life and works of Fléchier were examined in A.Fabre, *La jeunesse de Fléchier*, 1882, and *Fléchier orateur*, 1886.
22 On Massillon, see the two works by Blampignon, *Vie de Massillon. La jeunesse et la prédication*, 1879, and *L'Episcopat de Massillon*, 1884.
23 The *Quatrains du déiste* are reproduced in their entirety in Adam, *Les libertins au XVIIe siècle*, pp. 90–108: they comprise 424 lines. The manuscript in which they have been preserved (Bibliothèque nationale, Paris, f. latin, 10329) contains several passages that make no sense; these have been amended in the reproduced text.
24 On the influence in France of the philosophical school of Padua, see J.R.Charbonnel, *La pensée italienne au XVIe siècle et le courant libertin*, 1919.
25 *Theophrastus redivivus* was examined by J.S.Spink in an important article in *Revue d'Histoire littéraire*, 1937.
26 Extracts from the works of Des Barreaux, Dehénault, Saint-Pavin, Chapelle, and Mme Deshoulières can be found in Adam, *Les libertins au XVIIe siècle*.
27 Several accounts of the spread of Atheism among the aristocracy around 1700 can be found in Adam, *Histoire*, v, p. 12.
28 Among the Epicurian writings of Théophile, see particularly *Elégie à une dame* (ed. *cit.*, I, p. 216) and *Seconde satire* (I, p. 242).
29 See the definitive work by R.Pintard, *Le libertinage érudit*, 1943.
30 G.Mongrédien wrote an excellent work on Vauquelin des Yveteaux (1921) and published that poet's *Oeuvres complètes* in the same year.
31 There is a study of the life of Des Barreaux and a collection of his verse by Fr.Lachèvre, *Disciples et successeurs de Théophile de Viau*, 1911.
32 On Saint-Evremond, see the writings of R.Ternois, who is publishing an admirable edition of the writer's works; vol. 4 has already appeared.
33 Among the most characteristic of Saint Evremond, these passages are reproduced in Adam, *Les libertins au XVIIe siècle*.

6 SCIENCE AND PHILOSOPHY

1 The Académie des Dupuy is the central theme of the already mentioned work by R. Pintard, *Le libertinage érudit*.
2 The best source for a study of Père Mersenne is the monumental edition of his *Correspondance*, in progress since 1945.
3 On this most important question, see R. Lenoble, *Mersenne ou la naissance du mécanisme*, 1943.
4 On the Tétrade, see R. Pintard, *La Mothe le Vayer, Gassendi, Guy Patin, études de bibliographie et de critique*, 1943. Guy Patin of course did not belong to the Tétrade.
5 On Descartes, see particularly the article on him by M. René Poirier in *Dictionnaire des lettres françaises*.
6 On the spread of Cartesianism around 1660-70, see Adam, *Histoire*, III, pp. 18–23.
7 See Francisque Bouillier, *Histoire de la philosophie cartésienne*, 1868, I and II.
8 On Malebranche's part in the history of Cartesianism, see Bouillier, *op. cit.*, II, pp. 328–402.
9 On Nicolas Boindin, Jean-Baptiste Mirabaud, and Abbé Terrasson, see Ira Wade, *The Clandestine Organisation and Diffusion of Philosophic Ideas in France from 1700 to 1750*, Princeton, 1936.
10 On Henri Justel and his circle, see below, p. 135.
11 On the *Epigrammatum delectus*, see Adam, *Histoire*, II, p. 183, and III, p. 23.
12 On Henri Justel, see the excellent study by R. Ternois, *Revue de littérature comparée*, XIII, p. 588–605.
13 On the first 'cercles d'études' which were then coming into being, see Adam, *Le mouvement philosophique dans la première moitié du XVIIIe siècle*, 1967, p. 140.
14 On the opposition of the Cartesians to the philosophy of Newton, and its real significance, see the same work, pp. 47–55.
15 Nicolas Boindin has already been encountered (p. 132). Another philosopher of that generation was Claude Chesneau Dumarsais (1676–1751), who is treated by Werner Kraus in an article in *Revue d'histoire littéraire*, 1962, entitled 'L'énigme du Dumarsais'.
16 See Elisabeth Labrousse, *Pierre Bayle*, 2 vols., The Hague, 1963.
17 In 1931 Gilbert Chinard published an excellent edition of *Dialogues avec un sauvage Amériquain* by La Hontan.

7 ANCIENTS AND MODERNS

1 Urbain Chevreau confirmed Saint-Amant's lack of knowledge in this respect: 'Quoiqu'il ne sut ni grec, ni latin . . .', he wrote. Saint-Amant himself admitted his lack of Latin in his *Avertissement au Lecteur* at the beginning of the 1629 edition of his *Oeuvres*; but he immediately added: 'Une personne n'est pas moins estimable pour çela'.
2 The significance of these judgments becomes clearer when one realises

that, in line with the baroque aesthetics in whose era he grew up, he thought little of Virgil and explicitly preferred Lucan and Statius. See *Mémoires* by Racan, ed. Tenant de Latour.

3 Letter to Doneville, in Marcou, *Etude sur la vie et les oeuvres* de Pellisson, 1859, p. 475. In another letter (*ibid.*, p. 482), Pellisson returns to the same subject.

4 *Oeuvres complètes*, ed. *cit.* II, pp. 11–14.

5 Livet edition, I, p. 12.

6 *Lettre à un sot ami*, in *Oeuvres complètes* by Théophile, II, p. 328.

7 *Oeuvres* by Saint-Amant, Livet edition, I, p. 12.

8 Among the many interpreters of the baroque, Benedetto Croce placed particular emphasis on the relationship between the baroque and the birth of a new culture, and therefore of a new society. For that reason his account is better than those which came later and were purely aesthetic and metaphysical.

9 On the beginnings of the reaction against baroque style in prose, see Ch. Urbain, *Nicolas Coeffeteau*, 1883.

10 On the fashion in France of the pointe, and on the later criticisms of it, see Adam, *L'Age classique*, pp. 104–6.

11 On Ronsard during the last part of his life, see M.Raymond, *L'Influence de Ronsard*, 1927.

12 On Chapelain and his doctrine, see the excellent work by G.Collas, *Jean Chapelain*, 1911. A.C.Hunter edited (1936) the *Opuscules critiques*, which defined Chapelain's doctrine.

13 On 'coquette' poetry, which exactly reflected the taste of society when it was led by the financiers, see Adam, *Histoire*, II, pp. 53–4, and *L'Age classique*, p. 133.

14 The two main works on this topic are those of H.Rigault (1859) and H.Gillot (1914); but too schematic a treatment of the subject-matter led both writers into wrong interpretations of the facts.

15 Le Laboureur, preface to the poem *Charlemagne*.

16 A letter in Latin addressed to Habert de Montmort by the Cartesian lawyer Fleury.

17 Des Marests de Saint-Sorlin inserted a *Traité pour juger des poètes grecs, latins, et français* into the new edition of his *Clovis*.

18 Letter XXXVI (Droz edition, p. 94).

19 *Défense de la poésie et de la langue française*, 1675.

20 These ideas of Perrault are found in his *Critique de l'Opéra*.

Part Three

8 POETRY

1 Historians have taken to talking about poésie satyrique, poètes satyriques when they want to refer to the writers of the beginning of the seventeenth century, who were very different from Horace and Boileau, and whose characteristic tone was often audacious to the point of obscenity. F.

Fleuret and L.Perceau have provided an excellent anthology in *Satires françaises, au XVIIe siècle* 2 vols, where they have included pieces of different styles.

2 The works of Sigogne were published by F.Fleuret and L.Perceau, 1920.

3 Berthelot's *Oeuvres satyriques* were published by F.Fleuret in 1913. Practically nothing was known about him until G.Daumas published an erudite article based on unpublished material in *Revue des Sciences humaines*, Lille, 1950.

4 See J.Vianey, *Mathurin Régnier*, 1896. A critical edition by G.Raibaud of the *Oeuvres complètes* appeared in *Textes Français Modernes*, 1958.

5 See J.Rousset, *La littérature de l'Age baroque en France*, 1953, and *Anthologie de la poésie baroque*, 1961.

6 Alan Boase and François Ruchon published *L'Oeuvre poétique de Sponde*, Geneva, 1949.

7 On the reaction against the baroque as a style, see Y.Fukui, *Raffinement précieux dans la poésie française du XVIIe siècle*, Paris, 1964.

8 On Malherbe's work in the realm of poetic style, see R.Fromilhague, *La vie de Malherbe, Technique et création poétique*, 1954.

9 On the language of Malherbe, see principally F.Brunot, *La doctrine de Malherbe*, 1891.

10 The historical importance of this group was revealed by Maurice Cauchie in an article in the *Revue d'histoire de la philosophie* (now: *Revue des Sciences humaines*), Lille, 1942.

11 The evolution of poetic style has been particularly studied by Y. Fukui in the work cited above, note 7.

12 See the excellent work by J.Lagny, *Le poète Saint-Amant*, 1964.

13 Saint-Amant's preface to *Passage de Gibraltar, caprice héroi-comique*, 1640; the passage is reproduced in the anthology at the end of the earlier cited *Age classique* (pp. 194–5).

14 See in particular Urbain Chevreau, *Billets critiques*, pp. 248–9.

15 The most characteristic part of the *Métamorphose des Yeux de Philis en astres* is reproduced in Adam, *L'Age classique*, pp. 202–3.

16 The life of Voiture and his place in the society of his time are examined in the already cited Emile Magne, *Vincent Voiture et l'Hôtel de Rambouillet*, 2 vols, 1929, 1930.

17 Quoted by Magne, I, p. 8, note 1.

18 P.Festugière produced an excellent edition of Sarasin, *Oeuvres*, in 1926. It should be noted that the spelling is Sarasin, not Sarrasin as it still sometimes appears.

19 Among the writers of epics during this period, Père Le Moyne was the object of an excellent study in H.Chérot, *Etudes sur la vie et les oeuvres du P.Le Moyne*, 1887.

20 In a Latin dissertation, Père Mambrun pokes fun at such 'éplucheurs de syllabes' who reduce poetry to the concern of mere forms, *et hoc poetam esse contendunt*.

21 On burlesque poetry, see F.Bar, *Le genre burlesque en France au XVIIe siècle. Etude de style*, 1960.

22 Fr Lachèvre, in his *Les derniers libertins*, 1924, published *Poésies libertines, philosophiques et chrétiennes de Madame Deshoulières*.
23 On the life and works of La Fontaine, see Pierre Clarac, *La Fontaine, l'homme et l'oeuvre*, 1947, and P.A.Wadsworth, *Young La Fontaine*, 1952, which gives a detailed account of La Fontaine until about 1670.
24 On La Fontaine's relations with the Gassendists, see Adam, *Histoire*, IV, p. 52.
25 Pierre Clarac, *Boileau l'homme et l'oeuvre*, 1964.
26 See above, p. 59 on the 'gratification' policy instituted in 1663.
27 On the Académie of Lamoignon, see Adam, *Histoire*, III, pp. 15 and 114. After July 1667 Lamoignon's friends began to hold weekly meetings.
28 On this aspect of Boileau, which is vital to any real appreciation of his 'doctrine', see J.Brody, *Boileau and Longinus*, a Columbia University thesis, Geneva, 1958, and the article in *French Studies*, 1960, by W.G. Moore, 'Boileau and Longinus'.

9 THE THEATRE

1 The seventeenth-century theatre is studied as a whole in the great work by H.Carrington Lancaster, *History of French dramatic literature in the seventeenth century*, Baltimore, from 1929, 4 vols.
2 The topic was again treated by John Lough, *Paris theatre audiences in the seventeenth and eighteenth centuries*, 1957. The book does not, however, supersede the excellent work by P.Mélèse, *Le Théâtre et le public à Paris sous Louis XIV*, 1934, whose perspective is different.
3 *L'Ouverture des jours gras*, in *Variétés* by Fournier, II, p. 352.
4 Mairet, *Les galanteries du duc d'Ossone*, 1636, Preface.
5 Quoted by Lough, *Paris Theatre Audiences*, p. 19.
6 The best account of these theatre-loving merchants appears in Donneau de Visé's play *Zélinde, comédie, ou la Véritable critique de l'Ecole des Femmes et la critique de la Critique*, 1663.
7 On this change of taste, which was linked with changes in society, see the passage quoted in J.Lough, *Paris Theatre Audiences*, p. 131.
8 Quoted Lough, *op. cit.*, p. 77.
9 See the accounts in Adam, *Histoire*, V, p. 264.
10 The question as a whole, after 1660, is dealt with in P.Mélèse, *Le théatre et le public à Paris sous Louis XIV*, 1934; using original sources.
11 Hardy's plays are analysed in E.Rigal, *Alexandre Hardy et le théâtre français à la fin du XVIe siècle*, 1889; but it is desirable to use H.Carrington Lancaster's already cited work for a more up-to-date treatment of the subject. See also the book by Mme Deierkauf-Holsboer which is based on evidence from archives.
12 The main texts are Ogier's Preface to *Tyr et Sidon* by Jean de Schélandre (1628) and *Dissertation* by Chapelain. Ogier's preface is reprinted in the series 'L'Ancien Théâtre Français' in the *Bibliothèque elgévirienne*, VIII, p. 9 *et seq.*, and Chapelain's dissertation may be found in *Opuscules critiques* republished by A.C.Hunter, 1936.

13 On the parts played by Cardinal de la Valette and Comte de Cramail, see Adam, *Histoire*, I, pp. 434–7. Mairet defined his position in the Preface to *Silvanire*, 1631.
14 On Mairet's plays, see G.Bizos, *Etudes sur la vie et les oeuvres de Mairet*, 1877, but the dates he gives for the plays are wrong on grounds for which Mairet himself is responsible.
15 On heroism in Corneille, see J.Maurens, *La tragédie sans tragique*, 1966, and the thesis by André Stegmann, *L'Héroisme cornélien*, 1968.
16 On this period of Corneille's life and works as a whole, see G.Couton, *La Vieillesse de Corneille*, 1949.
17 See in particular the anonymous pamphlet *Le Parasite Mormon* (1650) which made cruel fun of the tragedy. On the names mentioned by the unknown author, see Adam, *Histoire*, II, p. 122, n.I.
18 Thomas Corneille, dedication of *Timocrate*.
19 See G.Reynier, *Thomas Corneille, sa vie et son oeuvre*, 1893, but the dates given for the plays are often wrong and can be rectified by referring to the work of H.Carrington Lancaster.
20 See E.Gros, *Philippe Quinault, sa vie et son oeuvre*, 1926.
21 R.Picard, *La carrière de Racine*, 1956, and P.Moreau, *Racine l'homme et l'oeuvre*, 1943.
22 Recent historians have tried in vain to cast doubt upon contemporary accounts of the origins of *Bérénice*. Abbé Du Bos and Louis Racine were absolutely clear that Henriette d'Angleterre had caused Racine to write the play. Also, on 5 October 1709, the Duchesse d'Orléans recorded that 'le roi et Madame Colonna' had provided the subject.
23 On the first operas in France, see Romain Rolland, *Histoire de l'Opéra en Europe*, 1895, and the works of H.Prunières, particularly his *Vie de Lully* (n.d.).
24 On the relationship between *Esther* and *Athalie* and the climate of the period, a subject long ignored, see J.Orcibal, *Autour de Racine, La Genèse d'Esther et d'Athalie*, 1950.
25 *Arlequin misanthrope*, 1696.
26 On the early period of that history, see H.Prunières, *L'Opéra italien en France avant Lully*.
27 The two works were splendidly republished in the twentieth century: Racan's *Bergeries* by L.Arnould, 1937, and Mairet's *Sylvie* by J.Marsan in 1905; both in the series *Textes Français Modernes*.
28 The probable date of *Le Menteur* is 1643; Spanish plays had been fashionable in Paris since 1638.
29 Preface to *Charme de la voix*.
30 This Charles Robinet, in 1654–5, had published a rhymed gazette called *La Muse héroique*; from 1656 to 1660 he published *La Muse Royale*.
31 The understanding of *Tartuffe* has been considerably enriched by two works: John Cairncross, *New light on Molière*, 1956, and *Molière, bourgeois et libertin*, 1963.
32 Donneau de Visé, *Lettre sur le Misanthrope*, reproduced in the 'Grands écrivains de France' edition of Molière, *Oeuvres*.

10 THE NOVEL

1 The work to be consulted on the subject as a whole is M. Magendie, *Le roman français au XVIIe siècle, de l'Astrée au Grand Cyrus*, 1932. The starting point for all research in this field is R.C. Williams, *A Bibliography of the Seventeenth-century Novel in France*, New York, 1932. The four main novels of the century (*Francion, Roman comique, Roman bourgeois, Princesse de Clèves*) have been published in one volume in the Pléiade series *Romanciers Français du XVIIe siècle*.

2 On the genre that was most fashionable at the time, see G. Reynier, *Le roman sentimental avant l'Astrée*, Paris, 1908.

3 See P.A. Wadsworth, *The Novels of Gomberville, a critical study of Polexandre and Cythérée*, New Haven, 1942.

4 See D. Dallas, *Le roman français de 1660 à 1680*, 1932.

5 See Wessie T. Tipping, *Jean Regnauld de Segrais*, 1933.

6 On the novels of Mme de Villedieu, see the useful book by Bruce A. Morrissette, *The life and works of Marie-Catherine Desjardins*, 1947. Marie-Catherine Desjardins is Mme de Villedieu's maiden name.

7 On this aspect of romanesque literature, see G. Reynier, *Le roman réaliste au XVIIe siècle*, 1914. The title is not very satisfactory since the novels were not *réalistes* but satyriques in the sense the word had at that time.

8 Until the twentieth century no copy of the first edition of *Francion* was available, nor was the actual text known; three copies have now been found, one of which is in the Bodleian Library in Oxford. Modern editions have, since 1910, provided the text of the first edition.

9 There is a good study on Gatien de Courtilz by B.M. Woodbridge, Paris, 1925. The name is frequently followed by de Sandras, Sandras being the name of his mother.

11 MORALISTS AND MEMORIALISTS

1 On the influence of the modern Neo-stoic school, see J. Maurens, *La tragédie sans tragique*, cited above.

2 See Magendie, *La politesse mondaine et les théories de l'honnêteté en France au XVIIe siècle*, 1925.

3 On La Rochefoucauld, see the excellent book by L. Hippeau, *Essai sur la morale de La Rochefoucauld*, 1967.

4 On Mme de Sablé and her circle, see W. Ivanoff, *Mme de Sablé et son salon*, 1927, with many important, hitherto unpublished texts.

5 Méré's works have been republished this century by L. Boudhors (1930).

6 G. Dulong, *L'Abbé de Saint-Réal*, 1921.

7 The social aspect, which is the relevant one in the present work, has been excellently dealt with in M. Lange, *La Bruyère critique des conditions et des institutions sociales*, 1909.

8 The words are those of Cousin, *Journal des Savants*, 28 March 1689.

Bibliography

In addition to the particular references contained in the Notes, a general bibliography is here given to provide suggestions for further reading on the various topics discussed in this book.

Part I Social Structure and Political Change

1 THE POLITICAL FRAMEWORK

For a general history of France in the seventeenth century the *Histoire de France* (volumes VI and VII) by Lavisse remains the most satisfactory work of reference.

The following can also be recommended: M.Reinhardt, *Henri IV ou la France sauvée*, 1943; V.L.Tapié, *La France de Louis XIII et de Richelieu*, 1952; P.Boissonnade, *Colbert, Le triomphe de l'Etatisme*, 1932; P.Goubert, *Louis XIV et vingt millions de Français*, Fayard, 1966.

On the relationship between political structure and thought: E.Thuau, *Raison d'Etat et pensée politique à l'époque de Richelieu*, Athens, 1966; J.E.King, *Science and Rationalism in the Government of Louis XIV*, Baltimore, 1949.

2 SOCIAL STRUCTURE

There is no better way of gaining insight into the mentality of the bourgeoisie than through the *Journal* of L'Estoile, the *Lettres* of Chapelain and those of Guy Patin.

The best studies of social classes in the seventeenth century are to be found in R.Mousnier, *Problèmes de stratification sociale* 1965, and in his introduction to *Lettres et mémoires au chancelier Séguier*, 1964.

P.Bénichou, *Morales du Grand Siècle*, 1948, seeks to link the moral ideas of the century with social class.

3 LITERATURE AND POLITICS

A. Adam, *Histoire de la littérature française au XVIIe siècle*, 5 vols. Each volume begins with a chapter on the political climate and its connections with literature.

On the question of government repression and control, see A. Adam, *op. cit.*, III, pp. 44–6, and V, pp. 29–33. The development of periodical literature is treated in the same work, V, pp. 33–8.

E. Coyecque, *Inventaire de la collection Anisson*, vol. 1, for decrees and general orders.

4 SOCIAL AND LITERARY LIFE

For the life of society see M. Magendie, *La politesse mondaine et les théories de l'honnêteté en France de 1600 à 1660*, 1925.

For the relationships between the world of letters and society see G. Mongrédien, *La vie littéraire au XVIIe siècle*, Taillandier, 1947.

For the rôle of the financiers see V. Chatelain, *Nicolas Foucquet, protecteur des lettres et des arts*, 1905.

For the principal salons see E. Magne, *Vincent Voiture et l'Hôtel de Rambouillet*, 2 vols, 1929–30; G. Mongrédien, *Mlle de Scudéry et son salon*, 1947; E. Magne, *Mme de la Suze et la société précieuse*, *1908*.

For Préciosité see R. La Thuillière, *La Préciosité*, vol. 1, 1966.

For the courts of the princes at the end of the century see G. Desnoiresterres, *Les Cours galantes*, 4 vols, 1860–64.

For the university see Ch. Jourdain, *Histoire de l'Université de Paris*, 1888, vol. 1.

Part II French Thought in the Seventeenth Century

5 RELIGION, SOCIETY, AND LITERATURE

H. Brémond, *Histoire littéraire du sentiment religieux*, 1916 *et seq.* (It should be noted that this great work completely distorts the perspective of the century, despite some interesting analyses of detail, because it entirely disregards the social, political and even philosophical context.)

Calvet, *La littérature religieuse en France de Charron à Pascal*, Vrin, 1933.

H.Busson, *La religion des classiques*, P.U.F., 1948.

François de Sales, as a spiritual adviser and writer, was the subject of a two-volume study by Francis Vincent in 1923.

For Port-Royal and Jansenism, the basic work is now J. Orcibal, *Les Origines du Jansénisme*, 4 vols, 1947–8. But Sainte-Beuve, *Port-Royal*, Pléiade, 3 vols, retains its importance.

For Bossuet one should use J.Lebarcq, *Oeuvres oratoires* 1890–7, and the excellent edition of his *Correspondance* by Ch. Urbain and E.Lévesque, 1909 *et seq.* The *Journal* by Abbé Ledieu, 1856–57, should also be read. New studies include A.Mortimort, *Le gallicanisme de Bossuet*, 1958. For Bossuet the preacher see J.Truchet, *La Prédication de Bossuet*, 2 vols, 1960, and *Bossuet panégyriste*, 1962.

For Fénelon see Ch. Urbain, *Lettres et écrits politiques*, 1921.

For independent religious thought see H.Busson, *Les sources et le développement du rationalisme dans la littérature française de la Renaissance*, 1922; H.Busson, *La pensée religieuse de Charron à Pascal*, 1933; Charbonnel, *La pensée italienne au XVIe siècle et le courant libertin*, 1917; R.Pintard, *Le libertinage érudit dans la première moitié du XVIIe siècle*, 2 vols, 1943; J.S.Spink, *French Free Thought from Gassendi to Voltaire*, London 1959; P.Vernière, *Spinoza et la pensée française avant la Révolution*, 2 vols, 1954, tome I.

Under the collective title *Le libertinage au XVIIe siècle*, Fr. Lachèvre has published a whole series of works by libertins. See also the anthology by A.Adam, *Les libertins au XVIIe siècle*, Buchet-Chastel, 1964; and Fr. Lachèvre's edition of the *Romans de Cyrano de Bergerac*, Classiques Garnier.

6 SCIENCE AND PHILOSOPHY

The best account of scientific life in the first half of the seventeenth century is to be found in the excellent editions of the *Correspondences* of Peiresc and Père Mersenne, 1945 *et seq.* See also R.Lenoble, *Mersenne et la naissance du mécanisme*, 1943.

For Gassendi see the three volumes of his works published by Bernard Rochot, 1944–62.

For Descartes see *Oeuvres*, edited by Ch. Adam and P.Tannery, 12 vols, 1897–1913. Also *Correspondance*, edited by Ch. Adam and G.Milhaud, 1936 *et seq.* Also the excellent selected texts chosen by F.Alquié, Classiques Garnier, F.Alquié, *Descartes, l'homme et l'oeuvre*, 1956.

For Saint-Evremond, the best critical edition of his *Oeuvres* is that begun by R.Ternois in *Textes Français Modernes*; H.T. Barnwell, *Les idées morales et critiques de Saint-Evremond*, P.U.F. 1957; L.Petit, *La Fontaine et Saint-Evremond, ou la tentation de l'Angleterre*, Privat, Toulouse 1953.

For Bayle see the critical edition by A.Prat, *Pensées diverses sur la Comète*, 2 vols, *Textes Français Modernes*, 1911–12; E.Labrousse, *Pierre Bayle*, 2 vols, 1963.

For Fontenelle see the critical edition by L.Maigron, *Histoire des oracles, Textes Français Modernes*, 1908; *Entretiens sur la Comète*, excellently edited by R. Shackleton, Oxford 1955; *De l'origine des Fables*, published with commentary by J.R.Carré, 1932; J.R.Carré, *La philosophie de Fontenelle, ou le sourire de la raison*, 1932; F.Grégoire, *Fontenelle. Une philosophie désabusée*, 1947.

On the intellectual climate at the end of the century see Paul Hazard, *La crise de la conscience européenne*, 1935.

7 ANCIENTS AND MODERNS

On the baroque style as a form of civilisation, Benedetto Croce, *Storia della Età barocca in Italia*, Laterza, Bari, 1929, can still be read with profit. Also V.L.Tapié, *Le Baroque*, P.U.F., and *Baroque et classicisme*, Plon, 1957.

On the origins of classical doctrine see F.Brunot, *La doctrine de Malherbe*, Masson, 1891; *Histoire de la langue française*, vol. 2.

On the theorists of classicism see Chapelain, *Lettres*, p.p. Tamizey de Lausque, 2 vols, 1880–83; *Opuscules critiques*, p.p. Hunter, Droz, 1936.

For the quarrel of the ancients see the old and debatable works of H.Rigault (1859) and H.Gillot (1914).

Part III Literary Forms

For the history of literature as such see A.Adam, *Histoire de la littérature française au XVIIe siècle*, 5 vols, Editions mondiales.

8 POETRY

For the Renaissance tradition see Marcel Raymond, *L'Influence de Ronsard sur la poésie française*, 1927.

For baroque poetry see J.Rousset, *La littérature de l'âge baroque en France*, José Corti, 1953; Yoshio Fukui, *Raffinement précieux dans la poésie française du XVIIe siècle*, Nizet, 1964; Marcel Raymond, *Baroque et Renaissance poétique*, Corti, 1955.

For the religious poets and *lyrisme officiel* see the excellent anthology R.Picard, *La Poésie française de 1640 à 1690*, S.E.D.E.S., 1964.

For burlesque see Francis Bar, *Le genre burlesque en France au XVIIe siècle*, D'Artray, 1960.

9 THE THEATRE

See the monumental work by H.Carrington Lancaster, *An History of French dramatic literature in the seventeenth century*, Baltimore, 4 vols, 1929 *et seq.*

For methods of production see H.Carrington Lancaster, *Le mémoire de Mahelot*, 1920; S.Deierkauf-Holsboer, *Histoire de la mise en scène dans le théâtre français de 1600 à 1654*, Nizet, 1933; and *Le théâtre du Marais*, 2 vols, Nizet, 1954 and 1958.

For the theatre and society see J.Lough, *Paris theatre audiences in the seventeenth and eighteenth centuries*, London, 1957; Mélèse, *Le théâtre et le public à Paris sous Louis XIV*, Droz, 1934; *Répertoire analytique des documents contemporains d'histoire et de critique* (1660–1715), Droz, 1934.

For the theatre and classical doctrine see R.Bray, *La formation de la doctrine classique*, Nizet, 1953; J.Schérer, *La dramaturgie classique*, Nizet, 1954.

For Corneille see *Oeuvres complètes*, 12 vols, *Grands Ecrivains de France*. It is preferable to use the critical editions of some of his works in *Textes Littéraires Français* and *Textes Français Modernes* whenever possible.

For Racine see *Oeuvres complètes*, 8 vols, *Grands Ecrivains de France*, 2 vols, R.Picard and R.Groos in Pléiade edition.

For Molière see *Oeuvres complètes*, 13 vols, *Grands Ecrivains de France; Le Moliériste* (1879–1889), an excellent review devoted to Molière studies.

10 THE NOVEL

Les Romanciers du XVIIe siècle, Pléiade, 1958. The volume

contains *L'Histoire comique de Francion, Le Roman comique, Le Roman bourgeois*, and *La Princesse de Clèves.*

For the novels see G.Reynier, *Le roman sentimental avant l'Astrée*, 1908; M.Magendie, *Le roman français au XVI siècle de l'Astrée au Grand Cyrus*, 1932; D.Dallas, *Le roman français de 1660 à 1680*, 1932; G.Reynier, *Le roman réaliste au XVIIe siècle*, 1914.

11 MORALISTS AND MEMORIALISTS

For La Rochefoucauld see *Oeuvres complètes*, Pléiade, 1959, new ed. 1964; E.Magne, *Le vrai visage de La Rochefoucauld*, 1923 (a biography); H.A.Grubbs, 'The originality of L.R.'s Maxims', in *Revue d'Histoire littéraire de la France*, 1929 (excellent interpretation of L.R.'s work); *La genèse des Maximes, ibid.*, 1932 and 1933; M.Moore, same review, 1952, on early version of maxims; Ivanov, *Le salon de Mme de Sablé*, is vital for an understanding of La Rochefoucauld's thought.

For Cardinal de Retz see *Mémoires, Grands Ecrivains de la France*, 1870–1887, or Pléiade 1950; L.Batiffol, *Le Cardinal de Retz*, Hachette, 1929.

For Méré see *Oeuvres complètes*, 1930 (letters omitted).

For La Bruyère see *Oeuvres complètes*, 3 vols, *Grands Ecrivains de France*, 1865–1878; M.Lange, *La Bruyère critique des conditions et des institutions sociales*, 1909.

For Mme de Sévigné see *Lettres*, Pléiade, 3 vols, new ed. 1963 (the authentic text of her letters does not unfortunately appear in *Grands Ecrivains de France*); Gérard-Gailly, *L'Enfance et la jeunesse heureuse de Mme de Sévigné*, 1926; J.Lemoine, *Mme de Sévigné, sa famille et ses amis.*

Index

Index

Index

Index

Index

Index

Index